KU-470-667

The Official Website of The New Life Mission
www.nlmission.com *or*
www.bjnewlife.org

Worldwide websites of

The New Life Mission

Please find your vernacular websites below.
You can download Christian e-books and request Christian books for free.
Feel free to visit our websites below right now!

A
www.nlmafghanistan.com
www.nlmafrikaans.com
www.nlmalbania.com
www.nlmamharic.com
www.nlmangola.com
www.nlmarabemirates.com
www.nlmarabic.com
www.nlmargentina.com
www.nlmarmenia.com
www.nlmaruba.com
www.nlmaustralia.com
www.nlmaustria.com

B
www.nlmbahamas.com
www.nlmbahrain.com
www.nlmbangladesh.com
www.nlmbelarus.com
www.nlmbelgium.com
www.nlmbengali.com
www.nlmbenin.com
www.nlmbhutan.com
www.nlmbolivia.com
www.nlmbotswana.com
www.nlmbrasil.com
www.nlmbriton.com
www.nlmbrunei.com
www.nlmbulgaria.com
www.nlmburkinafaso.com
www.nlmburundi.com

C
www.nlmcameroon.com
www.nlmcanada.com
www.nlmcebuano.com
www.nlmchichewa.com
www.nlmchile.com
www.nlmchin.com

www.nlmchina.com
www.nlmcolombia.com
www.nlmcongo.com
www.nlmcostarica.com
www.nlmcotedivoire.com
www.nlmcroatia.com
www.nlmczech.com

D
www.nlmdenmark.com
www.nlmdioula.com
www.nlmdominica.com
www.nlmdrcongo.com
www.nlmdutch.com

E
www.nlmecuador.com
www.nlmegypt.com
www.nlmelsalvador.com
www.nlmequatorialguinea.com
www.nlmethiopia.com

F
www.nlmfinland.com
www.nlmfrance.com
www.nlmfrench.com

G
www.nlmgabon.com
www.nlmgeorgian.com
www.nlmgerman.com
www.nlmgermany.com
www.nlmghana.com
www.nlmgreek.com
www.nlmgrenada.com
www.nlmguatemala.com
www.nlmgujarati.com

H
www.nlmhaiti.com
www.nlmhindi.com
www.nlmholland.com
www.nlmhonduras.com
www.nlmhungary.com

Turn over

© Some of these websites may not work because they are still under construction.

*W*orldwide websites of

 The New Life Mission

I
- www.nlm-india.com
- www.nlmindonesia.com
- www.nlmiran.com
- www.nlmiraq.com
- www.nlmisrael.com
- www.nlmitaly.com

J
- www.nlmjamaica.com
- www.nlmjapan.com
- www.nlmjavanese.com

K
- www.nlmkannada.com
- www.nlmkazakhstan.com
- www.nlmkenya.com
- www.nlmkhmer.com
- www.nlmkinyarwanda.com
- www.nlmkirghiz.com
- www.nlmkirundi.com
- www.nlmkorea.com

L
- www.nlmlatvia.com
- www.nlmluganda.com
- www.nlmluo.com

M
- www.nlmmadi.com
- www.nlmmalagasy.com
- www.nlmmalayalam.com
- www.nlmmalaysia.com
- www.nlmmarathi.com
- www.nlmmauritius.com
- www.nlmmexico.com
- www.nlmmindat.com
- www.nlmmizo.com
- www.nlmmoldova.com
- www.nlmmongolia.com
- www.nlmmyanmar.com

N
- www.nlmnepal.com
- www.nlmnewzealand.com
- www.nlmnigeria.com
- www.nlmnorthkorea.com
- www.nlmnorway.com

P
- www.nlmpakistan.com
- www.nlmpanama.com
- www.nlmperu.com
- www.nlmphilippines.com
- www.nlmpoland.com

- www.nlmportugal.com
- www.nlmportuguese.com
- www.nlmprcongo.com

Q
- www.nlmqatar.com

R
- www.nlmromania.com
- www.nlmrussia.com
- www.nlmrwanda.com

S
- www.nlmsaudiarabia.com
- www.nlmserbian.com
- www.nlmshona.com
- www.nlmsingapore.com
- www.nlmslovakia.com
- www.nlmslovene.com
- www.nlmsolomon.com
- www.nlmsouthafrica.com
- www.nlmspain.com
- www.nlmspanish.com
- www.nlmsrilanka.com
- www.nlmsuriname.com
- www.nlmswahili.com
- www.nlmswaziland.com
- www.nlmsweden.com
- www.nlmswiss.com

T
- www.nlmtagalog.com
- www.nlmtaiwan.com
- www.nlmtamil.com
- www.nlmtanzania.com
- www.nlmtelugu.com
- www.nlmthailand.com
- www.nlmtogo.com
- www.nlmtonga.com
- www.nlmturkey.com

U
- www.nlmuganda.com
- www.nlmukraine.com
- www.nlmurdu.com
- www.nlmusa.com

V
- www.nlmvenezuela.com
- www.nlmvietnam.com

Z
- www.nlmzambia.com
- www.nlmzimbabwe.com
- www.nlmzou.com

The Coverings of the Tabernacle

The first covering of the Tabernacle was made by weaving curtains with artistic designs of cherubim with blue, purple, and scarlet thread and fine woven linen. It reveals that the Messiah would come through the blue, purple, and scarlet thread and the fine woven linen and thereby save all those who believe in Him from their sins and condemnation.

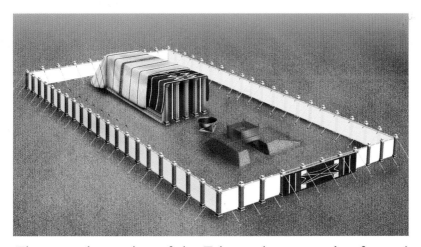

The second covering of the Tabernacle was made of goats' hair. This tells us that the Messiah to come would justify mankind by delivering them from their sins and the condemnation of these sins.

The third covering of the Tabernacle was made of ram skins dyed red. This manifests that the Messiah would come to this earth, take upon the sins of the world by being baptized, be crucified, and thereby become the sacrificial offering for the sins of His people.

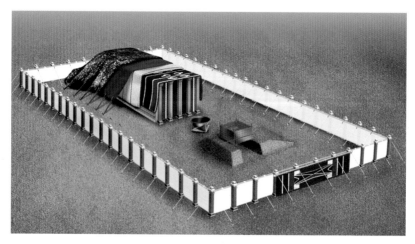

The fourth covering of the Tabernacle was made of badger skins. The badger skins shows us a portrait of Jesus Christ who lowered Himself all the way down to the level of human beings in order to save us from the sins of the world.

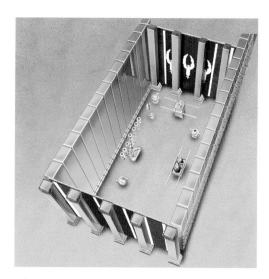

The holy place

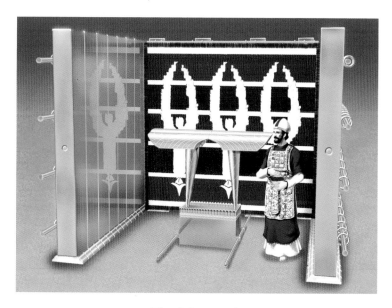

The Most Holy

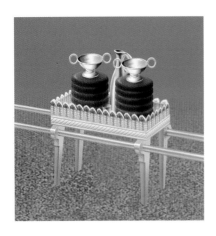

The Table for the Showbread

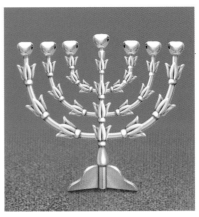

The Gold Lampstand

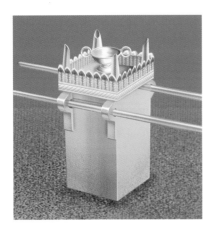

The Altar of Incense

The Ark of the Testimony

The TABERNACLE:
A Detailed Portrait of
Jesus Christ
(II)

FREE BOOK / DONATION
From THE NEW LIFE MISSION

http://www.bjnewlife.org
E-mail: newlife@bjnewlife.org

We, The New Life Mission, are looking for partners who are willing to co-work with us in mailing ministry or book distribution in order to effectively preach the gospel. If you are interested in these ministries, please read Paul C. Jong's free Christian book series first and then sign up for partnership at http://www.bjnewlife.org/english/join/join1.php in order to be a qualified partner.

Dear Readers of This Book:

The New Life Mission has been sending out Free Christian Books of Rev. Paul C. Jong through the homepage (www.nlmission.com or www.bjnewlife.org) in order to preach the gospel of the water and the Spirit throughout the entire world. We have been advertising our website on well known web search engines, such as, Google and Yahoo, which is on a cost-per-click pricing basis so that many more people can come to know the gospel of the water and the Spirit. However, this method of advertising has resulted in an increase costs for us in order to preach this genuine gospel to more souls. Moreover, the current global economic crisis has become an obstacle for our gospel ministry.

Therefore, we, the staff members of The New Life Mission, are requesting you to give our homepage address (www.nlmission.com or www.bjnewlife.org) to many people around you and bookmark our homepage on your computer so that you can access it easily while allowing us to save on these high advertising costs and still be able to preach the genuine gospel to many more souls. Your immediate cooperation will be highly appreciated as this will enable us to send out many more Free Christian Books to thirsty souls. This will be your first step in participating in this beautiful gospel ministry.

The TABERNACLE:
A Detailed Portrait of Jesus Christ
(II)

PAUL C. JONG

Hephzibah Publishing House
A Ministry of THE NEW LIFE MISSION
SEOUL, KOREA

The TABERNACLE: A Detailed Portrait of Jesus Christ (II)
Copyright © 2004 by Hephzibah Publishing House
All rights reserved. No part of this book may be reproduced or transmitted in any form or by any means, electronic or mechanical, including photocopying, recording or by any information storage and retrieval system, without the written permission of the copyright owner.
Scripture quotations are from *the New King James Version.*

ISBN 89-8314-354-1
Cover Art by Min-soo Kim
Illustration by Young-ae Kim
Printed in Korea

Hephzibah Publishing House

A Ministry of THE NEW LIFE MISSION
P.O. Box 18 Yang-Cheon Post Office
Yang-Cheon Gu, Seoul, Korea

♠ Website: http://www.nlmission.com
         http://www.bjnewlife.org
         http://www.nlmbookcafe.com
♣ E-mail: newlife@bjnewlife.org

Acknowledgement

This book is the second book of the two-volume series on the Tabernacle that follows my earlier publication of another two-volume series on Revelation. Needless to say, it is only by the grace of God this book is seeing its light. The more I write, the more I realize from the depth of my heart just how biblically sound the gospel of the water and the Spirit given to us by the Lord really is, how precious this gospel is, as well as how immensely thankful I am for having received the remission of my sins by believing in this gospel of the water and the Spirit.

Words fail me to express my profound gratitude to all the staffs and the coworkers of The New Life Mission who have labored tirelessly together in faith to bring this book out, and who have united their hearts to serve the gospel. I am sure that their precious, hard works will produce bountiful fruits all over the world. It is by the dedicated services of these faithful souls that this book could see its light, and it is by their services that I could follow the Great Commission of our Lord to spread the gospel to the ends of the earth. And I would also like to give my sincere thanks to Mr. Youngwon Cho for assisting us diligently with the translation of this book.

I give all glory and thanks to God for saving us all, and for permitting us the coworkers and His Church to serve the Lord's works. ✉

PAUL C. JONG

CONTENTS

CONTENTS

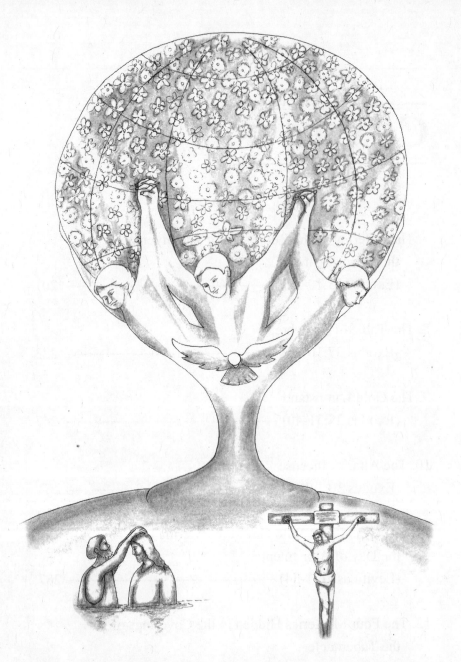

You can download Rev. Paul C. Jong's Christian Books on iPhone, iPad, or Blackberry by going to Amazon's Kindle e-bookstore (www.amazon.com).

Foreword

We Must Build the Sanctuary in Our Hearts Also

It is because those who still do not know and do not believe in the gospel of the water and the Spirit need this truth that I seek to testify the truth of the water and the Spirit revealed in both the Old and New Testaments. As I bear witness to the Tabernacle, it may seem like I am speaking of only basic principles, but it is my desire to preach to them the Word of the water and the Spirit that has solved away the sins of their hearts, for only then would those who are ignorant of the gospel of the water and the Spirit come to understand it and belong to God.

God called Moses and told him to build Him a Sanctuary where He would dwell. The place of God's dwelling is called the Sanctuary. In the door and coverings of this Sanctuary, the mystery of the salvation of Jesus Christ was hidden. When God commanded the people of Israel to build this Sanctuary, He meant that we also should build in our hearts a Sanctuary where He can dwell.

What must we do for our part if we want to have the holy God dwell with us? We must first, of course, know how God has washed away our sins through the gospel Word of the water and the Spirit. And we must believe in it. To do so, we must first see our fundamental selves. From our very birth, we had no choice but to be born as sinners. How, then, can the Spirit of the Holy Lord dwell in the hearts of people like us? For the Spirit of the Lord to dwell in the hearts of sinners, they must have the faith that believes in the gospel of clear truth. In

Free book request www.bjnewlife.org

other words, the Holy Spirit dwells in us only when we have washed away our sins by knowing and believing in the gospel of the water and the Spirit. That the Holy God can dwell in our hearts is made possible by believing in the everlasting truth of the water and the Spirit. This truth, that the Holy Spirit dwells in the hearts of those who have received the remission of sin, is fulfilled by the will of God.

The Sanctuary Where God Wants to Dwell

However, many people who have not yet received the remission of sin are ignorant of this truth. They do not know just how much God wants to dwell in their hearts. Why do you think God commanded Moses to build the Tabernacle? He did so because He wanted to dwell in our hearts. The problem is that many people, in their ignorance of this truth (the gospel of the water and the Spirit), spend huge sums of money to build colossal and extravagant church buildings and are deluded to believe that these are the Temples where God dwells.

Such people are willing to offer all the money that they had made throughout their entire lifetime to God, for they mistakenly think that their churches can become the Temples of the Holy God only if they construct luxurious and huge buildings. But would God be pleased if we build a big, beautiful church and offer it to Him? Would He really bless us if we do this? Would this church then become the Sanctuary that is dwelt by God? That is not true at all. This is only a product of the ignorant faith and thoughts of those who do not know the truth of the gospel of the water and the Spirit and have fallen into a great delusion.

The Sanctuary where God wants to dwell is not a big

church building, but it is your hearts that have been washed from sin. God wants to dwell in the hearts of the righteous who have received the remission of sin and become holy. To make this possible, then, do we have to give our prayers of repentance and be sanctified? No, this is not the case. Yet so many of today's Christians think and believe in this way. Is this not immensely unfortunate and saddening?

God said, *"Let them make Me a sanctuary, that I may dwell among them. According to all that I show you, that is, the pattern of the tabernacle and the pattern of all its furnishings, just so you shall make it" (Exodus 25:8-9).* As God said, He has washed away the sins of those who believe in the gospel of the water and the Spirit and blessed them as the ones in whom His Spirit can dwell. They are the ones whom God turns into His workers. God has shown us His workers the pattern of the Temple, and He has told us to build the Sanctuary according to this pattern, to what He has shown us. By this, God is telling us to receive the remission of sin through the gospel of the water and the Spirit, the mystery of the Tabernacle.

To build the Tabernacle through Moses, God commanded the people of Israel to bring Him offerings. As written in Exodus 25:3-7, *"And this is the offering which you shall take from them: gold, silver, and bronze; blue, purple, and scarlet thread, fine linen, and goats' hair; ram skins dyed red, badger skins, and acacia wood; oil for the light, and spices for the anointing oil and for the sweet incense; onyx stones, and stones to be set in the ephod and in the breastplate."* Accepting these offerings, Moses built the Sanctuary of God with these materials through the workers who received wisdom from God.

As God had commanded Moses to build the Tabernacle in the Old Testament, in the New Testament, God wants us to also build a Sanctuary in each of our hearts so that He may dwell in us. The materials of faith with which we can build this Sanctuary in our hearts are the Word of the gospel of the water and the Spirit. With the materials of this gospel of the water and the Spirit, we must wash away all our sins and be cleansed. By telling us to build Him a Sanctuary, God is telling us to empty our hearts and believe in the gospel of the water and the Spirit. We must all cleanse our hearts by believing in the gospel of the water and the Spirit.

This, then, raises the question of what kind of faith we must have for God to dwell in sinners' hearts. The answer is simple and clear. For the Holy God to dwell in sinners' hearts, they must first know what the gospel Word of the water and the Spirit is telling them, and then they must believe in it. Only when they believe in the gospel of the water and the Spirit can their hearts be cleansed and receive the remission of sin, and only then can the Holy Lord finally dwell as the Holy Spirit in the hearts of such people who have received the remission of sin. And when the righteous who have received the remission of sin cast aside their stubbornness and decide to believe in the gospel of the water and the Spirit, which is the providence of God, God then comes to dwell in their hearts.

This is why 1 Corinthians 3:16-17 states, *"Do you not know that you are the temple of God and that the Spirit of God dwells in you? If anyone defiles the temple of God, God will destroy him. For the temple of God is holy, which temple you are."* God is holy and completely sinless. He cannot abide in a sinner's heart. Therefore, He can only come into our hearts just when they are perfectly cleansed by the gospel Word of the water and the Spirit. The Bible clearly says that only those who have received the remission of sin can receive the gift of the Holy Spirit (Acts 2:38).

This Word of truth is greatly blessing to those of us who

have been born again, but for those who have not yet receive the remission of sin, it is extremely difficult to understand. "How can the Holy God dwell in human hearts?" For theologians and ministers who have not been born again, such a question cannot be untangled forever. If we pose this question to the people of today who are yet to be born again and ask them for its exact answer, whether they are ministers, deacons, or elders, a satisfactory answer would be hard to come by. Of course, those who know and believe in the truth of the water and the Spirit have the answer to such an easy question.

What, then, must we do now? Actually, the Sanctuary that enables God to dwell in our hearts is built when we believe in the gospel of the water and the Spirit with our hearts. There is no other way to build the Sanctuary but this. Our hearts can turn into a clean Sanctuary where God can dwell only when we believe in the gospel of the water and the Spirit, thereby washing away all the sins of our hearts and standing before God.

When we cleanse away all the sins of our hearts by believing in the gospel of the water and the Spirit, God then comes to dwell in them. It is by believing in the gospel of the water and the Spirit that you can build the holy Temple in your hearts. It is highly likely that until now, at least some of you have probably been giving your prayers of repentance to cleanse your hearts, trying to build the Temple by yourselves. But now is the time for you to abandon this false faith and be transformed by the renewing of your minds by believing in this gospel of the water and the Spirit.

The Gospel of the Water and the Spirit Is the Real Substance of the Sacrificial System of the Old Testament

In the Old Testament, the gospel of the water and the Spirit is revealed as the sacrificial system of the Tabernacle. The core truth that must not be left out of the Old Testament's sacrificial system is that there must be the unblemished offering of sacrifice, priests, the laying on of hands, and bloodshed. Sinners brought the sacrificial animal consecrated by God, passed their sins onto it by putting their hands on its head, and drew its blood and gave it to priests. The priests then gave the offering to God on their behalf, cutting the offering into pieces and putting its blood on the horns of the altar of burnt offering.

On the Day of Atonement, the High Priest also had to give a sin offering for himself and his household before giving the offering for the people of Israel. Because God determined that the High Priest should first be remitted of his sins and the sins of his household before giving the offering for his people, he did all these things exactly as set by God. He then brought two goats as the sacrificial offerings, cast lots for them, passed the sins of the people of Israel onto the first goat by putting his hands on its head. Killing the goat, he then brought its blood into the Sanctuary to sprinkle, and gave Him the sin offering.

Then he gave the other goat as the sin offering for all the sins of his people. He had to lay his hands on the head of the live goat, and then confess over it all the iniquities of the children of Israel, and all their transgressions, concerning all their sins, putting them on the head of the goat, and then send it away into the wilderness by the hand of a suitable man (Leviticus 16:20-21). Here, we should pay particular attention to the very critical action of the High Priest—that is, *he laid his hands on the head of the live goat*. What is the consequence of this action? The Bible states that with this action, all the sins of the Israelites were put on the sacrificial animal. The Old Testament's sacrificial system set by God was all manifested as the gospel of the water and the Spirit in the New Testament.

We Must Satisfy God's Desire with Our Faith

What God wanted to do for the people of Israel was to deliver them from Egypt and lead them into the land of Canaan after living in the wilderness. God wanted to dwell among His people and be worshipped by them. It was to become their God and to make them His people that He had delivered them from Egypt. Like this, the providence of God for you and me is so clear and definite. He wants to deliver each and every one of us from the slavery of sin and make us His people. Yet many people are completely oblivious to this and just wasting their time in vain, a situation that is truly sad.

The sacrificial system shown in Leviticus speaks exactly about the ministries of Jesus who has saved us by being born unto this earth, being baptized, dying on the Cross, and rising from the dead again. This is the truth that has enabled us to wash away our sins and stand before God by faith. It is only when we become sinless and serve God that we can live this world by faith and spread the gospel to all its souls as we walk with God. When the path to receive the remission of sin is that clear, we can only pity those who are still wandering in their ignorance of this truth.

For God to dwell in the hearts of sinners, they must first build the holy house of faith where God can dwell. How, then, can they build this house? With straw or wood? With bricks? But God does not want to dwell in such physically constructed places, for He is the Spirit. To participate in the works of God and build a house for Him, we must build it with the materials that He has specified to us.

In the Old Testament, God commanded the people of Israel to build the Temple with what He had told them—that is, with gold, silver, bronze, blue, purple, and scarlet thread, fine woven linen, goat's hair, ram skins dyed red, badger skins, and acacia wood. Like this, it is with the gospel Word of the water and the Spirit, the materials of faith set by God, that we must also build the holy house of faith in our hearts. This house must be built in our hearts. We must not build this house of heart where God can dwell based on our own thoughts and opinions.

If we want to build the house of faith dwelt by God, we must surely believe in the gospel of the water and the Spirit planned and decided by God even before the foundation of the world to blot out our sins. If we build the pillars of the court of the Tabernacle with mud, God will not then dwell in our hearts. To become the Temple dwelt by God, we must change our faith to what He wants, so that we may, by knowing and believing in His gospel, receive the remission of sin, please Him, and be loved by Him as we live our lives of faith. To do so, we must open our minds, and our faith must also follow the gospel of the water and the Spirit. Led by those who know the pattern shown by God, and who believe and follow it as it is, we must surely believe in the gospel of truth as set by God.

Like this, for you and I to have the Lord dwell in our hearts, we must infallibly believe in the baptism that the Son of God received and His blood. We must believe exactly as how He has saved us—that is, the Son of God came to this earth, was baptized, died on the Cross, and rose from the dead again.

By believing in this truth, we must cleanse away all the sins of our hearts. We must understand and believe so, for only then can God dwell in the hearts of those who believe. For us to be delivered from our sins, there is no other way but to believe in the gospel of the water and the Spirit.

Jesus Is the Door of Our Salvation

Jesus said, *"I am the way, the truth, and the life" (John 14:6)*. If we want to receive the remission of sin from God, then we must invariably believe that Jesus is the Son of God. We have to believe in our hearts that Jesus Christ took away all our sins onto His body, was condemned for them, and thus has saved us with His baptism and His blood on the Cross. We cannot thank God enough for this salvation. If we do not believe like this, all our faith is in vain, no matter how devoted we might have been.

We can never receive the remission of sin by anything else but the truth of the gospel of the water and the Spirit. The Apostle Paul said that when the last day comes, God will test our works with the true gospel to see how exactly we have believed in Him. Paul said that if our works are burnt and disappear, then such works of faith are all in vain (1 Corinthians 3:11-15). We cannot fail to come before God by believing in the gospel Word of the water and the Spirit, the Word of real truth.

When God tests our faith in the last day, all the works that we have built with our carnal lives of faith will be burnt by fire. The result would be the same if we build the Temple with hay, stones, bricks, or wood. With what, then, must we build the House of God? Invariably, it is with what God has told us—

that is, acacia wood, silver, gold, bronze, blue, purple, and scarlet thread, fine woven linen, precious stones, and so on—that we must build the Temple.

This tells us that we must believe in the gospel of the water and the Spirit, that our Lord came to this earth and has saved us, and thereby receive the remission of sin. When Jesus said that He is the way, the truth, and the life, He meant that He has blotted out our sins with the gospel of the water and the Spirit, the real truth. He is also the door to Heaven. As the gate of the court of the Tabernacle was made woven of blue, purple, and scarlet thread, and fine woven linen, Jesus the King of kings came to this earth in the flesh of a man, was baptized to bear all the sins of the world, shed His blood to death to atone them, and has thus opened the way to Heaven for us. By believing in this Lord, we have become the people of God who have received new life by faith, the ones who have received eternal life. But sinners still do not know this truth, and so even today they continue to build the house of their faith with hay that, in the end, would all be burnt down.

The True Workers of God Are Building the Temple According to the Pattern That God Has Shown to Them

This is why my heart felt the need to show the truth of the Tabernacle to Christians. The first volume of my Tabernacle series was oriented toward the Jewish people. Now, it is to the Gentiles that I am preaching the gospel of the water and the Spirit manifested in the Tabernacle that God has set for them. Just a few more additional discussions would sufficiently explain the gospel of the water and the Spirit manifested in the

Tabernacle.

If we untangle and explain the truth manifested in the Tabernacle, then we would have done all that we have to do for everyone. If they still do not believe, then there is nothing more that we can do, but regardless of whether they believe or not, we the workers of God will continue to spread the gospel of the water and the Spirit throughout the whole world. When we fulfill this work, it will make it possible for many Christians who have not been born again to be saved from all their sins. You and I still have the duty to tell the truth of the water and the Spirit. This is why we are working so hard to spread the gospel.

If we become idle with this work and fail to spread the gospel, then when those who believe only in the blood of Jesus are punished to hell, God will find their sins with us (Ezekiel 33:6, 1 Corinthians 9:16). Placing His confidence in us, God has entrusted us with this precious gospel. If we turn into indolent and wicked servants, and as a result people are able to neither hear nor see this gospel of the water and the Spirit, then we will be entirely responsible for this. God will then rebuke us, chiding, "Why have you not spread My gospel?" This is why we continue to work to bring the gospel of the water and the Spirit to people. When we do all that we are supposed to do, then we are no longer responsible for the fate of unbelievers who are cast into hell. It would be their own fault, for they did not believe even as they knew the truth.

What we must do now is preach the gospel of the water and the Spirit throughout the whole world. This is not just what I must do, but it is what all of us must do together. If people do not believe even as we had preached to them the gospel of the water and the Spirit, this is beyond our power, and God will not blame us, either.

Free book request www.bjnewlife.org

Already, many people are demanding us to provide them with the final evidence of this truth from His Word, asking, "Is the gospel of the water and the Spirit proven in the Tabernacle also?" If we testify to them what God spoke in the Tabernacle also, then they will have nothing more to say before this evidence, and our hearts will also be relieved and rejoice, for we would then truly have done all that we are supposed to do. We can only hope that each and every one of them would believe and be born again, so that their hearts may be cleansed and become the Temple of God's dwelling.

While we cannot be responsible for whether or not they believe in the gospel of the water and the Spirit, we must still fulfill our small duty to spread the gospel, which is in fact our solemn responsibility. It is to fulfill this small duty that we are preaching the gospel of the water and the Spirit. This is never an easy task. To make a single book, it takes devotion, faith, and patience that can withstand long and profound suffering, as a mother goes through her birth pain.

The fact is that it was for the Lord to dwell in our hearts that, in the Old Testament, He blotted out the sins of the people of Israel through the offering of sacrifice, the laying on of hands, and its blood under the sacrificial system, and, in the New Testament, Jesus came to this earth, was baptized by John, carried the sins of the world, was crucified, shed His blood and died on the Cross, rose from the dead again, and has thereby become our perfect Savior. It is by believing in this Jesus with our hearts that we can receive the remission of sin and have the holy God dwell in our hearts. There is no other truth but the gospel of the water and the Spirit.

The Gospel of the Water and the Spirit That Has Been Sowed Throughout the World Will Soon Bear Abundant Fruits

It is my most sincere hope to accomplish this before the Lord, who will return to this earth soon. I yearn for the Lord to come quickly and take us away. We all long for the day when the Lord would come to us and give us eternal life, just as He Himself had risen from the dead again. If we happen to fall asleep before the Lord returns, He will wake us, clothe us in spiritual bodies, and take us up to the Kingdom of Heaven. We eagerly wait for this day to come soon, for the day when the Lord will rapture us, take us to the Millennial Kingdom that He made for us, make us reign for a thousand years, and then enable us to live in the everlasting Kingdom of God in Heaven. Is this not the case? This is why I hope for the gospel to be spread throughout the whole world

The gospel of the water and the Spirit began to be preached from the Early Church period. Had this gospel maintained its momentum and continued to be preached for 2,000 years until now, the end of the world would already have come. But with the end of the Early Church period, the gospel of the water and the Spirit was interrupted and laid dormant. And as it is only now that this gospel has been resuscitated again and is preached around the world, the history of its spreading is rather short. As God said that He would bring both early and latter rains of the Holy Spirit, everyone will now hear the gospel of the water and the Spirit that we are spreading, and they will receive the remission of sin and eternal life as a result.

At this point in time when the final destination of mankind is nearing, we should in fact consider it an honor that God is spreading this gospel through us, and we should thank Him for the fact that we are taking part in this marvelous work of the spreading of the gospel and living our lives in its service.

Originally, our existence was such that we all deserved to be dumped into a trashcan and cast into a pit of fire. Born as the descendants of Adam, our common fate as human beings was one where all of us could not avoid but be cast into hell. Yet through His Son, God has washed away our sins and delivered us from our condemnation—how thankful and believable is this? You should all realize just how truly fortunate we are, for even as everyone else in this world is being swept away by the filthy and polluted floodwater of the world and carried to the sea of death to face the final demise, we have been delivered. We can only thank God with our faith for saving you and me, who had been bound to hell, from our sins.

This mission that we are doing will also be all finished soon. Backed by the works that we have already done, our mission to spread the true gospel is gaining its momentum, and as it picks up the pace, even more people in even more countries will surely receive the remission of sin. It is my hope that we would all follow God's will and spread the gospel to its full soon, and for the Lord to return before long. I know very well that the day when we will enjoy God's glory is not too far away. Truly, it will come soon. When we finish spreading the gospel throughout the whole world and God calls us, we will joyfully enter the Kingdom filled with His love and live in it forever.

Now is the time for us to lead all the souls of the world to the gospel of the water and the Spirit, so that they, too, could worship God the Father in the Spirit and truth (John 4:23). What all of us must do now is to faithfully fulfill, by our faith in the Lord, our duty to build the Sanctuary of faith according to the pattern of God that the Lord has entrusted to us—by believing, in short, that we would bear even more fruits than what we have worked for. I give all my thanks to God who has delivered us from sin. ✉

You can download Rev. Paul C. Jong's Christian Books on iPhone, iPad, or Blackberry by going to Amazon's Kindle e-bookstore (www.amazon.com).

SERMON

1

You can download Rev. Paul C. Jong's Christian Books on iPhone, iPad, or Blackberry by going to Amazon's Kindle e-bookstore (www.amazon.com).

We Are Not of Those Who Draw Back to Perdition Because of Our Sins

< John 13:1-11 >

"Now before the Feast of the Passover, when Jesus knew that His hour had come that He should depart from this world to the Father, having loved His own who were in the world, He loved them to the end. And supper being ended, the devil having already put it into the heart of Judas Iscariot, Simon's son, to betray Him, Jesus, knowing that the Father had given all things into His hands, and that He had come from God and was going to God, rose from supper and laid aside His garments, took a towel and girded Himself. After that, He poured water into a basin and began to wash the disciples' feet, and to wipe them with the towel with which He was girded. Then He came to Simon Peter. And Peter said to Him, 'Lord, are You washing my feet?' Jesus answered and said to him, 'What I am doing you do not understand now, but you will know after this.' Peter said to Him, 'You shall never wash my feet!' Jesus answered him, 'If I do not wash you, you have no part with Me.' Simon Peter said to Him, 'Lord, not my feet only, but also my hands and my head!' Jesus said to him, 'He who is bathed needs only to wash his feet, but is completely clean; and you are clean, but not all of you.' For He knew who would betray Him; therefore He said, 'You

are not all clean.'"

All the Word of the Bible is a mystery to the false teachers who are not yet born again. They therefore try to interpret God's Word in their own way with man-made thoughts. However, they themselves are not even convinced of what they are teaching. As a result, even among those who believe in Jesus, there are not many who have the conviction of their salvation.

Why is this the case? It is because they say that they believe in Jesus even as they do not clearly know the gospel of the water and the Spirit. Such Christians think that they would not be destroyed because they believe in Jesus. But they need to realize that when looked from a biblical perspective, it is only an accomplished fact for them to be destroyed unless they are born of water and the Spirit.

It is a generally held belief for people to think that although they do not know the truth, because they believe in Jesus blindly, they would at least not be destroyed. However, as they do not understand the scriptural Word correctly, they cannot realize from the Word that they are actually misbelieving, even as they have not been properly saved.

So if people interpret the Word of the Bible literally and come up with their own doctrines based on their own thoughts, then such people, even if they believed in Jesus, cannot receive the remission of sin and will ultimately end up in hell because of their sins. As such, the Bible is not something to be unraveled in our own way, but we must wait for God to bring us our understanding through His born-again saints with the Word of the truth. We must also realize that all the Word of God is explained within the gospel of the water and the Spirit.

Jesus said, *"Unless one is born of water and the Spirit, he cannot enter the kingdom of God" (John 3:5)*. Those who know and believe this passage correctly can indeed be delivered from all sins and enter the Kingdom of Heaven. Jesus said that only those whose hearts have been cleansed from sin by believing in the gospel of the water and the Spirit can enter Heaven. But if people believe without understanding the gospel of the water and the Spirit given by the Lord—that is, the truth manifested in the blue, purple, and scarlet thread and the fine woven linen of the Tabernacle—they will then be destroyed for their sins.

Just how utterly dismaying would it be if we were to be destroyed for our sins even as we believed in Jesus? It saddens me deeply to think that although there now are so many people in this world who believe in Jesus as their Savior, many of them cannot answer confidently when asked if they are really convinced that they have been saved from all sins. It is no mistake to say that all sinners, regardless of whether they profess to believe in Jesus or not, are to be destroyed for their sins. How many people would really be destroyed even as they believe in Jesus?

Matthew 7 tells us that although many who believe in the Lord would say to Jesus that they had prophesied, cast out demons, and done many wonders in His name, they will still be forsaken by Him. Jesus said that He would declare to such people, *"I never knew you; depart from Me, you who practice lawlessness!" (Matthew 7:23)* Our Lord said that not everyone who calls on His name would enter Heaven. Like this, the Lord will rebuke those who have misunderstood the gospel of the water and the Spirit.

Yet many people do not even realize that they have misunderstood and misbelieved in Jesus, a situation that is deeply saddening to our Lord. There are too many people who, oblivious to the fact that the Lord is actually rebuking them for their flawed faith, are heading toward their own destruction.

This is why our hearts lament for today's nominal Christians. They believe in Jesus only vaguely, still unable to reach a clear and biblical definition of what the true gospel of the water and the Spirit is. This is why it is such an important and urgent task for us to preach the gospel of the water and the Spirit to all of them.

It is critically important for all of us to know and believe in the gospel truth of the water and the Spirit. How, then, can we know the gospel truth of the water and the Spirit? By hearing, of course, the teachings on the gospel of the water and the Spirit contained in the Word of God. We really must know and believe in the gospel of truth and be called by God as His saints. It is by doing so that we can enter the Kingdom of God by faith, receive the remission of sin by faith, and become His own children by faith.

This is why Christianity focuses on salvation received by faith. The religions of the world prize one's own acts. But the real truth tells us that salvation is the gift of God, not of human works, lest anyone should boast (Ephesians 2:8-9). True Christianity points out the way to be saved from sin and enter Heaven only by knowing and believing in the gospel of the water and the Spirit.

Today's main passage from John 13 is also about the gospel of the water and the Spirit. Knowing that the time had come for Him to die on the Cross, Jesus sought to wash the feet of His disciples. This was right before the Feast of the Passover. The Feast of the Passover is of deep import to Jews. As it was the day when the people of Israel escaped from Egypt and were saved from their slavery, it had become a great holiday for

Jews. So the people of Israel recalled the Old Testament's Feast of Passover and held it in remembrance by performing Passover rituals together.

During the supper, Jesus gathered His disciples together and sought to tell them something holding great significance. By washing the feet of His disciples before He Himself died on the Cross, He wanted to teach them the truth that has washed their actual sins. With the advent of the Feast of Passover, Jesus knew that He would be captured as the Lamb of Passover, be crucified, die, and rise from the dead again. So Jesus wanted to teach His disciples that as the Lamb of sacrifice, He has washed away even their actual sins. Put differently, He washed the disciples' feet in order to give them a very important teaching before dying on the Cross.

The Reason Why the Lord Washed Peter's Feet

Let us see what Jesus said when He sought wash the disciples' feet and Peter refused: *"If I do not wash you, you have no part with Me" (John 13:8).* How critical and fearsome is this saying? However, Jesus really wanted to teach His disciples what kind of faith it took to wash away their actual sins, and how important it was for both His disciples and Himself that He should wash their feet before He died on the Cross.

So Jesus rose from the meal, laid aside His garments, took a towel and girded Himself, then poured water into a basin and began to wash the disciples' feet. It then came to Simon Peter's turn, but Peter kept declining. He said to Jesus, *"Lord, are You washing my feet?"* Peter was awe-stricken that Jesus would want to wash his feet. Because he had believe in Jesus and served Him as the Son of God, it was hard for him to accept such a preposterous situation. This is why Peter asked how come the Lord sought to wash his feet, thinking that if anyone should wash feet, it should be Peter himself washing the Lord's feet, and that it was neither proper nor courteous for him to let the Lord wash his feet. So literally shocked by this, Peter said, *"Lord, are You washing my feet?"* and refused to be washed.

Jesus then said in verse 7, *"What I am doing you do not understand now, but you will know after this."* This meant, "You don't understand now why I am doing this. But after I die on the Cross, rise from the dead and ascend to Heaven, you will then realize the reason why I washed your feet." And then Jesus said forcefully, *"If I do not wash your feet, you have no part with Me."* Unless Jesus washed Peter's feet, Peter and Jesus would have nothing to do with each other. Having no part with Jesus meant having no relationship with Him, and so Peter had no choice but to put forth his feet before Jesus. Jesus then put Peter's feet into the basin, washed them, and then wiped his feet with the towel.

When the Lord said to Peter, *"If I do not wash your feet, you have no part with Me,"* Peter, shocked by this, said, "Then wash me even more so that I may have part with You. Wash my hands, my head, and my whole body!" Hearing this, Jesus then said, "He who is bathed needs only to wash his feet. He is completely clean. You are completely clean, but not all of you."

Jesus often mentioned what made people momentarily perplexed and confused. Unable to comprehend what Jesus said, people tend to misunderstand, misbelieve, and do some bizarre things. Those who have not received the remission of sin by not believing in the gospel of the water and the Spirit cannot properly understand what Jesus said to Peter here.

Why? Because those who do not have the Holy Spirit cannot understand the correct meaning of the Word of God.

Not just anyone can realize the truth revealed in the Bible, even if he/she is a genius gifted with prodigious worldly brilliance. While such people clearly understand the Word of the Scriptures in its literal sense, unless they know the truth of the water and the Spirit, they just cannot fit all the puzzles together and find out with what kind of faith they can wash their actual sins no matter how hard they try.

The Lord said, *"He who is bathed needs only to wash his feet, but is completely clean; and you are clean, but not all of you" (John 13:10).* This passage is a very difficult passage to understand for many Christians today, for they cannot convince themselves with this passage whether they have already been remitted from all their actual sins or not. Actually, they hold this passage as the basis of the doctrine of prayers of repentance, one of the so-called orthodox doctrines in Christianity.

They interpret this passage like this: "Once we believe in Jesus as our Savior, then we are forgiven of all our sins including original sin. But, because we are too insufficient to not to sin everyday, and thus become sinners again, we have to ask God's forgiveness to be remitted from of these actual sins. By doing so, we can be cleansed of our sins, and restore our relationship with Him again."

Nonsense! Can you really cleanse your actual sins by offering prayers of repentance? What about the sins that you might fail to ask for forgiveness from your carelessness? How could these sins be forgiven then?

The Church, the body of God, is in fact the gathering of those who believe in the gospel of the water and the Spirit given by our Lord. So when Jesus said that the body is completely clean, but not all of the disciples are clean, He had said this in reference to Judas who did not believe in Him. It was because He knew that Judas did not believe in Him that He said, "not all of you."

We must believe that the Lord has washed away all our sins once for all with the gospel of the water and the Spirit, the pivotal truth of the Bible. So if we fail to know the key points of the Word and try to understand the Word of God in our own way, we can fall into great fallacies. Even now, many people, having fallen into great fallacies, are giving up all their belongings and even being martyred when they do not even believe in Jesus correctly, but in the end, they will ultimately be destroyed for their sins.

The Reason Why Jesus Has to Wash Our Feet

Why could Peter have anything to do with Jesus only if Jesus washed his feet? The reason was because Jesus could become Peter's true Savior only if He blotted out all the sins of his entire lifetime. Jesus came to this earth, took upon the sins of mankind through the baptism that He received from John, died on the Cross, rose from the dead, and thereby washed away Peter's sins and all the sins of His disciples once for all. Jesus wanted to imprint this truth on their minds. But because the disciples had thought of His washing of their feet only as a matter of ethics, they did not know the reason why Jesus washed their feet.

They had to realize that not only their present sins but the future sins that they would commit later would also threaten to kill them spiritually. So they had to realize that even the sins that they would commit in the future were already all passed onto Jesus by faith. Because Peter would have no part with Jesus unless this was the case, Peter had to realize the great lesson of Jesus washing his as well as the other disciples' feet. Jesus had to teach Peter the truth that by being baptized, He has washed "every and each sin" committed by Peter from his insufficiencies and weaknesses. This is why Jesus had to wash Peter's feet, and Peter had to have his feet washed by Jesus. Peter could have a part with Jesus only if he believed that all the sins committed by him during his lifespan on account of his weaknesses and insufficiencies were also washed away once for all when Jesus was baptized by John.

We can understand the truth of the water and the Spirit by hearing the Word of God. It is by knowing and believing in the Word of the gospel of the water and the Spirit that has remitted all our sins that we can be cleansed from all our actual sins also. Jesus said, "He who is bathed needs only to wash his feet." Because Jesus has already washed away all our sins and made us clean, those who believe in this are the ones who have been remitted of all sins.

Jesus Christ has in fact washed away all sins by being baptized in the Jordan River and taking upon all our sins. And by going to the Cross, being crucified, shedding His blood, dying, and rising from the dead again, He has become our eternal Savior. With the baptism that He received and the blood of the Cross, the Lord has become our perfect Savior. Like this, through the gospel of the water and the Spirit, our Lord has enabled all those who believe in Him to be washed from all their sins once for all by faith.

Those who know this truth and believe in it can be perfectly remitted of their actual sins also. Seen from God's viewpoint, it is true that the entire mankind has been washed from all sins by Jesus' righteous acts. All that we have to do to be actually washed of all our sins is receive this grace freely by having faith in the gospel of the water and the Spirit. Is this not the case? Of course it is! By our faith that believes in this truth, we have become those who have already been bathed.

Jesus said that those who have thus been bathed need to wash only their feet, because although we sin everyday on our part, Jesus already took upon all sins when He was baptized and has wholly saved us. By being baptized, Jesus has washed away all the sins of our entire lifetime, and it is by affirming this everyday on our part that we can be resolved of our actual sins.

This is what this passage is telling us. The reality is that even those who have received the remission of sin by believing in the gospel of the water and the Spirit—that is, Jesus accepted all sins through the baptism that He received from John, died on the Cross while shouldering the sins of the world, and rose from the dead again—still live their lives while sinning, for they too have the flesh. However, God already took upon even all the actual sins that people commit day in day out after believing in Jesus, for He is mighty.

Transcending time, from eternity to eternity, God has at once fulfilled this work that has blotted out all the sins of mankind. Like this, Jesus accepted all the sins of our entire lifetime through John after being baptized, died on the Cross while carrying them all, rose from the dead again, and has thereby washed away all our sins. Yet in spite of this, how do we believe? Despite believing in this truth, everyday we are still troubled by the sins that we commit in our lives and our insufficiencies.

This is why everyday we must reaffirm, with our faith, the truth that Jesus took upon all these sins that we commit throughout our entire lifetime while we walk on this earth. By being baptized, Jesus has washed away the sins of the world once for all, but we must affirm this truth with our faith day after day, time after time.

As Peter, to remain united with Jesus by faith, had to remember that Jesus had washed his feet, for us to stay within His salvation, we, too, must affirm everyday the truth that He has already blotted out all our sins with His baptism and the blood of the Cross. But those who do not believe in this truth cannot wash away any of their sins forever. Those who have not washed all their sins by not believing in the gospel of the water and the Spirit are the ones who have no part with Jesus. Though everyday they ceaselessly try to wash away their sins, their sins are not washed, for the sins that they try to wash by giving prayers of repentance are not such light sins. Every sin is followed by God's fearful judgment.

As such, those who try to wash away their sins with their own prayers of repentance, instead of washing them by believing in the gospel of the water and the Spirit, will experience and realize that not even a penny's worth of their sins is washed away. Could we wash away our sins by giving such prayers of repentance everyday? Even if we ourselves believe that we have washed away our sins with our prayers of repentance, these sins actually still remain in their entirety.

Only those who have bathed their whole bodies by believing in the gospel of the water and the Spirit are qualified to wash their feet as they live their lives, and only they are also clothed in the grace that enables them to wash away their sins with faith everyday and thereby keep their cleanness forever.

By being baptized, Jesus took upon all our actual sins once for all. We therefore believe that with His baptism, Jesus also took upon all the sins that we commit from our insufficiencies as we live our lives, and that He bore all their condemnation as well. Jesus told us, in other words, that there must be no such a thing as stumbling or dying from falling into our own weaknesses.

After Jesus washed the disciples' feet, all that now remained of Him was to die on the Cross, rise from the dead again, and ascend to Heaven. Jesus would now no longer be at the disciples' side, but as according to the written Word, He would be at the right hand of the throne of God the Father. And He will come again.

But if Jesus had died on the Cross without teaching His disciples about this, how could they have remained on this earth and spread the gospel of the water and the Spirit? Jesus' disciples would have lived while committing actual sins, for they were weak and insufficient, and not knowing what to do when they commit the sin of jealousy, avarice or hatred, they would not have been able to live by faith. How could they then have spread the gospel to others? They could not have done this. This is why Jesus certainly had to tell His disciples that He had already washed away even all these sins, and this is why He washed their feet.

Like the Remission of Sin Manifested in the Tabernacle

When we open and enter into the gate of the court of the Tabernacle, we would first see the altar of burnt offering and the laver of bronze. The first lesson that the Tabernacle provides us for our lives of faith is that if we have sin before God, the condemnation of sin awaits us. Our lives of faith, as indicated by the altar of burnt offering also, fundamentally begin with the condemnation of sin and death. We are to be condemned before God for our sins, but the Lord came to this earth to take upon our sins.

As the Old Testament's offering of sacrifice accepted the iniquities of sinners with the laying on of hands, shed its blood and died, and its flesh was placed on the altar of burnt offering and burnt with fire, thereby being vicariously condemned for the iniquities of sinners by bearing the judgment of fire, so did Jesus do this for us. Instead of us dying, Jesus received the laying on of hands from John, shed His blood and died on the Cross, and thereby paid the wages of our sins with His own death.

We sin everyday, and we will continue to sin until the day we die. You and I were the ones who could not but die for our sins. But to save such people like us from our sins and condemnation, the Lord forsook the throne of the glory of Heaven and came to this earth, took upon our sins by receiving baptism from John on His own body, gave up His body on the Cross, was crucified, and shed His precious blood, rose from the dead, and has thereby become our true Savior. Realizing and recognizing the law of death, that we must be condemned and die for our sins, is the starting point of faith.

Only those who know and believe that they must die for their sins can become the ones who can take the bath of the washing of sin and receive the remission of sin by passing all their sins onto Jesus by faith. True faith begins from such a belief. And we who have begun from this belief have become whole by confirming our faith that Jesus Christ has blotted out all the sins that we commit on a daily basis and washed away even the sins that we are to commit in the future.

Even the High Priest and his sons shown in the Tabernacle gave their burnt offering every morning and evening. They regularly brought their offering of sacrifice, laid their hands on

its head, drew its blood, and offered it to God. This is why
there was no chair in the Tabernacle. They, in other words,
continued to give offerings at all times that there was no time
for them to sit down and rest. Like this, we were such people
who sinned ceaselessly and could not avoid His judgment for
those sins, but Jesus Christ has wholly saved us from all our
sins with the baptism that He received and His bloodshed.

We must begin our faith by believing that we cannot but
always die for our sins. For such people like us, Jesus came to
this earth and took upon our sins once for all by being baptized.
Having taken upon our sins with His baptism, Jesus Christ then
carried all sins to the Cross and paid the wages of these sins
with His bloodshed by giving up His own life. And rising from
the dead again, He has become our everlasting Savior.

Romans 6:23 states, *"For the wages of sin is death, but
the gift of God is eternal life in Christ Jesus our Lord."* We
really were someone who had to die for our sins, but Jesus
Christ has saved us perfectly. In other words, by being baptized,
dying on the Cross, and rising from the dead again, our Lord
has given us the remission of sin and eternal life. Do you
believe this? It is from here that faith begins.

By any chance, do you not think, "I can follow Jesus no
more because I am too insufficient"? Do you perhaps think that
you are just too trashy and too carnal, and so even as you
believe in the gospel of the water and the Spirit, it is too hard
for you to plow ahead? This is the faith that draws back to
perdition.

Let us turn to Hebrews 10:36-39: *"For you have need of
endurance, so that after you have done the will of God, you
may receive the promise: 'For yet a little while, And He who is
coming will come and will not tarry. Now the just shall live by
faith; But if anyone draws back, My soul has no pleasure in*

him.' But we are not of those who draw back to perdition, but of those who believe to the saving of the soul." It is said that we are not of those who draw back to perdition. Those who believe in this truth are heavily persecuted, despised, and face many difficulties. But the inheritance of Heaven, which does not decline forever, awaits us. All things in Heaven are waiting for us their owners.

Hebrews 10:34-35 says, *"For you had compassion on me in my chains, and joyfully accepted the plundering of your goods, knowing that you have a better and an enduring possession for yourselves in heaven. Therefore do not cast away your confidence, which has great reward."* That is right. For you and I who believe in the gospel of the water and the Spirit, the enduring inheritance of Heaven awaits us. God has given Heaven as His gift of inheritance to those who have received the remission of sin.

This is why He told us not to cast away our confidence in His promise. Knowing that we are to receive great reward for our faith, we must not draw back to perdition, but we must make our faith even more firm and do not cast away our confidence. We must have the faith that believes in the gospel of the water and the Spirit, the real truth, fight our spiritual battle until the end, save souls and overcome.

We the saints must surely possess this faith that believes in the gospel of the water and the Spirit. We must have this faith, that even though we are so insufficient that we sin everyday as long as we live on this earth, the Lord has still saved us wholly by being baptized by John and shedding His blood on the Cross for us. It is by this faith that we can have great confidence and live our lives in uprightness until the end of the world. We must come before God by faith, run the race of faith with this true gospel, spread the gospel, and live our lives by serving the gospel. This is why the Bible tells us, *"For you have need of endurance, so that after you have done the will of God, you may receive the promise" (Hebrews 10:36).*

"'Now the just shall live by faith; But if anyone draws back, My soul has no pleasure in him.' But we are not of those who draw back to perdition, but of those who believe to the saving of the soul" (Hebrews 10:38-39). We who live with faith in the gospel of the water and the Spirit, are the ones who can also save others from all sins. When this is the case, despite having the faith that can save others from all sins, how could we draw back to perdition? If we do not keep looking toward the gospel of the water and the Spirit, then our faith will decline and we will end up falling into the swamp of death to die completely. Having received the remission of sin, our task now is to continue to run with our faith following the will of God, not to fall into our own weaknesses, remain where we are, and end up dying.

We who believe in the gospel of the water and the Spirit are not of those who draw back to perdition. We are the ones who have the kind of faith that can save other people' souls also. When we are such people, how could we just fold down and die because of our weaknesses? We could never do so. Those who believe in the gospel of the water and the Spirit are never the ones to draw back to perdition. No matter how insufficient and weak you and I may be, we are the righteous who live our lives of faith with great conviction in the gospel of the water and the Spirit.

You and I must think about from where our faith began, come out of perdition and live by faith. Fundamentally, we had been someone who could not but die for our sins, but by believing in the gospel of the water and the Spirit, the gospel through which our Lord has saved you and me from all sins, we have received our eternal salvation.

In other words, because we began our faith by completely acknowledging all our weaknesses, insufficiencies, incapacity and evilness for 100 percent, when we, having received the remission of sin, walk on this earth while sinning, we will not overcome unless we pass all our sins onto Jesus Christ by believing in the gospel of the water and the Spirit and wash them away with the faith in His baptism. This is why we must realize for sure that we are not of those who draw back to perdition, and really live our lives by faith.

Sometimes, bound by our own circumstances and situations, we may fall into various trials and difficulties, and as we are weak, our lives of faith may also collapse, unable to keep on moving. But we are not to die. It was to teach this to Peter that He said to him, *"If I do not wash you, you have no part with Me."* Jesus wiped out all Peter's sins. Just as the Lord was baptized and took upon all the sins committed by Peter throughout his entire lifetime, died on the Cross, rose from the dead, and thereby saved him, the Lord has also saved you and me from all our sins and condemnation.

Unless He had done so, how could you and I have anything to do with Jesus? Were it not for the gospel of the water and the Spirit, how could we have been saved from all our sins and lead others to be saved also? We could not have done any of this were it not for the gospel of the water and the Spirit. This truth is what Jesus wanted to teach Peter.

You and I have heard and understood this teaching, but how are we really? Don't we often feel depressed in spirits owing to our insufficiencies? Do we then fall into our own weaknesses or not? Because we see that we are so insufficient and weak, we are prone to fall into self-contempt easily. You may even talk to yourself, "How can I follow Jesus to the end?

I'd better stop following Him at this point! I am sure the Lord also thinks it better for me to quit His Church." Were it not for the gospel of the baptism that Jesus received, we would therefore have ended up falling into eternal perdition.

Believe in the truth that, even as you and I essentially had no other choice but to die for our sins, our Lord has already delivered us from our sins and condemnation. Even if our flesh is too weak and we cannot but sin again even after receiving the remission, we must still acknowledge the perfect and everlasting salvation of Jesus completed by the baptism that He received and His bloodshed.

You and I must confess our faith, "Fundamentally speaking, I cannot but die for my sins. That is right. But didn't the Lord come to this earth for me and took upon all my sins by being baptized? Didn't Jesus accept all my sins passed onto Him through His baptism? And didn't He die on the Cross? Didn't He rise from the dead again, and doesn't He now live? Since my sins were passed onto Jesus Christ, no matter how I am insufficient, and no matter how my insufficiencies are revealed, I am still sinless. I am therefore not of those who draw back to perdition and die." By thus believing in this way, we must cast aside our weaknesses.

Even if we have insufficiencies yet again tomorrow, by believing in the baptism that Jesus received in the gospel of the water and the Spirit, we can always cast aside our weaknesses. By our faith, we must cast aside the spiritual death and curses that visit us from our weaknesses.

We have to ruminate on this truth as often as we can, saying, "The Lord has saved me. Since all my sins were passed onto the Lord, do I still have sin or not? Of course I don't!" By thus believing, we can cast aside our weaknesses and sins, affirm the gospel of the water and the Spirit once again, and validate the fact we have been perfectly saved by faith. This is how we can run toward God everyday.

All Sins Disappeared When Jesus Was Baptized

Brothers and sisters, how important was this Word that Jesus spoke to Peter and His disciples? He washed their feet in order to make them stand steadfastly on the gospel of the water and the Spirit even after His death, especially when they would fall into their weaknesses. If Jesus had not washed the feet of Peter and the other disciples, what would have happened to the disciples when Jesus died on the Cross, rose from the dead again in three days, and ascended to the Kingdom of God? How would the disciples have resolved their weaknesses when they were revealed? They had to resolve them by the faith that believes in the baptism that Jesus received, and if they had not believed so, then it would have been difficult for them to resolve their weaknesses.

We must solve the problem of our weaknesses and actual sins with the faith that knows and believes in the truth manifested in the blue, purple, and scarlet thread and the fine woven linen, the ministries of Jesus. Had Jesus not taught His disciples about the power of the baptism that He received, His disciples would also have despaired and died spiritually. They would not have had the strength to possess the faith to dedicate their entire lifetime to the gospel, commit their lives to save the others' souls, and, in the end, even to be martyred, and they would therefore ultimately have failed to defend their faith and despaired.

But according to the oral tradition handed down to us, it is said that the twelve disciples of Jesus all preached the gospel and they were all martyred. Among the twelve disciples of Jesus, the name of the disciple who had the most doubt was Thomas. But even this Thomas went to India and was martyred there.

Where, then, was this faith that enabled all the disciples of Jesus to be martyred? This faith filled with confidence, that Jesus took upon all the sins of their entire lifetime by being baptized, that they had become perfectly clean as all their sins were passed onto Jesus, and that they had wholly become God's own children and would inherit Kingdom—it was precisely because they had this faith that they could spread the gospel of the water and the Spirit on this earth and go to God when He called them. All of us, in other words, can also be martyred with this faith when God so desires.

When Peter denied Jesus for three times at the High Priest's courtyard, he came to realize even more keenly what Jesus meant when He had said to him, "If I do not wash you, you have no part with Me." After Jesus ascended to Heaven, Peter and the other disciples of Jesus came to realize why Jesus had washed their feet, and to believe in and preach the gospel of the water and the Spirit with great conviction.

Today's Christians, if they do not know this truth held in the baptism of Jesus, will also find it hard to live their lives of faith and eventually quit believing in Him. If we are bound by our own weaknesses, our consciences would be corrupted from our inability to resolve this problem, and because of our corrupted consciences, we would no longer be able to come out to church. This is true for each and every member of His Church, even for our children.

Brothers and sisters, if you were bound by sin, would you be able to worship God? Today, even those who have not been born again go to church, give their prayers of repentance for their sins, and worship God, and they do so because they believe in Jesus only as a matter of religion.

But for those who believe in the gospel of the water and the Spirit, if they feel that their souls have sin because of their weaknesses and for being bound by them, they cannot come before God and worship Him. In times like this, we must cleanse our souls by believing in the power of the baptism that Jesus received, by believing that Jesus accepted all our sins through His baptism.

Those nominal Christians who are ignorant of the truth of the gospel of the water and the Spirit do not know the path of faith, either, and so they blindly try to be remitted of their sins through their prayers of repentance. Just as those who follow the religions of the world blindly supplicate to their gods, pleading, "I beg you, please forgive my sins and bless me and my family. I will do anything; I will give you more offerings, I will do good deeds; please forgive my sins," such nominal Christians are merely following a religion of their own making.

Jesus said to Peter, "What I am doing you do not understand now, but you will know after this. If I do not wash you, you have no part with Me." Had Jesus' disciples not realized the truth hidden in this Word even after this, they could not have been born again in this gospel of the water and the Spirit given by Jesus and do the works that saved even others from sin. Had Jesus, while washing Peter's feet, not planted in him the conviction of perfect salvation through the power of the baptism that He received, Peter would not have been able to be martyred and fulfill his role as the leader of God's Church.

Were it not for the truth of the gospel of the water and the Spirit, neither would we have been able to come before God and give Him the worship of faith because of sin, because of the sins that we continue to commit. Those who have been cleanly remitted of their sins by believing in the gospel of the water and the Spirit can come to His Church. And they are able to wash away their sins by faith wherever they are. Just as the Lord said that those who whose whole bodies are clean need to wash only their feet, whenever we sin out of our weaknesses, we must remember and believe that such sins of ours were also passed onto Jesus when He was baptized.

Our sins were passed onto Jesus when Jesus was baptized (Matthew 3:15). If the sins that were in our hearts were passed onto Jesus, do we or do we not have sin? We have no sin. Because our sins were passed onto Jesus once for all through His baptism, we have become clean as our sins were blotted out by faith, and because we are clean, no matter how insufficient we may be, we are still priests before God. This is why those who believe in the gospel of the truth of the water and the Spirit can swiftly come out of their weakness and go to God by faith, do His works by faith, thank Him for the salvation that He has given them, give Him the praises that glorify Him, and spread the gospel of the water and the Spirit to others also.

"What I am doing you do not understand now, but you will know after this." Did you know this truth when you first received your remission of sin? You might not. However, we all have heard this teaching and come to know it. Although you and I sin everyday and our insufficiencies are revealed, just as Jesus had washed Peter's feet, He has also washed our feet everyday.

At the beginning, we were rejoiced when we first believed that the sins that had been in our hearts from long ago and the sins that we had committed recently were all passed onto Jesus, but we have seen how our insufficiencies are revealed and how we are bound by our weaknesses even after receiving the remission of sin. In such times, it is by knowing and believing that Jesus took upon even such sins through His baptism that we can actually pass onto Him all the sins that we would commit in the future also.

Do the righteous, then, sin freely because of this? They never do so. Romans 1:17 says, *"The just shall live by faith."* Some people had stood against the gospel of the water and the Spirit, saying absurdly, *"Let us do evil that good may come"* *(Romans 3:8)*. Can the born-again sin more freely after they have received the remission of sin? Absolutely not!

When we think by believing in the gospel of the water and the Spirit, brothers and sister, do we have sin or not? Of course we don't! Also, even if we have insufficiencies, are we imperfect or perfect by faith? We are perfect. When Jesus told us that our whole bodies are clean, He meant that through His baptism, blood, and resurrection, He has made us perfectly clean.

We, too, came to know the power of the gospel of the water and the Spirit after believing in Jesus. As such, we must apply this power of the gospel of the water and the Spirit to our lives everyday. As we apply this faith everyday, we may perhaps become tired of it later on, wondering how long we have to do this. But, at this very moment, to where must we return once again? We must return to the Lord by believing that although we basically could only die for our sins, the Lord has saved us from all sins by taking upon our sins through His baptism, dying on the Cross, and rising from the dead again.

Remember that the priests had to give burnt offerings in the court of the Tabernacle everyday and wash their hands and feet at the laver of bronze every time they passed by it. Like them, we must think of the first love of the Lord and ruminated on it with our faith. We could not but die fundamentally, but the Lord took upon our sins and washed them away, and by being condemned for our sins on the Cross, He has brought the condemnation of sin to its complete end. In this way, with the baptism and blood of the Lord, He has saved us perfectly from all our sins and condemnation.

Everyday, we must engrave in our hearts this love that has wholly saved us, who could not but only die, and come before God by the faith that believes in this. We had no choice but to die, but because of the Lord, we have been perfectly saved and become the perfectly righteous children of God. When the Lord has given us such faith, should we not always have this faith with us?

We are the pilgrims who live on this earth only for a while and then leave. The word 'pilgrims' means travelers. Travelers mean those who move from one place to another. We are the travelers who stay in a place for only a short while and then leave for another place when we have finished our mission there. We are the pilgrims who are to return to the Kingdom of Heaven after living in this world for only a short while. As we live our lives as pilgrims to pass through this earth and go to the Kingdom of Heaven, there are times when we just wish to call it quits and flop down on the ground. There will be times when you, too, would also want to flop down, both carnally and spiritually. Times like these might come because while you yourselves are whole, your circumstances are not be so ideal, or while your circumstances are fine, the evil thoughts of your flesh keep rising.

To us who are like this, our Lord has given the Word that is so necessary for us. *"You do not understand now, but you will know after this."* Yes, now do we know. As we live our lives as pilgrims, whenever our many insufficiencies are revealed, and whenever we are bound by our weaknesses and trapped by our circumstances, we must remember that we have wholly received the remission of sin by believing in the baptism of Jesus who has blotted out even these things, and in the blood of the Cross. By believing in the gospel of the water and the Spirit, we have received the remission of sin perfectly.

When we look at the Tabernacle, we discover just how elaborate it is. As manifested in the altar of burnt offering as well, the wages of sin is death. Because we sin everyday, we had to be condemned and put to death everyday for these sins of ours. In the altar of burnt offering is manifested the truth that Jesus Christ came as the sacrificial Lamb, received the laying on of hands and died in our place. Passing the altar of burnt offering, the laver of bronze appears, where we ruminate on the gospel of the water and the Spirit to cleanse away our sins that we commit everyday. This gospel of the water and the Spirit is the perfect truth that has saved us from our original and actual sins.

What is the gift of God that is in Jesus Christ our Lord? Is it not the remission of sin and eternal life? The Lord has saved us perfectly. He has wholly saved us, we who were to die for our sins at anytime. All the sins that we commit throughout our entire lifetime have been cleansed away by our faith in the water and the blood, and by the Word, that the Lord has washed even our feet. Because the Lord took upon all our sins when He was baptized and all the sins that we commit in our entire lifetime were passed onto Him, Jesus Christ, carrying our sins, was condemned for them on the Cross and died, rose from the dead, and has thereby become our perfect Savior. It is when we wholly believe in this Jesus Christ that we become whole. And although our flesh may be insufficient, as we have the perfect faith, we will live spiritually blessed lives and enter the eternal Kingdom of God.

Are You Not Like Peter Now?

Just as Jesus had washed Peter's feet, has He not also washed your feet? It is right that Jesus has also washed our feet everyday. This is why Jesus took upon all our sins by being baptized, and for these sins, He died on the Cross in our place. And He rose from the dead again in three days. Like this, through His baptism, His blood on the Cross, and His resurrection, Jesus has become our perfect Savior. We believe in this Jesus Christ wholly.

It is by faith that we worship God wholly, and it is by faith that we do His works wholly. Our acts cannot be perfect. It is our faith that makes us perfect. This is why we must live as the disciples of Jesus by believing in the gospel of the water and the Spirit. We are not the ones to draw back to the perdition of faith. Though we may be insufficient, we can run by faith, and we must in fact run even more by faith. *"The just shall live by faith." "Seek first the kingdom of God and His righteousness."* Given the fact that we have become upright by faith, and thereby the ones who save other people's souls, if we do not dedicate ourselves to God-given mission of saving others, we will then fall into the swamp of perdition and despair and end up dying in our sins.

The sinless are rejoiced while doing His righteous works. They are rejoiced to spread the gospel of God that saves other souls. But the sinful are not rejoiced to do what is right. For those who have received the remission of sin, doing what is right becomes their spiritual bread. Spreading the gospel throughout the whole world is the right thing to do that saves other souls, but at the same time, it is also our own bread of life. From doing what is right, our hearts are filled with the Spirit, and new strengths spring up in us. As our spirits grow and mature, we become braver. So to live like Abraham, to be blessed by God and to share these blessings with others, we must love righteousness, love what is right, and love to spread the gospel. Even though we are weak, unless we continue to do these righteous works, our souls will die. We the just will surely die spiritually if we stop working for His righteous mission. This is why Jesus said, *"Blessed are those who hunger and thirst for righteousness, for they shall be filled" (Matthew 5:6).*

Jesus also said, *"Blessed are the pure in heart, for they shall see God" (Matthew 5:8).* Those who have received the remission of sin and believe that the Lord has completely washed away all our sins come to see God. And they come to believe in God, to follow, and to spread heavenly blessings throughout the whole world.

We have become perfect by faith. We could not but die for our sins, but the Lord came to this earth, was baptized, and died on the Cross in our place, and has thereby saved us perfectly. This is the truth, and the way to the Kingdom of Heaven. Realizing it is realizing the path of faith. There is no other way but this. We cannot enter Heaven by our good deeds. Only by realizing and believing in what the Lord has done for us can we enter Heaven.

By and large, if we were to divide people into two kinds, there are those who are used for what is right, and those who are used for what is evil. Those who are used for what is evil are not the ones who have properly received the remission of sin. By believing in what the Lord has done for us, we have become the instruments of righteousness, but those who have not received the remission of sin still cannot but remain as the instruments of the Devil, regardless of their own will.

At this hour, I say to you confidently that God has given us His perfect salvation, the perfect faith, and the perfect remission of sin. Are your deeds insufficient even as you believe in this gospel, and, by any chance, are your hearts drawn back by this? There is no need to be so, for the righteous can live by faith. Didn't the Lord, who cannot possibly be ignorant of our insufficiencies and weaknesses, already take upon all these things with His baptism?

Let me give you an everyday example of how insufficient we are. We play soccer together sometimes. When my team was in trouble, with the ball coming down from high toward our goalpost, I often just tossed it out or grabbed it with my hands. Was I a goalie? Of course not. I just wanted to win. On such a situation, all of us, the ministers, saints, and workers of God all alike do everything possible to try to win. You can forget about going easy; to win, we make all kind of foul plays. The game is so fiercely fought that everyone does everything possible just to win, so much so that there seems be no other game that reveals the naked, essential self-portrait of human behavior better than soccer. If our team is in trouble, we don't hesitate to makes foul moves, to play tricks, and to insist on our ways.

All these things are permissible for us, but if the other team wrongs us, we cry foul and demand the referee to issue a yellow card, but even the referee's ruling cannot be expected to have any effect at all. This is who we really are. We always want what is advantageous for what is ours, for our team, and for ourselves, and we only want what benefits us. Yet God has saved such people like us. Though we are still full of blemishes and rampant with lawlessness, as far as our faith is concerned, we have become the ones who have been born again without blemish.

The Lord has completely saved us from all our sins. This is why we call the Lord as the God of salvation, and the God of salvation as the Lord. The Lord is our God of salvation. Peter confessed, *"You are the Christ, the Son of the living God" (Matthew 16:16).* And the Lord approved his blessed faith as God-given one. The word Christ here means the One who took our sins upon His own body and blotted them all out. Jesus Christ is the Son of the living God. As the Son of God and our Savior, He has saved us perfectly. So, be bold in your hearts nonetheless, even if you may feel too insufficient and weak to serve the gospel.

Your souls, hearts, and bodies should not be drawn back and stooped; instead, straighten them out by faith and become the bold, great people of righteousness who are spreading God-given faith wide and far. Look at me. I have nothing to show in my flesh, but am I not spreading the gospel throughout the world? Are you not like this also? Do not think that those who seemingly appear to have no insufficiency are really free of any shortcomings. Sinners are only hypocrites. Hypocrites, too, are the same human beings as you are, and so how could their flesh be so good, dignified, and clean? What is always insufficient is the flesh of human beings. You have to realize that those who are showing off their virtuousness, especially in Christian communities, are merely showing off their hypocritical and fraudulent nature.

Our God has saved us perfectly. Therefore, we can serve the gospel of the water and the Spirit by our faith that has perfected us, empowered by this perfect righteousness of God. We thank God for enabling us to be saved by faith, through the truth of salvation that He had planned even before the foundation of the world. All your sins were already washed away when Jesus was baptized and shed His blood on the Cross. I hope you all believe in this truth. ✉

SERMON

2

You can download Rev. Paul C. Jong's Christian Books on iPhone, iPad, or Blackberry by going to Amazon's Kindle e-bookstore (www.amazon.com).

The Screen and Pillars of The Holy Place

< Exodus 26:31-37 >
"You shall make a veil woven of blue, purple, and scarlet thread, and fine woven linen. It shall be woven with an artistic design of cherubim. You shall hang it upon the four pillars of acacia wood overlaid with gold. Their hooks shall be gold, upon four sockets of silver. And you shall hang the veil from the clasps. Then you shall bring the ark of the Testimony in there, behind the veil. The veil shall be a divider for you between the holy place and the Most Holy. You shall put the mercy seat upon the ark of the Testimony in the Most Holy. You shall set the table outside the veil, and the lampstand across from the table on the side of the tabernacle toward the south; and you shall put the table on the north side. You shall make a screen for the door of the tabernacle, woven of blue, purple, and scarlet thread, and fine woven linen, made by a weaver. And you shall make for the screen five pillars of acacia wood, and overlay them with gold; their hooks shall be gold, and you shall cast five sockets of bronze for them."

The Holy Place

I would like to meditate on the spiritual meanings contained in the pillars of the Holy Place and the colors of its

Free book request www.bjnewlife.org

screen. The Tabernacle that we are considering here measured 13.5 m (45 feet) in length and 4.5 m (15 feet) in width, and it was divided into two rooms called the Holy Place and the Most Holy. Inside the Holy Place, there were a lampstand, the table of showbread, and the altar of incense, while inside the Most Holy, the Ark of the Testimony and the mercy seat were placed.

Consisted of the Holy Place and the Most Holy, the Tabernacle was surrounded on all sides by boards of acacia wood measuring about 70 cm (2.3 feet) in width and 4.5 m (15 feet) in height. And at the door of the Tabernacle, five pillars of acacia wood overlaid with gold were placed. The door itself, through which one entered into the Tabernacle from the outer court, was made of a screen woven of blue, purple, and scarlet thread and fine woven linen.

In the outer court of the Tabernacle, there were sixty pillars standing, each measuring 2.25 m (7.5 feet) in height. The gate of the court, which was placed at its east, was also woven of blue, purple, and scarlet thread and fine woven linen, and only by passing through this gate of the outer court could anyone enter into the Tabernacle's court. In this court of the Tabernacle were the altar of burnt offering and the laver.

Passing by these two, one would then come upon the door of the Tabernacle, measuring as tall as 4.5 m (15 feet) in height. This door of the Tabernacle had five pillars, whose sockets were made of bronze. Like the gate of the court of the Tabernacle, the door of the Tabernacle was also made of a screen woven of blue, purple, and scarlet thread and fine woven linen and hung on the golden hooks placed on the top of the five pillars. This screen was the divider that separated the inside and outside of the Tabernacle.

What We Must First Consider Is the Pillars of the Door of the Tabernacle

The five pillars of the door of the Tabernacle measured 4.5 m (15 feet) in height. On these pillars, a screen woven of the four threads of blue, purple, and scarlet colors and of fine woven linen was placed.

First of all, let us focus on the fact that the five pillars of the door of the Tabernacle measured 4.5 m (15 feet) in height. What is the meaning of this? It means that God Himself paid a great price of sacrifice in order to blot out our sins and make us His children. Because you and I are such insufficient and weak beings in our fundamentals, we live in this world committing so many transgressions. Because you and I are the worst sinners who cannot but commit sin every moment in this world, we have many blemishes and transgressions. These pillars of the door of the Tabernacle show us that in order to deliver us from such blemishes and sins of the world, God sacrificed His only begotten Son, Jesus Christ, as the wages of our own sins, and that He has indeed thereby delivered us from the sins of the world.

For our blemishes and sins committed in this world, in other words, Jesus Christ gave up His own body as a sacrificial offering before God and paid off the wages of the sins of the world more than sufficiently, thereby saving us. If a person committed a trespass, and sinned unintentionally in regard to the holy things of the Lord, then he had to bring a ram as a trespass offering, and he had to add one-fifth to it and give it to the priests (Leviticus 5:15-16). This means that Jesus Christ gave Himself up to save you and me from our sins and has thereby paid off the wages of our sins more than sufficiently. Our Lord came to this earth to blot out our sins and gave

Himself up as our own trespass offering for these sins of ours.

The offerings of the Bible, such as burn offerings, sin offerings, and peace offerings, were given so that the people who sinned could make their sins disappear by laying their hands on their sacrificial offerings and thereby passing their sins onto them. Of such offerings, the trespass offering was one in which a sacrificial offering was given to blot out one's blemishes. This trespass offering was given, when one harmed another through negligence, in order to compensate the victim and restore the relationship. And the trespass offering involved adding 20 percent of restitution to the total restitution including fines and reparations. This was the basic requirement of the trespass offering. It was an offering that was given for the particular purpose of atoning one's blemishes when he harmed someone else (Leviticus 5:14-6:7).

Are you and I so far apart from sin? Do we not live our entire lifetimes while sinning? We cannot avoid but do so, for you and I are the descendants of Adam. We ourselves know just how many shortcomings we have, and how we live our lives while committing so many sins. How many evils have we done against each other and against God? It is only because we are too slow and insufficient to recognize these evils as sins that we often forget about them as we live our lives. But you and I cannot avoid but recognize before God that we have done so many trespasses against each other and against God, that we are simply sinners before Him.

To deliver such sinners from all their sins, God wanted to send Jesus Christ as their own trespass offering. By having Jesus Christ bear the condemnation of our sins through the price of His sacrifice, God has given us the gift of salvation. When God the Father sent His Son to this earth and had Him be baptized and crucified, all to save us from all our sins and make us His own people, how could we ever compare ourselves to the preciousness of this sacrifice? To save us sinners from all our sins, our Lord was sacrificed to pay all the wages of sins, and has thereby saved us from the sins of the world. How could this be anything else but the amazing grace of God? How deep, wide, and high is the love of God? The very fact that the pillars of the door of the Tabernacle were as high as 4.5 m (15 feet) tells us about God's love for us given through Jesus Christ.

To deliver such worthless beings as us from the condemnation of sin, our Lord has saved us through His own sacrifice—I thank Him for this truth. When we could not avoid but be bound to hell for the punishment of our sins, and when the Lord gave up His own body for us to save us from these sins of ours, how could we possibly not thank Him? We give thanks to Him! By being baptized by John, Jesus took upon our sins on His precious body, paid the wages of our sins with the blood of the Cross, and has thereby saved us from all our sins and condemnation. We can therefore only thank Him with our faith in this gospel. This is the profound meaning of salvation contained in the pillars of the door of the Tabernacle.

Each of the five pillars of the door of the Tabernacle was 4.5 m in height. The number "5" implies "God's grace" in the Bible. Therefore, that there were five pillars implies the gift of salvation that God has given us. By loving us and clothing us in His love of salvation, God made us not to lack anything at all to become His own people. In the Bible, gold refers to the faith that believes in God who has saved us through His blue, purple, and scarlet thread and fine woven linen. By gold, in other words, the Bible speaks of the "faith" that believes wholeheartedly in the truth that God Himself came to this earth, took upon our sins by being baptized, died on the Cross, rose from the dead, and has thereby made us perfectly righteous. This is why the pillars of the Holy Place were all overlaid with gold.

That the sockets of the pillars of the Tabernacle's door were made of bronze manifests that the Lord, being condemned vicariously, has saved us, who truly could not avoid but be bound to hell because of our sin, through His baptism and the blood of the Cross. Because we were so full of blemishes, we had been worthless beings who really could not avoid but be put to death, and yet to make us His own people, the absolute and holy God sacrificed Himself, who is far worthier than us, and has thereby made us the children of God the Father. This is why gold refers to the faith that believes in this truth. This is how we must understand the colors of the door of the Tabernacle, and we must also meditate on it, thank for it, and believe it in the center of our hearts.

The Bronze Sockets of the Pillars of the Tabernacle

In the Tabernacle, only the sockets of the pillars of its door were made of bronze. This means that on this earth you and I have committed many sins against each other and against God, and that we therefore could not avoid but be condemned for these sins. The truth hidden in these bronze sockets makes us think about the altar of burnt offering. The first thing that sinners encountered when entering into the court of the Tabernacle through its gate was this altar of burnt offering where burnt offerings were given.

The word "altar" here has the meaning of "ascending." The altar of burnt offering refers to none other than the truth that Jesus Christ was baptized and then sacrificed on the Cross vicariously instead of us all sinners. The altar of burnt offering was the place where the offerings that had accepted sins through the laying on of hands were put to death as the punishment of these sins. Priests put the blood of these sacrificial offerings on the horns of the altar of burnt offering, poured the rest of the blood on the sand ground below it, and burnt their flesh on the altar by fire. It was the place of death where the offerings that took upon sins were killed.

The altar of burnt offering was placed between the gate of the court of the Tabernacle and the Tabernacle itself. As such, whoever sought to enter the Tabernacle had to first pass through this altar of burnt offering. Without going through the altar of burnt offering, therefore, there was absolutely no way to enter the Tabernacle. It goes without saying that the altar of burnt offering is precisely the shadow of the baptism of Jesus Christ and the Cross. And the baptism of our Lord and the Cross are what remits the iniquities of all the sinners who come before God.

As such, without first bringing their sins and stopping at the altar of burnt offering, and without remembering that the sacrificial offering has saved them from their sins by taking upon these sins through the laying on of hands and shedding its blood of sacrifice at this place, no sinner can ever go before God. This faith is the way to go before God, and at the same time it is what leads us to the blessing of the remission of our sin and of bearing the punishment of sin (that is, dying to sin).

When the people of Israel brought an offering to remit their sins, they first passed their sins to the offering by laying their hands on its head, killed it and drew its blood of sacrifice, and then put this blood on the horns of the altar of burnt offering and poured all the remaining blood at the base of the

Free book request www.bjnewlife.org

altar. The ground under the altar of burnt offering was earth. Earth here refers to the hearts of human beings. As such, it tells us that sinners receive the remission of sin by believing in their hearts that the offering of sacrifice accepted their sins and died in their place, all in accordance to the law of salvation. The horns of the altar of burnt offering tell us of the sins that are written in the Book of Judgment spiritually.

Sinners of the Old Testament's time could receive the remission of their sins by believing in the fact that they had laid their hands on the head of the sacrificial offering and thereby passed their sins onto it, and that this offering then shed its blood and was given on the altar of burnt offering. If there had not been the laying on of hands and the death and burning of the sacrificial offering, which made it possible for sinners to atone their sins, the way for them to go before God would have been completely blocked, and they would no longer have been able to go before the holy God. In short, there was no other truth except this sacrificial system that enabled them to go before God.

Like this, without our faith in the baptism of Jesus Christ, His death, and His sacrifice of atonement, there is no way for us to receive the remission of our sins and go before God. No matter how the people of Israel might have brought the most beautiful, perfect, cute and unblemished lamb to their priests, if their hands had not been laid on its head, if it had not thereby accepted their sins, and if it had not bled and died, then this would have had no effect whatsoever.

When it comes to our faith, if we do not believe that the baptism that Jesus Christ received from John and the precious blood that He shed on the Cross have remitted all our sins, then we cannot say that we have received the perfect remission of sins. The baptism that Jesus received and His death on the

Cross clearly stand between sinners and God the Father, and they have therefore become the interceding factors that save sinners from their iniquities.

The altar of burnt offering is a model that contains the plan of salvation that the Almighty God Himself in Heaven had arranged and fulfilled in Jesus Christ. Moses built the Tabernacle according to the method of salvation and the pattern that God had shown to him on the Mountain Sinai. When we look in the Bible, we can see that this instruction was repeatedly given. As Exodus 25:40 states, *"And see to it that you make them according to the pattern which was shown you on the mountain."*

People could make a cross and hang Jesus Christ on it, but beyond this, they could not do anything else. They could bind Him by the hands and drag Him to Calvary. They crucified Him while they didn't know what they were doing before God. Sinners could go this far because these things had to be fulfilled all according to the providence that God had already planned. However, it is Jesus Christ who has saved all sinners through His baptism and the blood of the Cross once for all, by being baptized by John the Baptist and thereby taking upon sins of the world, washing them all away at once, and shedding His blood on the Cross.

As such, before the death of the Lord Jesus Christ on the Cross, His baptism received from John was the most critical event absolutely indispensable to our salvation. His bearing of sins and their condemnation was determined by God even before the creation. In John 3, Jesus told Nicodemus that this is the gospel of the water and the Spirit. Therefore, the baptism of Jesus and the Cross are the providence of God planned and determined beforehand in Jesus Christ.

Jesus Himself said, *"For God so loved the world that He*

gave His only begotten Son, that whoever believes in Him should not perish but have everlasting life" (John 3:16). And on the baptism of Jesus, Peter also said, "There is also an antitype which now saves us—baptism" (1 Peter 3:21). It is also written in the Book of Acts, "Him, being delivered by the determined purpose and foreknowledge of God, you have taken by lawless hands, have crucified, and put to death" (Acts 2:23).

The baptism that Jesus received and the blood of the Cross were all fulfilled by the purpose and plan of the Almighty God. As such, because no one can enter the Kingdom of God without accepting this truth into their hearts and believing in this truth, we must realize that God demands from us faith, and we must have it. Without the faith that believes in the gospel of the water and the Spirit, no one can be saved. And had Jesus not decided, of His own volition, to be baptized by John, to deliver Himself to the hands of sinners, and to shed His blood on the Cross, then sinners would never have been able to crucify Him. Jesus was not coerced to be dragged to Calvary by others, but it was entirely out of His own will that He took upon the sins of the world by being baptized, shed His blood on the Cross, and thereby has saved sinners from all their sins.

Isaiah 53:7 states, "He was oppressed and He was afflicted, Yet He opened not His mouth; He was led as a lamb to the slaughter, And as a sheep before its shearers is silent, So He opened not His mouth." Therefore, the baptism of the Lord Jesus Christ and His death on the Cross were entirely out of His own will, and through them He has saved, once for all, those who believe in His baptism and the blood of the Cross from all their sins. On these works of the Lord, the writer of the Book of Hebrews also writes, "Now, once at the end of the ages, He has appeared to put away sin by the sacrifice of Himself" (Hebrews 9:26).

In the altar of burnt offering that shows us the shadow of the baptism of Christ and His death on the Cross, we can really witness the spiritual gift of salvation of Heaven. The death of the sacrificial offering at the altar of burnt offering implied none other than the very baptism and death of Jesus that was required because of the sins of everyone. In the Old Testament, sinners were atoned of their iniquities through their sacrificial offering that took upon their sins with the laying on of their hands and died in their place. In the same manner, in the New Testament, before the Son of God was killed at the hands of the cruel at Calvary, He first took upon the sins of the world by being baptized by John, and it is because of this that Jesus had to be crucified, pour out His blood, and die.

As such, God planned and predestined Jesus to be laid on of hands and to be crucified to death, all in order to bring peace between these murderers who killed His Son and Himself. God planned the law of salvation constituted by the laying on of hands and death, and according to this law, He allowed the people of Israel to receive the remission of their sins by giving Him sacrificial offerings.

In other words, God Himself became the peace offering solely to save sinners. How immeasurably profound, wise, and righteous this salvation of God is! His wisdom and truth are amazingly marvelous, simply unfathomable by us. Who can even dare to imagine His providence of salvation constituted by the laying on of hands and the bloodshed and manifested in the altar of burnt offering? Like Paul, all that we can do is just marvel, *"Oh, the depth of the riches both of the wisdom and knowledge of God! How unsearchable are His judgments and His ways past finding out!" (Romans 11:33)* The gospel of the water, the blood, and the Spirit is the only righteous gospel with which God has saved sinners perfectly.

The Horns of the Altar of Burnt Offering

On the four corners of the altar of burnt offering placed in the court of the Tabernacle, bronze horns were attached. In the Bible, these horns show the judgment of sin (Jeremiah 17:1; Revelation 20:11-15). This shows us that the gospel of the Cross is based on the baptism that Jesus received. The Apostle Paul therefore said, *"For I am not ashamed of the gospel of Christ, for it is the power of God to salvation for everyone who believes" (Romans 1:16).* Also, in 1 Corinthians 1:18, it is written, *"For the message of the cross is foolishness to those who are perishing, but to us who are being saved it is the power of God."*

Those horns of the altar of burnt offering clearly declare that God's righteous judgment and salvation have been wholly fulfilled through His baptism, His death on the Cross, and His resurrection.

The Two Poles Put in the Rings of the Altar of Burnt Offering

All the utensils of the Tabernacle built in the wilderness were movable. This was a method suitable to the nomadic nature of the life of the people of Israel. They had to roam in the wilderness until they settled down in the land of Canaan. Because their life of pilgrimage continued while they were passing through the wilderness, God made them prepare two poles to hook through the altar of bunt offering, so that their priests could carry the altar when the people of Israel were commanded by God to move forward.

As Exodus 27:6-7 states, *"And you shall make poles for*

the altar, poles of acacia wood, and overlay them with bronze. The poles shall be put in the rings, and the poles shall be on the two sides of the altar to bear it." As two poles were put through the four bronze rings of the altar of burnt offering on its two sides, the Levites could bear it on their shoulders and transport it when the people of Israel were on the move. The altar of burnt offering manifests the baptism of Christ and the Cross. As such, just as the Levites lifted up the altar of burnt offering with its two poles and carried it in the wilderness, the gospel of His baptism and the Cross is also delivered throughout the whole wilderness of this world by His servants.

Another issue that we must examine before we move on is the fact that there were *two* poles that enabled the Israelites to move the altar of burnt offering. Likewise, the gospel of the water and the Spirit is also composed of two parts. One is the baptism that Christ received from John, and the other is the punishment that the Lord Jesus Christ bore on the Cross. When these two are united, the salvation of the remission of sin is completed. The altar of burnt offering had two poles. Put differently, it had handles. One pole was not enough, for with only one pole, the altar could not be balanced when moving.

Like this, the gospel of the water and the Spirit is also constituted in two parts. These are the baptism that Jesus Christ received from John and His bloodshed on the Cross. In other words, the baptism of Jesus and His death on the Cross are mutually complementing elements that together constitute the righteous truth. The baptism and blood of Jesus have righteously accomplished sinners' remission of sin. Of these two (the baptism of Jesus and His death on the Cross), if one is ignored, then it is the same as ignoring the other. There can be no salvation without the baptism of Christ and His bloodshed.

His resurrection, of course, is also important. Without the

resurrection of Christ, His death would be in vain, having no result whatsoever. If we were to believe only in a dead Christ, then He would not be able to save anyone, not even Himself. But Christ, who was baptized, bled to death on the Cross, and overcame death to live again has become the true Savior to those who believe in the gospel of the water and the Spirit and come forth to God. And He has also become their eternal Lord of salvation and Protector.

Spreading only the death of Christ without His resurrection is only a contradiction and an imposture. And without the resurrection of Christ, His Cross would only have been a failure of God. It would also turn Jesus into merely an insignificant criminal. Not only this, but it would moreover make God a liar, resulting in a mockery of the Word of the Bible. As Christ was baptized by John, He died on the Cross, rose from the dead again, and has thereby become the true Savior to those who believe in Him.

The gospel that leaves out the baptism of Jesus from the whole gospel, which many of today's Christians are following, betrays God, deceives people and leads their souls to hell. And believing in such a gospel is ignoring and rejecting the Word of the everlasting truth of God. The false prophets who are teaching only the Cross of Christ are turning Christianity into just one of the many religions of the world. This is the reason why the gospel that they are following is totally different from the true gospel of the water and the Spirit.

Christianity is the sole religion that believes in the only God and the living Christ. However, even as Christianity may appear to be above all other religions of the world and proclaim itself as the real truth, if it only expounds on its monotheistic belief while leaving out faith in the gospel of the water and the Spirit, then it is not a faith of love and truth, but only a religion of arrogance.

The Location of the Altar of Burnt Offering

Here, let us once again consider the location where the altar of burnt offering was placed in the court of the Tabernacle. Of all the furnishings of the Tabernacle, the altar of burnt offering was the largest. It was also the first of the instruments of the Tabernacle that priests came upon in sequence when they sought to enter the Holy Place for worship. The altar of burnt offering is the starting point of faith in God, and it requires people to follow His formula in order to approach Him. In other words, the altar of burnt offering manifests the truth that people must solve the problem of all their sins by becoming believers rather than disbelievers, for not believing in the baptism that Jesus received from John and the Cross cannot allow anyone to go before the living God.

It is by believing in the baptism and death of the Son of God that we have been saved from our sins, not by disbelieving. We have been saved from our sins and received new life only by believing in the baptism and bloodshed of the Son of God. Because this very gospel of the water and the Spirit is so important, fundamental, and the most perfect, we must continue to repeatedly meditate on it in our hearts. We must recognize this gospel and believe in it. We must believe in our hearts that we had been all bound to hell, and we must also believe, together with this faith, that the Lord took upon all our sins by being baptized and bore the condemnation of our sins by shedding His blood on the Cross.

Along with this altar of burnt offering, that the sockets of the pillars of the Tabernacle's door were made of bronze tells us that we must admit the fact that we all deserve, because of our blemishes, to be cast into hell. And according to the judgment of God, which declares that *"the wages of sin is death,"* it is clear that we are all hell-bound because of our sins.

Yet to save such lowly beings as us, who truly must go to hell, from the judgment of all our sins, our Lord incarnated and came to this earth, took the sins of mankind upon His own body by being baptized, carried the sins of the world to the Cross, was condemned by shedding His blood, and has thereby saved you and me perfectly from our sins and condemnation. Only those who believe in this truth can join God's Church and become His people. The screen and pillars of the door of the Tabernacle show us that only those who have this faith can become God's people and enter His Kingdom.

We Must Believe in the Truth Manifested in the Four Colors of the Screen Door of the Tabernacle

Do you believe that the Lord has saved us by coming to this earth through His ministries of the blue, purple, and scarlet thread and the white, fine woven linen? The purple thread means that Jesus is God Himself; the blue thread means that Jesus, God Himself, became a man and took upon our sins by being baptized on this earth; and the scarlet thread means that Jesus Christ, who thus accepted al our sins, sacrificed His precious body by being crucified. It is critically important for us to believe that the baptized and crucified Jesus rose from the dead again and has thereby saved you and me perfectly.

Only those who truly believe in this truth can become the workers of God's Church. The pillars of the door of the Tabernacle refer to workers. They show us that only those who believe in this way are God's people, and that only such people can be used by God as His workers and pillars.

The white, fine woven linen tells us that those who have become God's people, the righteous, are the ones who truly have no sin at all in their hearts. The righteous are those who have received the remission of their sins by believing in the truth of the blue, purple, and scarlet thread. Our Lord came to this earth and has saved all sinners through the baptism that He received from John and the blood of the Cross. Since the Lord has saved us by giving up His own precious life, we cannot but believe in Him who came by water and blood (1 John 5:6).

The purple thread refers to the fact that Jesus is the King of kings. In other words, we must believe that the Lord has saved us, who are lowly and full of blemishes, by giving up His precious life, and that He has thereby made us God's people. Now, if only we believe in this truth in our hearts, then by our faith in the perfect salvation, we can all become the righteous who are sinless. We must thank God for giving us this gift of faith, so that we may have such faith.

In fact, that we have come to believe in this truth is, in itself, a gift from God. Our salvation from sin is also a gift of God. Has God not delivered us from our sins by giving us His precious life, far worthier than us? Because Jesus was baptized, died on the Cross, rose from the dead, and has thereby given us the gift of salvation, all those who now believe in this gospel can receive this gift of salvation and become God's own people. When it comes to salvation, there is absolutely no work of our own. There is nothing for us to do but just believe in Jesus Christ who came by the blue, purple, and scarlet thread. This salvation is God's gift for us.

Faith in Jesus begins by first thinking about "whether or not we are truly bound to hell." Why? Because when we first recognize and admit our sinful true selves, we cannot avoid but believe in the truth that Jesus became our own trespass offering for our sins. That we can be saved even when sinning is all that we can do is made possible by the gift of salvation give by the Lord who sacrificed Himself in our stead. Have we been saved by just believing in Him? Have we thereby become God's people by faith? Do we really have such faith? Can we confess that our salvation is God's gift, not of our works? Did we really admit that we had been all bound to hell before we believed in the gift of salvation given by God? We must reexamine these issues one more time.

The Tabernacle Is a Detailed Portrait of Jesus

The truth manifested in the Tabernacle seals off the mouths of false prophets. When we open the Word of the Tabernacle and speak about it before them, their deception is all revealed.

The pillars of the door of the Tabernacle were all overlaid with gold. This shows that nowhere in the Tabernacle has any human trace. Everything inside the Tabernacle were overlaid with gold. The pillars of its door were overlaid with gold, and the covering above the pillars were also overlaid with gold. However, the sockets of the pillars were made of bronze. This tells us that because of our sins and blemishes, you and I were all bound to hell. Is this not true? Is this not really the case? Do you really believe that you also were bound to hell because of your sins of blemishes committed everyday? That you were bound to hell for your sins is a righteous judgment rendered by God. Do you then admit this judgment? You must! This is not a mere knowledge, but you must accept it by believing in it.

The Bible says, *"For with the heart one believes unto righteousness, and with the mouth confession is made unto salvation" (Romans 10:10)*. When we recognize in our hearts that we were bound to hell, and when we believe in the truth that the Lord has saved us by giving us the gift of salvation fulfilled by His works manifested in the blue, purple, and scarlet thread, then we can all enter and live in the Holy Place. We believe that the Lord came to this earth, that He, who is far more precious than us, took upon our sins by being baptized, that He shed His blood and died on the Cross, and that by doing so He has washed away all our sins and saved us from our condemnation. By saving us through the blue, purple, and scarlet thread, the Lord has made us righteous.

We must truly believe in this in the center of our hearts. Only those who believe in this truth in the center of their hearts can become God's people and His workers. Accepting this truth only as one of man-made thoughts is not the true faith. "Oh, so the Tabernacle had this meaning. I've often heard about the blue, purple, and scarlet thread in my church, and so their meaning may be interpreted like that!" Even though you had believed in the truth only in your thoughts like this until now, now is the time when you must sincerely believe in the gospel of the water and the Spirit in your hearts.

The sockets of the pillars of the Tabernacle's door were made of bronze. But bronze sockets were used only for the five pillars of the door of the Tabernacle; the pillars for the veil of the Most Holy, in contrast, had no bronze socket, but the four sockets of these pillars were all made of silver. In the Bible, silver denotes God's gift and grace, while gold denotes the true faith that believes in the center of the heart. Bronze, on the other hand, denotes the judgment of sin. Were we not all bound to be judged by God for our sins? Each and every one of you had to be judged for your sins and blemishes before God and people. Is this not the case? I am not saying that only you were like this. Rather, I admit before God that I myself was like this. I ask this not only to you, in other words, but also to myself. And as for myself, I fully recognize before God that I had been bound to be judged by Him for my blemishes, and that in accordance to His Law, I had also been bound to hell because of my sins. I admit this clearly.

For such a being as me, the Lord came to this earth. He came in flesh as a man, took all my sins upon His own body by being baptized, bore all the condemnation of my sins by dying on the Cross, and has become my perfect Savior by rising from the dead again. This is what I believe. And when I believed so, my salvation that God had planned even before the creation was all fulfilled. It was fulfilled as I believed in this in the center of my heart.

Your hearts are like this also. By believing in this truth, your salvation that God had planned in Jesus Christ even before the foundation of this world is also fulfilled in your hearts. The plan of God to make you His people is fulfilled when you believe in this plan in the center of your hearts. It is by believing in your hearts that the true salvation comes about in the center of our hearts. Salvation is not achieved by our thoughts of the flesh. Salvation does not come about by any theological doctrines. Rather, it comes about only by faith in the truth.

This Salvation Had Been Planned in Jesus Christ Even before the Creation

Salvation is a gift that has been given to us in Jesus Christ through His baptism and the blood of the Cross. This salvation was actually fulfilled on this earth about 2,000 years ago. And no one is excluded from this gift of salvation, because Jesus had fulfilled God's plan of salvation to blot out the sins of everyone. As such, those who believed in this salvation in the center of their hearts have all become God's children. All their sins have been blotted out, as white as snow, and they have all received the remission of their sins for free.

Yet there are many people in this world who have not received the remission of sin. Who are these people? They are the ones who do not believe in the truth even as they know it. Those who have not confessed in the center of their hearts that they are bound to hell, and those who have not recognized the gospel of the water, the blood and the Spirit—such people have nothing to do with the Lord.

God's salvation is given only to those who know their own sinful nature and recognize that they are bound to be condemned and cast out to hell because of their sins. Where were the five pillars of the screen door of the Tabernacle, which were woven of blue, purple, and scarlet thread and fine woven linen, all raised on? They were raised on bronze sockets. You and I had been bound to hell because of our sins. Only when we admit this fact can our salvation be raised on this recognition. *"For God so loved the world,"* for you and I, the Lord came to this earth, was baptized by John the Baptist, shed His blood on the Cross and was sacrificed, and has thereby given us salvation from our sins.

As such, you and I must truly believe in the gospel of the water and the Spirit in the center of our hearts. At least once, our hearts must recognize, "I am truly bound to hell, and yet the Lord has saved me through the water and the Spirit." We must then believe in our hearts to be saved. As Romans 10:10

states, *"For with the heart one believes unto righteousness, and with the mouth confession is made unto salvation."*

We must truly believe in our salvation in the center of our hearts and confess it with our mouths: "The Lord has saved me through the blue, purple, and scarlet thread. I had to be cast out to hell and condemned, but the Lord has washed away my sins on my behalf, took upon my sins, bore all my condemnation in my stead, and has thereby saved me wholly. He has perfectly made me God's child." In this way, we must believe in the center of our hearts and confess with our mouths. Do you believe?

Do you, by any chance, still not admit the fact that you were bound to hell, even as you believe in the truth of the blue, purple, and scarlet thread, and even as you believe that the Lord has saved us in this way? The Bible says, *"All have sinned and fall short of the glory of God" (Romans 3:23).* The true faith is believing that even as all have sinned and therefore all had to go to hell, the Lord came to this earth, was baptized, died on the Cross, rose from the dead again, and has thereby perfectly made us righteous.

How amazing is this salvation? Is it not simply marvelous? The Tabernacle was not made in whatever way, but it was built according to God's Word in elaborated detail. Through the Tabernacle, God foretold us in detail that He would save us by giving us His precious life. He tells us, through the Tabernacle, that Jesus has given us precious salvation by being baptized and dying on the Cross, and what we must do is believe in this in the center of our hearts. Who can give you salvation for your sake? You can be saved by believing in Jesus Christ who came in the flesh of a man just like yourselves.

If somebody took upon your sins and was condemned

vicariously in your place, you would have more than enough reason to be thankful, but the Lord Jesus who is a million times nobler and richer than us made His precious sacrifice for our sake—just how grateful is this? How precious a gift is the fact that the exalted Lord has given us salvation with His blue, purple, and scarlet thread? How priceless is this gift? How could we not possibly believe it in our hearts?

This is why all who admit their sinfulness must believe in this truth. The ones who are qualified to believe in this truth are those who admit that they cannot avoid but be cast out to hell. Only those who recognize that they truly are sinners, and that they are bound to hell for sure, are qualified to believe in God's precious salvation, as well as to receive it by faith. And those who believe in the truth in their hearts can become the workers of God's Church.

We are just lowly beings who have nothing to boast of, even when we compare ourselves to those who have become famous in this world even with their marginal abilities. When this is the case, how could we ever dare to boast of ourselves before the holy, perfect, and omnipotent God? All that we can do before Him is just admit that the Lord has saved us even as we could not avoid but die because of our blemishes.

The Bible tells us, *"For the wages of sin is death, but the gift of God is eternal life in Christ Jesus our Lord" (Romans 6:23)*. Indeed, we had to pay the wages of death because of our sins. But because our Lord has saved us, who had been bound to hell, we can now enter Heaven by this faith. If we take out this faith, we are all bound to hell for the hundredth time. Is this not the case? Of course it is. We all deserve to be cast out to hell.

But because the exalted Lord with unfathomable love came to this earth, was baptized, and shed His blood and was condemned on the Cross, we have now escaped from our certain destination of hell. Because the Lord has given up His precious life for our sake, we have received the remission of sin. When this is the case, how could we not believe that the Lord has saved us from all our sins once for all, and that He has therefore given us the gift of salvation? How could we refuse to become righteous? How could you not believe in this? Just as the pillars for the screen door of the Tabernacle were overlaid with gold, so too must we completely wrap our hearts in faith. We must cover ourselves completely and wholly in faith. We must believe in the gospel of the water and the Spirit in the center of our hearts. Without believing in this true gospel in the center of our hearts, we cannot go before God.

It is by faith that we could become sinners truly bound to hell. It is by faith that we could also become righteous before God. It is by faith, in other words, that sinners can receive the remission of their sins—by believing that the Lord has saved us through His water and blood. This is how the Word of our Lord, *"as it is appointed for men to die once, but after this the judgment" (Hebrews 9:27),* is fulfilled.

When we were born into this world once, we were already to be condemned for our sins. However, God has given us the gift of salvation through our Lord Jesus Christ. By believing in the gospel of the water and the Spirit in the center of our hearts, therefore, we have been able to become God's children. God has given His unconditional love of salvation to all who believe. But He will judge and condemn those who do not believe in this gospel for their sins of unbelieving (John 3:16-18).

We Must Believe in These Two Facts of Salvation

We had been sinners who were bound to be condemned and put to death for our sins, but by believing in the salvation of the blue, purple, and scarlet thread and the fine woven linen that God has planned and given to us, we have received the remission of our sins. Truly, we must confess to God, "I am truly bound to hell," and we must also confess, "But I believe that the Lord has saved me through the water and the blood." We must believe in the gospel of the water, the blood and the Spirit; that is, in the truth of the blue, purple, and scarlet thread and the fine woven linen. It is by believing in this truth in the center of our hearts that we have been saved. It is by believing in the gospel that we are saved.

We have been saved by believing in the gospel of the water and the Spirit. People can become God's own people only when they believe that the Lord has saved all human beings who were bound to hell through the blue, purple, and scarlet thread and the fine woven linen. Do you believe? Only faith in the blue, purple, and scarlet thread and the fine woven linen is the true faith.

This is the spiritual meaning manifested in the screen door of the Tabernacle. Do you believe? When people come to believe in the truth in their hearts, then they can speak correctly about the true faith. The real faith is not just confessing the truth only with lips while not believing in the heart, but it is to confess one's faith with his/her mouth while believing in the truth in the center of the heart. All of you must believe in the salvation of the blue, purple, and scarlet thread and the fine woven linen that have saved you eternally.

We cannot thank God enough no matter how hard we serve Him. How could we then forget about our salvation?

How could we forget that the Lord has saved you and me, who could not avoid but be bound to hell, from all our sins? How could we forget the gospel of the water and the Spirit when our blemishes are revealed everyday? How could we ignore this gospel when there is no other way to be saved but through this very gospel? We are always thankful. We are always rejoicing. We cannot but always praise Him.

Those who do not know this truth say that God made human beings only as toys and is making fun of them. Standing against God, they say, "God must be bored. He made us as His toys and is playing with us. He knows that we would sin, and yet He just watches us committing sins, and now He says that He has saved sinners. Isn't He just toying with us? He makes us, and then He just plays with us in whatever way He feels like. Didn't God make us as His toys then?" A countless number of people think like this. They bear a grudge against God, saying that if He truly loved them, He should have made them as perfect beings, instead of making them as insufficient sinners. There are so many people who remain ignorant of God's heart and point their accusing fingers at Him.

We Are Creatures Made by God

Like plants and animals, human beings are also creatures made by God. But God did not make us human beings like plants and animals. Even before He made us, God had decided to make us His own people in Jesus Christ His Son and allow us to join His glory, and it is for this purpose that God created us. The purpose of creation for human beings was different from that of other creatures. What, then, was this purpose with which God made people? It was for them to live forever in His

Kingdom in all glory and splendor, unlike the plants and animals that are made to simply praise the glory of God. The purpose of God's creation of human beings was to enable them to know their own sinful selves, to recognize and believe in the Savior who has saved them as the Lord of creation, and thereby become whole and enter the Kingdom of God in the future.

God did not make us as robots or toys, but He made us so that we would become His children by recognizing the Creator, believing in the Savior, and being born again through the gospel of the water and the Spirit. As such, following this purpose of our creation, we will receive and enjoy glory. Although on this earth we sacrifice ourselves to serve other souls with the gospel, in the Kingdom of God, we will be served. What do you think God's fundamental purpose for mankind was? It was to enable human beings to enjoy the splendor and glory of God forever. God's purpose in creating human beings was to make them His people and allow them to partake in His own splendor and glory.

Why were we born? What is the purpose of life? Where did we come from, and where are we heading? Such philosophical questions have not been answered yet, and so people are still in anguish trying to solve the problem. Not knowing their own future, some people even turn to fortunetellers and sorcerers. All these are the results of the failure of mankind to recognize the very God who created us and to believe in the salvation that He has given them.

However, to make us His own children, God made us differently from all other creatures. And He has saved us through the water and the Spirit, having planned our salvation even before the creation with the blue, purple, and scarlet thread and the fine woven linen. By saving us with the law of salvation manifested in the blue, purple, and scarlet thread,

Free book request www.bjnewlife.org

God has indeed fulfilled His purpose for us.

Therefore, we must now know and believe in this purpose of God to give us eternal life in Jesus Christ. If we do not know this, then the mystery of life will forever remain unsolved. Why were we born in this world? Why must we live? Why must we eat? Why must we live our lives fatefully? How can we solve the problem of life and death, of aging and illnesses? Why must we go to hell for our sins? Why is life so tragic? Why is life so painful? All such questions can find their answers from God through the gospel of the water and the blood that has saved us in Jesus Christ.

God allowed us to be born unto this earth and has made us hope for the Kingdom of Heaven in the midst of our tiring and hard lives, so that He would save you and me, who had been bound to hell, from all our sins, and so that we would receive eternal life. When we believe in the gospel of the water and the Spirit, the mystery of life is all solved.

God Had a Great and Splendid Plan for You and Me

Just as God planned, He sent His Son Jesus Christ to this earth, passed all our sins onto His precious body by having Him be baptized, condemned and put Him to death for our sake, and has thereby saved us, who were facing eternal destruction, from all our sins, condemnation, and curses. Now, we must believe in this truth, and we must give our thanks to God for moving us from the unavoidable fate of destruction to the Kingdom of the Son of God, and for enabling us to enjoy eternal life. The truth of salvation from God, in other words, is the gospel of the water and the Spirit, which is manifested in the screen woven of blue, purple, and scarlet thread and fine woven linen, and hung on the doors of the Tabernacle.

The bronze sockets of the pillars of the Tabernacle's door shows us our fundamental sinful selves, and thereby enables us to believe in the gospel of the water and blood of Jesus. The pillars of the door of the Tabernacle and the screen woven of blue, purple, and scarlet thread and fine woven linen manifest the mercy of God that has saved us, who had been all bound to hell, from our condemnation through the precious sacrifice of Jesus Christ. By thus believing in the gospel of the water and the Spirit, I have been saved from all my sins. Do you also believe so?

Do you believe in the truth manifested in the Tabernacle? You and I are all lucky. It is a truly great blessing, for even as there are many people who are heading straight to hell, we have found the truth and are now living in Jesus Christ. We had indeed been worthless and useless in this world, where, being born into it, we could not avoid but only sin and be bound to hell, to live cowardly lives and be cast out to hell. But even so, our Lord came to this earth, was baptized, died on the Cross, rose from the dead, and has thereby forever saved us from our sins. We cannot but be amazed at the fact that not only do we have nothing to do with hell any longer, but we have also become enabled to do valuable, useful, and just works.

Those who can enter into the Holy Place are the ones who have received the remission of their sins once for all. Our Lord did not just blot out our past sins, but by being baptized, He took upon all the sins of our entire lifetime, and by dying on the Cross, He has blotted out all our sins forever. Therefore, only those who believe in salvation thus fulfilled all at once are the ones who have the faith of priests, and only such people can enter into the Holy Place.

Free book request www.bjnewlife.org

Strictly speaking, according to the Tabernacle system, ordinary priests could not enter the Most Holy, but only the High Priest could. And the everlasting High Priest is none other than Jesus Christ. Only those who believe that Jesus Christ has thus saved us can enter into the House of God, even into the Most Holy along with Jesus Christ.

"Now where there is remission of these, there is no longer an offering for sin. Therefore, brethren, having boldness to enter the Holiest by the blood of Jesus, by a new and living way which He consecrated for us, through the veil, that is, His flesh, and having a High Priest over the house of God, let us draw near with a true heart in full assurance of faith, having our hearts sprinkled from an evil conscience and our bodies washed with pure water" (Hebrews 10:18-22). Those who recognize themselves as evil ones destined to hell and receive the remission of all their sins by being cleansed *with pure water* (Jesus' baptism) and *the blood of Jesus* can enter the Kingdom of God to dwell with Him forever.

It is not because we have daily repented our sins that our sins have been cleansed, but it is because the Lord came to this earth, took upon our sins of the world once for all by being baptized, was condemned on the Cross that He has forever blotted out all our sins. *"For thus it is fitting for us to fulfill all righteousness."* Jesus was baptized and took upon the sins of mankind once for all, carried the sins of the world to the Cross and died on it, and rose from the dead again and has thereby saved us forever once for all. Only those who believe in this truth in the center of their hearts can enter into the Holy Place. We receive the remission of our sins once for all by believing that our Lord has saved us all at once, and that He took care of all the sins of our entire lifetime and of the entire universe.

Do you believe that the Lord took upon our sins once for

all by being baptized? And do you believe that He shouldered the sins of the world, died on the Cross, rose from the dead again, and has thereby become our perfect Savior all at once? Through His 33 years of life, our Lord has blotted out all the sins of this world forever. He has made them all disappear, leaving not even a single spot. I believe this in the center of my hearts. I believe that when He was baptized, He took upon the sins of the world once for all, that He bore the condemnation of all my sins once for all by shedding His blood on the Cross, and that He has become my perfect Savior by rising from the dead and living again once for all. It is by this faith that I have been saved from all my sins.

By believing in this, we all can enter the Kingdom of Heaven, and while we are living on this earth, we must meditate on this faith everyday. Why? Because the Lord took away even the sins that we are yet to commit. But every time we sin, we must confess. And we must believe in the center of our hearts that the Lord took upon even those sins with His baptism. We must recognize that the Lord took care of the sins of the world by believing once again. Why? Because if we do not ruminate on the gospel of the water and the Spirit over and over again, our hearts will be defiled. Because the Lord took away even the sins that we have not yet committed, whenever our weaknesses are revealed, we must thank Him with our faith in His ministries of the blue, purple, and scarlet thread.

We must all believe that the Lord came to this earth and took upon our sins all at once. Once for all, all our sins were passed onto Jesus Christ, for He accepted all the sins of the world through His baptism. As Jesus Christ has given us eternal salvation by being baptized and dying on the Cross, we must believe in this truth firmly and bravely. Our Lord Jesus says that we can take the Kingdom of God with our firm belief in His baptism received from John. Jesus said, *"From the days of John the Baptist until now the kingdom of heaven suffers violence, and the violent take it by force" (Matthew 11:12).* It is by this faith that we have been remitted of all the sins of the blemishes of our bodies, thoughts, minds, and flesh. By believing that our Lord took upon all these sins with His baptism and bore all the condemnation of sins, we must be saved from all our sins to take the Kingdom of God.

No matter how insufficient you might be, if you just have this faith, you are the people of faith. Though you are insufficient, the Lord has saved you perfectly, and therefore you must believe in this. As our Lord lives forever, so is our salvation perfect forever. All that we do is just believe in our salvation that the Jesus Christ has given to us. That is right! We have been saved by believing in Him in our hearts.

Because the Lord is our perfect Savior, He has solved away all the problems of our sins. Do you believe that our Lord was baptized, shed His blood on the Cross, died once, rose again from the dead, and has thereby given us eternal salvation? How marvelous is this salvation? Although we are insufficient in our deeds, we can still enter the Kingdom of God by believing in this truth. It is by faith that we will be able to enter the Kingdom of God and enjoy all the glorious majesty and splendor of God. Those who believe in the gospel of the water and the Spirit are qualified to enjoy them. But without this faith, no one can even set a foot into the Kingdom of God.

The truth that has saved us through the blue, purple, and scarlet thread and the fine woven linen had been planned by God in Jesus Christ even before the creation. As God determined to save us, He came to this world, was baptized and took upon our sins once for all, carried the sins of the world to the Cross and was condemned all at once, died once, rose from the dead once, and has thereby given us eternal salvation. This is our salvation made of His ministries of the blue, purple, and scarlet thread and the fine woven linen, and we must believe in this salvation. Only then do we become God's people perfectly by faith. Only then do we become God's workers by faith. We will enter into the perfect Kingdom of God and live forever.

The perfect God has saved us perfectly, but we are still insufficient everyday, for our flesh is insufficient. But how is it? When the Lord was wholly baptized, did He actually take upon our sins or not? Of course He did! Because our Lord took away our sins with His baptism, we recognize that all our sins were indeed passed onto Him with His baptism. Do you recognize that your sins were really passed onto Jesus? By thus doing so, Jesus carried our sins and the sins of the world to the Cross, was crucified, and thereby completely fulfilled God's plan of salvation. Though we are insufficient, we can enter the Kingdom of God by believing. By believing in what? We can enter the Kingdom of God by believing in His ministries of the blue, purple, and scarlet thread and the fine woven linen.

After we have received the remission of sin, it is the insufficient who have good faith and are doing well in the Church. God's Church is not a place where the strong reign, but it is where the insufficient reign by faith. Why? Because in God's Church, we can still follow the Lord by faith only when we know we are insufficient. It is a place of the caring and healing of wounds. As Heaven is a place where a toddler can *"put his hand in the viper's den" (Isaiah 11:8)* and shall not be bitten, the paradise on this earth is none other than God's Church. This is the amazing mystery of God's Church.

It is by faith that we enter the Kingdom of God. It is the violent of firm faith who take the Kingdom of Heaven. Do you believe in this truth in your hearts? I, too, believe, and this is

Free book request www.bjnewlife.org

why I give my thanks to God.

And it is because I am thankful to God that I am serving this gospel. I live for this truth and serve the gospel, for there are still many people who do not now the truth of the blue, purple, and scarlet thread. But right now, setting aside the question of whether others serve this gospel or not, what is needed is for you to first believe in it yourselves.

I hope and pray that you would all believe in the truth that Jesus has saved you from your sins once for all, and thereby be saved from all your sins. ✉

SERMON

3

You can download Rev. Paul C. Jong's Christian Books on iPhone, iPad, or Blackberry by going to Amazon's Kindle e-bookstore (www.amazon.com).

Those Who Can Enter into The Most Holy

< Exodus 26:31-33 >

"You shall make a veil woven of blue, purple, and scarlet thread, and fine woven linen. It shall be woven with an artistic design of cherubim. You shall hang it upon the four pillars of acacia wood overlaid with gold. Their hooks shall be gold, upon four sockets of silver. And you shall hang the veil from the clasps. Then you shall bring the ark of the Testimony in there, behind the veil. The veil shall be a divider for you between the holy place and the Most Holy."

The Materials of the Tabernacle

The Tabernacle was a small fold-up house covered with four kinds of coverings. It was made of various materials—its wall, for instance, were made of 48 boards of acacia wood. The height of each board was 4.5 m (10 cubits: 15 feet), and the width was 67.5 cm (1.5 cubits: 2.2 feet). All the boards were overlaid with gold.

The coverings of the Tabernacles were made of the following materials: the first covering was made of curtains woven of blue, purple, and scarlet thread and fine woven linen; the second covering was made of goats' hair; the third covering was made of ram skins dyed red, and the fourth covering was made of badger skins.

Free book request www.bjnewlife.org

As we have already examined, all the doors of the Tabernacle were woven of blue, purple, and scarlet thread and fine woven linen.

The colors of the four threads used for the veil door of the Most Holy manifest the works of Jesus Christ that have saved people from sin. As these four colors are the light of truth manifesting that Jesus Christ would give us the gift of the remission of sin, they are something for which believers are utterly thankful and grateful.

The Materials of the Doors of the Holy Place and the Most Holy

The materials of the doors of the Holy Place and the Most Holy were fabrics woven of blue, purple, and scarlet thread and fine woven linen. All the doors of the Tabernacle were made of these fabrics. One would come upon the veil door of the Most Holy after passing through the door of the Tabernacle that led into the Holy Place. The door of the Most Holy shows us that the Lord has remitted our sins with His four ministries manifested in the blue, purple, and scarlet thread and fine woven linen.

The blue, purple, and scarlet thread and the fine woven linen used for the Holy Place and the Most Holy are a shadow revealing that the Messiah would come to this earth, be baptized, shed His blood, and thereby complete the works of salvation. Among these, the blue thread is the shadow that manifests the baptism that Jesus would receive, and the scarlet thread is the shadow of the sacrifice that He would offer for the sins of the world that He took upon. To wash away our sins, our Lord was baptized and bore the condemnation of sin. This

Free book request www.nlmission.com

is what the veil door of the Most Holy implies.

The Floor of the Tabernacle

The Tabernacle was built on plain sand, the ground. The ground here refers to the hearts of people. That the floor of the Tabernacle was made of sand and ground also tells us that Jesus came to this earth in the flesh of a man to blot out the sins of our hearts. Because Jesus went experienced all the weaknesses of mankind, He washed all their sins with the baptism that He received and the precious blood that He shed on the Cross. Our Lord came to this earth to shine the bright light of truth to this world and resolve mankind's fundamental problem of sin. Jesus is the God of creation who made the whole universe and all things in it, and He is the light of salvation who came to this earth to deliver mankind from all their curses and sins.

The Pillars of the Most Holy

The pillars of the Most Holy were made of four columns of acacia wood. In the Bible, the number 4 means suffering. The pillars of the Most Holy show us that people cannot be saved unless they believe in the shining light of salvation manifested in the blue, purple, and scarlet thread and the fine woven linen. They manifest, in other words, that we can discover the bright light of salvation by believing in the gospel of the water and the Spirit fulfilled by God Himself through His suffering.

Whoever wants to enter into the Most Holy and stand

before the presence of God must believe in the shining gospel of the water and the Spirit, the gospel of salvation that God has prepared. But those who come to God without believing in the gospel set by God will face His fierce wrath. Those who stand before God must have the faith that believes in the bright truth manifested in the blue, purple, and scarlet thread and the fine woven linen. Through the shining light of truth, all of us must come out to the most holy place where God dwells.

The gospel of the remission of sin revealed in the Old Testament is the truth of salvation manifested in the blue, purple, and scarlet thread. The very gospel of the remission of sin revealed in the New Testament was fulfilled through the baptism that Jesus received, the blood of the Cross, and His resurrection. We can enter into the Most Holy only when we have the faith that believes in this most holy gospel.

We Must Believe in Our Salvation Manifested in the Blue, Purple, and Scarlet Thread

Hebrews 11:6 states, *"But without faith it is impossible to please Him, for he who comes to God must believe that He is, and that He is a rewarder of those who diligently seek Him."* God will live forever. And to give us eternal life, He has blessed us to receive the remission of sins through our faith in Jesus Christ who came to this earth in the flesh of a man, was baptized and crucified, died, rose from the dead again, and has thereby become our Savior. By washing away all the sins of our old selves with His vicarious judgment for our sins, and giving our souls the faith that believes in the gospel of the water and the Spirit, the Lord has clothed us in the holiness of absolute perfection.

By clothing us in new life, our Lord has enabled us to go before God and pray to Him. Moreover, He has also given us the grace of being able to stand before the presence of God and call Him our Father. All these things are the gifts of God that have come about by the salvation that He has given us. By bringing this salvation to us through the truth of the blue, purple, and scarlet thread, God has made us have the faith that enables us to be saved and to stand before Him.

If you and I were to die tomorrow, are we confident enough that we would all go to Heaven? Let us think about our future for a moment here. When people die, they all stand before the judgment seat of God. This can only mean that we must solve the problem of all the sins we had committed on this earth—how, then, can we resolve this issue? If we just blindly believe in Jesus as our Savior, does this not mean that we believe in a mere religion?

There was a time in my life when I had been ignorant of the gospel of the water and the Spirit and tried to solve the problem of my sins by blindly believing only in the blood of the Cross. At that time, I had believed obstinately that Jesus was crucified and died for people like myself, and that He solved away all the problems of sin. But with this faith, I could not solve the problem of the daily sins that I committed. Far from it, it was by believing in the salvation manifested in the blue, purple, and scarlet thread here that my spirit was wholly born again.

Are all our sins really blotted out when we blindly believe in Jesus as the Savior? The faith that enables us to go before the holy God is not found by believing in Him blindly, but it is found by knowing and believing in the truth. No matter how fervently we might believe in Jesus as our Savior, if we do not know the gospel of truth that has saved sinners with the blue, purple, and scarlet thread, then we just cannot meet the holy God. It is only when we have the faith that believes in the gospel of the water and the Spirit that we can meet the holy God. What materials of faith, then, constitute the truth that enables us to stand before God as the saved? What is the gospel that enables us to have such a faith? This gospel is the shining gospel of the water and the Spirit.

Our Lord came to this earth, took upon the sins of the world by being baptized by John, was crucified, shed His blood, rose from the dead in three days, and thereby fulfilled His perfect salvation for those of us who believe. If our souls desire to be cleansed of sin, it is only when we believe in the baptism that Jesus received from John (Matthew 3:15) and the blood of the Cross (John 19:30) that we can enter into the bright dominion of truth. Unless we believe in Jesus Christ who has come of the shining gospel of the water and the Spirit as our Savior, we can never have hearts that are as clean as white snow.

Sometimes, looking at the weaknesses of our flesh, we lament over them. But even so, because of the gospel of the water and the Spirit, we still come to give our thanks to God, for the Lord has blotted out all our sins with His baptism and blood. You and I could never have become holy in any other way, yet by believing in the gospel of the water and the Spirit, we have become holy. Our Lord has perfectly saved us from sin. By believing in the gospel of the blue and scarlet thread, we can discover the brilliant light of truth that has saved us from all our sins. With the gospel of the water and the Spirit, the Lord has made us sound and holy.

In Matthew 19:24, our Lord said, *"It is easier for a camel to go through the eye of a needle than for a rich man to enter the kingdom of God."* Those who are rich in spirit cannot be saved, for they do not believe that they can receive the remission of sin by believing in the gospel of the water and the Spirit. Only those who truly are poor in spirit desire to enter Heaven, ask for God's help, throw away their own righteousness and instead believe in the righteousness of God for 100 percent can receive eternal life by believing in the gospel of the water and the Spirit. The gospel of the water and the Spirit has shone the bright light of salvation so that we may be able to meet the most holy God. On our own, we can never become holy, but when we believe in the gospel of the water and the Spirit given by the Lord, we can indeed become holy and come into the bright dominion of truth.

We Must Abandon Religious and Doctrinal Faith

In John 3:3, Jesus Himself said, *"Unless one is born again, he cannot see the kingdom of God."* To this, Nicodemus asked in reply, *"How can a man be born when he is old? Can he enter a second time into his mother's womb and be born?" (John 3:4)*

To those who are not born again, being born again only by faith seems impossible. Sometimes, even His disciples didn't understand His Word and even doubted about it. Thus, the Lord once said to His disciples, *"With men this is impossible, but with God all things are possible (Matthew 19:26)."* Of course, it is impossible for human beings to enter the Kingdom of God with their religious faith, but it is possible for them to enter the Kingdom by believing in the gospel of the water and the Spirit. Although we cannot become holy by ourselves, those who believe that the Lord came to this earth, took the sins of the world upon His body through His baptism, was crucified, rose from the dead again, and has thereby shone the bright light of salvation that has forever blotted out all our sins—God has enabled them to enter His Kingdom.

The truth manifested in the blue, purple, and scarlet thread used as the materials of the Tabernacle is intricately related to the gospel of the water and the Spirit that Jesus accomplished in the New Testament. The gospel of the water and the Spirit, in other words, is the same as the truth manifested in the blue, purple, and scarlet thread. The blue, purple, and scarlet thread is a shadow of His actual salvation, and the gospel of the water and the Spirit is the real substance of this shadow.

We can therefore discover the bright truth of salvation through the gospel of the water and the Spirit and rest in it. There is peace in the shining gospel of the water and the Spirit, like a weaned child playing, resting, and sleeping peacefully in the arms of the mother. It is by discovering the most holy light in the gospel that we have been able to meet the most holy God. It is by believing in the shining gospel of the water and the Spirit that we can find the salvation that God has given us. It is only those who believe in this salvation given by God that can receive everlasting rest.

In short, believing in the most holy gospel of the water and the Spirit is the only faith that enables us to enter into the Most Holy. The faith that believes in this bright gospel of the water and the Spirit enables us to take the remission of sin as ours. Our Lord came to this earth, and with the truth of the gospel that has blotted out our sins once for all through His baptism and the Cross. He has now fulfilled the promise He had made to us with the blue, purple, and scarlet thread and the fine woven linen. Only those who believe in Jesus as their Savior and in the gospel of the water and the Spirit can receive eternal life and enter Heaven.

Had this true gospel of the water and the Spirit been preached since 30 years ago, it would indeed have swept across the world. But it is the providence of God for this truth to be spread in the end times. Our Lord said in Revelation that countless people would be saved from their sins in the end times. He also said that there would be many martyrs, and that during the time of tribulation a myriad of people would demonstrate their faith by trusting in the Lord and embracing their martyrdom. Our Lord, in other words, has focused on the end times as the time to harvest many souls. God's plan is for only those who truly believe in this gospel of truth to receive the gift of salvation from all sins.

It is because you have been fortunate enough to hear the gospel of the water and the Spirit now in this age that you have been able to be saved from all sins. I am truly thankful to God for giving us this gospel of the water and the Spirit. What would have happened to all of us had we not heard the gospel of the water and the Spirit? But it is a fact that even now not everyone accepts the gospel of the water and the Spirit. This truth is not something that can enter into just anyone's heart.

In fact, we see that although there are many Christians throughout this world, many of them neither know nor believe in the gospel of the water and the Spirit. How, then, can these people who are ignorant of the true gospel be delivered from sin? That is why God has allowed us to spread the true gospel through Christian literature.

There are many throughout the world who testify that they have come to know what the gospel of the water and the Spirit is only after reading the gospel literature that we have been spreading. They all had known only the blood of the Cross before knowing this gospel of the water and the Spirit, but now they are thanking the Lord for being able to reach a clear understanding of the gospel of the water and the Spirit and believe in it. Also, there are many who testify that they did not know such a great significance was hidden in the fact that Jesus was baptized by John. They now believe in this gospel and cannot thank God enough for it.

We can see that like the gospel of the water and the Spirit, the gate of the court of the Tabernacle was also made of blue, purple, and scarlet thread and fine woven linen. These four colors are the same as the gospel of the water and the Spirit. And in the same manner, the shining gospel of the water and the Spirit is also manifested in the screen door of the Holy Place and the veil door of the Most Holy. The first covering of the Tabernacle, moreover, was also woven of the same four colors; blue, purple, and scarlet thread and fine woven linen. This truth refers to the baptism and blood of Jesus. That is why Jesus declared Himself to be the way to the Kingdom of Heaven. By coming to this earth and saving sinners with the truth of the gospel of the water and the Spirit, He has made those who believe sinless.

The way to the Kingdom of Heaven is found in the faith that believes in the baptism and blood of Jesus. With the blue, purple, and scarlet thread and the fine woven linen, Jesus has saved us from sin perfectly. Where do you think you can find this truth? If you believe in the baptism that Jesus Christ received and the blood of the Cross, you will then be saved from all sins and receive eternal life once for all.

What, then, is the difference between the faith that believes in Jesus Christ somehow and the faith that believes exactly in the gospel of the water and the Spirit? Because it is with the gospel of the water and the Spirit that the Lord has saved sinners from their iniquities, believing in this gospel is believing in the Lord correctly. Because the Lord has saved sinners with His baptism and the blood of the Cross, believing in this Lord as the Savior is the same as being saved from sin by believing in the gospel of the water and the Spirit that He fulfilled. Believing in just His name somehow does not mean that we would be remitted of our sins and enter Heaven.

Rather, it is by believing exactly that Jesus Christ was baptized by John for our sake, shed His blood on the Cross, bore the condemnation of all sins, and rose from the dead that we can receive our remission of sin and become God's own people. God allows only those who have the faith that believes in the most holy gospel of the water and the Spirit to enter the Kingdom of Heaven. But those who do not believe in the gospel of the water and the Spirit cannot enter the Kingdom of Heaven, for they have not been born again.

By believing in the gospel of the bright light of the water and the Spirit manifested in the Tabernacle, we have been able to receive the most holy faith while living on this earth. Although our deeds are insufficient, when we have such faith, how could anyone say that we have not been made righteous? When we have become holy by believing in the gospel of the water and the Spirit, how could we still have sin? Some people wonder how we can say that we are sinless when we are still in the flesh that continues to sin.

But this is their own thoughts of the flesh. Those who know and believe in the gospel of the water and the Spirit agree that human beings have imperfect bodies and therefore they cannot help but sin until they die. However, they also believe that they have been forever remitted of all their sins, including the sins that they will commit in the future, within the perfect salvation of Jesus' baptism and His Cross.

That you and I can share such Word of spiritual faith and have the most holy faith while living on this earth is because of the fact that the Lord has given us our salvation manifested in the blue, purple, and scarlet thread and the fine woven linen. It is because the Lord has given us the faith that enables us to believe in the truth of the gospel of the water and the Spirit as His gift for us. With our faith in the Lord, we can have fellowship with one another and live our lives while serving the Lord and loving one another—this is where our true happiness lies.

We cannot help but thank God for this gospel. How wonderful it is that I could have come to know the gospel of the water and the Spirit and believe in it! When I didn't have a whit of knowledge on Jesus' baptism, through the Word of truth, God has given my heart the faith that believes in this gospel of the water and the Spirit. By believing in the gospel of the water and the Spirit, we have all received the blessings of Heaven.

Because of the True Gospel in My Heart, I Preach It with True Thanksgiving

While reading the Bible, a question began to rise in my mind: why was Jesus baptized? Because this question kept rising, I sought to find its answer through the Bible, but no one was able to teach me. That was why I had been highly interested in this subject until I came to know the gospel of the water and the Spirit.

I often read the passage from Matthew 3:13-17, especially where Jesus said to John before being baptized, *"Permit it to be so now, for thus it is fitting for us to fulfill all righteousness,"* but I could never understand its meaning. So I often asked others about the reason why Jesus was baptized by

John the Baptist in the Jordan River, but I never heard a completely satisfying answer. Nonetheless, God enabled me to realize the purpose of the baptism that Jesus received from John. This was a spiritual revolution for me, as if a blind man received his sight. Thus, it was after I perceived the meaning of Matthew 3:13-17 that I came to realize the truth manifested in the blue, purple, and scarlet thread that saved me from my sins.

Before I grasped this truth, I had believed in only the blood of the Cross as my salvation, but the reality was that I still had sin and therefore was a sinner. At that time, I believed that I could be remitted of only original sin by the blood of Jesus, and my actual sins still remained in my heart. I had not known the faith that makes one completely sinless—that is, I had been completely oblivious of the baptism that Jesus received from John. However, God illuminated my heart with the bright light of the remission of sin, as light is turned on in a dark room. "Ah, the baptism that Jesus received from John is closely related with the laying on of hands of the sacrificial system in the Old Testament! So this is what the gospel of the water and the Spirit is!"

But what then? Astounded by my recognition, a great turmoil began to rise in my heart after realizing this truth: if no other gospel but this gospel of the water and the Spirit is the only true gospel, what would happen to this world? I had thought that the faith of the evangelicals had been biblically sound. But now, I eventually came to realize that all gospels other than the gospel of the water and the Spirit are the false ones coming from Stan.

So, all that I have done from then on is believe and preach that there is no other true gospel but the gospel of the water and the Spirit. Some people have criticized me for this. God has also shown me, a man of many shortcomings, the truth of salvation manifested in the blue, purple, and scarlet thread, and He has also enabled me to believe and preach that this truth is the real gospel. There are many similar gospels in this world, but there is only one true gospel. This is why I have decided to spread the gospel of the water and the Spirit throughout the whole world.

When I think about how I came to preach the truth of the remission of sin, and how I came to know, believe in, and spread the most holy gospel of the water and the Spirit, I come to realize just how greatly I have been blessed by God. All that I did was just believe that Jesus took upon the sins of the world by being baptized by John and shed His blood on the Cross, and yet all my sins have disappeared! The gospel of the water and the Spirit is the real truth, and I thank the Lord for giving me this gospel. I am a man who has indeed been greatly blessed by God. Those of you who believe in the gospel of the water and the Spirit are also such blessed people.

I believe that all these things are the blessings that God has bestowed on me. As the Apostle Paul confessed, *"But by the grace of God I am what I am, and His grace toward me was not in vain," (1 Corinthians 15:10)* I cannot but praise His grace bestowed on me. In all honesty, were it not in God's Church, where could you have heard the gospel of truth manifested in the blue, purple, and scarlet thread? Anyone who hears and believes in the Word of the blue, purple, and scarlet thread and the fine woven will be cleansed in the heart. What, then, do those who do not believe in the gospel of the water and the Spirit think about this gospel? For them, the truth of the water and the Spirit is only tiresome.

Do you have the faith that believes in the blue and scarlet thread of the veil door of the Most Holy? When you hear this Word, do not just think that you already know it, but examine yourselves to see if the truth is found in your hearts. Now, you must be, in other words, the ones who believe in the gospel of the water and the Spirit according to the Word of the Scriptures. It would be fortunate and blessed if you can come into God's Church, hear the Word of God, and have the privilege to enter Heaven.

But if this is not the case, if you are unable to know the gospel of the water and the Spirit, to have the true faith, and to enter the Kingdom of Heaven, all from hearing only mundane and trite man-made stories, what benefit could this possibly bring you? If the gospel that you believe in is different from the gospel of the water and the Spirit, how could your souls have any relevance before the Lord? The Word of God and your faith must be exactly the same, just as the faith of the Apostle Paul and our faith are the same. The gospel of the water and the Spirit that Peter believed in is also the same as the gospel that we believe in (1 Peter 3:21).

I am so thankful to God for allowing us to believe in the true gospel of the water and the Spirit in these end times. And when you hold the truth of the gospel of the water and the Spirit in our books and share it with others, they, too, will come to receive the remission of sin and thank God in their joy. We must realize that all the patterns and utensils of the Tabernacle provide are a detailed portrait of the Lord of salvation who has blotted out all our sins, and we must thank God for this truth.

We are blessed to be saved and to enter Heaven when we believe in the truth revealed in the veil door of the Most Holy. Moreover, God has enabled us to spread throughout the whole world the truth of the remission of sin made of the blue, purple, and scarlet thread and the fine woven linen. God has entrusted us with this work. From our respective places of duty, we are faithful to the works that have been assigned to each of us, and God is blessing us for this faithfulness.

I give my thanks to God. I glorify Him with my faith, believing that the gospel of the water and the Spirit manifested in the blue, purple, and scarlet thread and the fine woven linen used for the gate of the Tabernacle's court is the same as the four colors revealed in the veil door of the Most Holy. Now, it is my sincerest hope that you would all be the ones who have been saved from all sins by faith, who are able to enter the Most Holy where God dwells forever. Is your faith standing firm on this truth also? ⊠

SERMON

4

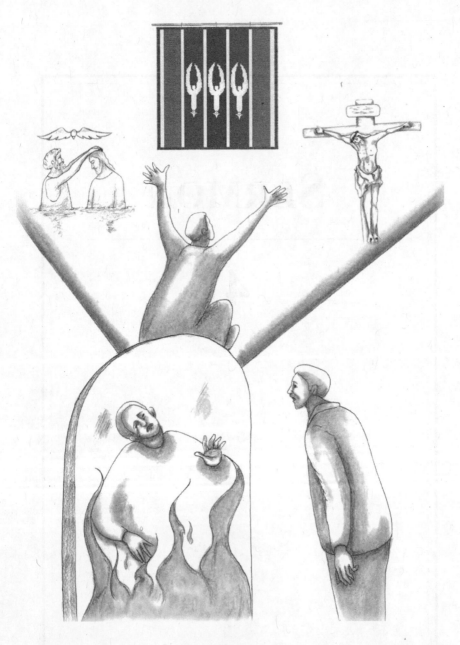

You can download Rev. Paul C. Jong's Christian Books on iPhone, iPad, or Blackberry by going to Amazon's Kindle e-bookstore (www.amazon.com).

The Veil That Was Torn

< Matthew 27:50-53 >

"And Jesus cried out again with a loud voice, and yielded up His spirit. Then, behold, the veil of the temple was torn in two from top to bottom; and the earth quaked, and the rocks were split, and the graves were opened; and many bodies of the saints who had fallen asleep were raised; and coming out of the graves after His resurrection, they went into the holy city and appeared to many."

The Most Holy was the place where God dwelt. And only the High Priest could enter into the Most Holy once a year, on the Day of Atonement, carrying the blood of the sacrificial goat for the remission of the sins of the Israelites. He did so because the Most Holy of the Tabernacle, the House of God, was a holy place where he could not enter unless he took the blood of the sacrifice, on whose head his hands were laid, to blot out the iniquities of sinners. Put differently, even the High Priest could not avoid God's condemnation unless he had received the remission of his sins by offering a sacrifice before entering into His presence.

When was the veil of the Temple torn? It was torn when Jesus shed His blood and died on the Cross. Why should He shed His blood on the Cross to die? Because Jesus the Son of God, coming to this earth in the flesh of a man, had taken upon all the iniquities of sinners by being baptized by John in the Jordan River. Because Jesus had taken upon all the sins of the world through His baptism, Jesus could end all the condemnation of sin only if He shed His blood on the Cross and died. This is why the veil that had separated the Most Holy from the Holy Place in the House of God was torn from top to bottom. This means that the wall of sin that had separated God from mankind fell down once for all.

In other words, through the baptism that Jesus received and the blood that He shed on the Cross, He has made all sins disappear. With the baptism and blood of Jesus Christ, God the Father has blotted out all our sins once for all and opened the way to Heaven, so that anyone can now enter Heaven by believing in the these baptism and bloodshed of Jesus.

When Jesus died on the Cross, darkness fell on where He was for three hours. Having shouldered all the sins of the world through His baptism in the Jordan River, Jesus, crucified and nearing His death, cried out, *"Eli, Eli, lama sabachthani?"*, which meant, *"My God, My God, why have You forsaken Me?"* *(Matthew 27:46)*. He then said His last words, *"It is finished!"*, and then died. And in three days He rose form the dead again, bore witness for 40 days, and then ascended to Heaven before the eyes of His many disciples and followers.

Did the Father Really Forsake Jesus?

The pain that Jesus suffered was so intense that He felt as if His Father had forsaken Him. The suffering of the condemnation of sin was that much great. Because Jesus took upon the sins of the world by being baptized by John, it is true that He was momentarily averted by the Father when He bore the condemnation of sin on the Cross. God the Father had to punish anyone who had sin, and because all the sins of the world had passed onto Jesus, Jesus had to be pierced and shed

His blood on the Cross as the punishment for these sins.

Because Jesus, who is God Himself in His essence, took upon all the sins of mankind by being baptized, the sins of the world were shifted onto His own holy body. So Jesus, having taken upon the sins of the world, now had to be averted by God the Father for a moment, suffer death on the Cross to pay the wages of all our sins, and thereby save mankind from all sins. This is why Jesus had to be subjected to the extreme suffering of the condemnation of sin, and why God the Father could not but turn His face away from His Son briefly.

But this does not mean that Jesus was forsaken by the Father forever. Rather, it just means that Jesus had to bear the vicarious condemnation of our sins, and therefore He had to be forsaken by the Father only momentarily. But as Jesus shouted out in His pain, *"My God, My God, why have You forsaken Me?"* it was because Jesus suffered such extreme agony of sin that we have been saved from the condemnation of sin. We had been someone who had to be abandoned by God for our sins, but Jesus took upon our sins, suffered the pain of the condemnation of sin on the Cross, and, moreover, was even forsaken by the Father for a while for our sake.

As you might already know, after the construction of the Temple during the reign of the King Solomon, the Tabernacle was substituted by the Temple. But the basics of the Tabernacle system were still applied to the Temple exactly as they were applied before its construction. So there was also a veil that separated the Most Holy Place from the Holy Place of the Temple. And at the very moment when our Lord shouted out on the Cross, *"Eli, Eli, lama sabachthani?"* this veil of the Temple was torn from top to bottom. The truth spoken by this event is that because the Lord has washed away our sins with the baptism that He received and the precious blood that He shed on the Cross, the gate of Heaven has now been flung open, so that all who believe may enter it. Now, by believing in the gospel of the water and the Spirit, we can all enter Heaven by faith.

Through the revelation of the Tabernacle system, the people of the Old Testament also believed in Jesus to come as the Messiah, and therefore they were also remitted of all their sins and became God's children. In the New Testament, all God's righteousness of the remission of sin was fulfilled once for all when our Lord was actually baptized in the Jordan River and died on the Cross. The reason why we have thankful hearts, having heard and believed in the gospel of the remission of sin that the Lord has given us, is because we have the gospel of the water and the Spirit.

On our own, we could not be freed from sin, but because of the truth of salvation that God has given us through the water and the Spirit, we have been able to be remitted of our sins by believing in this truth. By believing in the gospel of the water and the Spirit that Jesus has given us, our sins have disappeared and we are now able to enter the Kingdom of Heaven by faith. Given this, how could we not thank God? We can only thank Him, for we now know that the gate of Heaven was broken down from top to bottom the moment our Lord died. This is the joyful news telling us that our Lord took upon all the sins of mankind through the baptism that He received in the Jordan River, bore the condemnation of sin with His blood of the Cross, and has thereby delivered from sin all those who believe.

The fact that the veil of the Temple was torn from top to bottom when Jesus died on the Cross teaches us the truth that now in this age, those who have been cleansed from sin by believing in the gospel of the water and the blood can all enter

Heaven. This is the definitive evidence of the truth of salvation that the Lord has permitted to us. Because we were sinners, there was a wall of sin that had blocked us, disabling us from coming before God, but with His baptism and blood, Jesus has made this wall of sin disappear once for all. That God tore the veil of the Temple from top to bottom signifies that anyone who believes in the baptism through which the Son of God took upon all the iniquities of sinners and in the blood of the Cross can now be perfectly cleansed from their sins and thereby enter Heaven unimpeded. God has saved us from sin like this.

Jesus tore the veil of the Temple from top to bottom as the evidence of these works of salvation that He fulfilled. Therefore, Hebrews 10:19-22 states, *"Therefore, brethren, having boldness to enter the Holiest by the blood of Jesus, by a new and living way which He consecrated for us, through the veil, that is, His flesh, and having a High Priest over the house of God, let us draw near with a true heart in full assurance of faith, having our hearts sprinkled from an evil conscience and our bodies washed with pure water."*

When Jesus died on the Cross, the entrance of the Most Holy was opened wide as its veil was torn, and this open door of the Most Holy here is the God's Word of the gospel that opened a new and living way to Heaven. Here, the Bible tells us again that all the sins of our hearts and bodies were blotted out through His baptism (the pure water) and His blood, and therefore, we can be cleansed by our full assurance of faith in His perfect salvation.

For this, I give all my thanks to God. We could not enter Heaven no matter how much we tried, but for such people as us, Jesus has saved us from all our sins with these righteous acts of His baptism and His bloodshed on the Cross, and He has flung the gate of Heaven wide open, all so that only those who believe in the gospel of the water and the Spirit may enter Heaven. Now it has become possible for us to be cleansed from our sins and enter Heaven by the faith that believes in the gospel of the water and the Spirit.

Because the Lord has opened the gate of Heaven for us by being baptized and crucified, we are now able to wash away our sins and enter Heaven by believing in this truth. How could we then not thank God? We cannot thank Him enough for His love of sacrifice. The veil-door of the Most Holy was torn across by the baptism that Jesus received to take upon our sins and the sacrificial offering of His body that He made to be vicariously condemned for these sins of ours.

There Is Only One Way to Enter Heaven

Because we believe in the baptism of Jesus and the blood of the Cross, we will enter Heaven. There is no other way to enter Heaven but by believing in this gospel of truth. It is only by believing in what Jesus has done for us that we can enter Heaven, for God has done such works for those who believe in the gospel of the water and blood of Jesus.

This is why Christians cannot enter Heaven through their own efforts, devotion, or other such hypocritical attempts. God has determined that only those who have been cleansed from their sins by believing in the baptism that Jesus received and His bloodshed can enter Heaven. Those who believe in this truth are the ones who believe that Jesus is the Son of God, God Himself, and the everlasting Savior who has saved them from sin through His baptism and bloodshed. It is to such people that God has permitted the washing of sin. Only through the baptism that Jesus received and the suffering that He endured on the Cross, God the Father has enabled those of us who believe in these to enter the Kingdom of Heaven by faith.

Do we need money to enter Heaven? If this were the case, we would be attaining our salvation by paying for it, and so this cannot be the salvation that is given freely by the Lord. For us to enter Heaven, we need nothing else apart from the faith that believes in the gospel of the water and the Spirit. In other words, to enter Heaven, no payment, act, or effort of our own is ever needed. Nothing that is of human character is necessary to enter Heaven. For us to be qualified to enter Heaven, God does not demand any effort, act, will, compensation, or goodness from us.

There is only one thing that is absolutely necessary for us to enter Heaven, and this is the faith that believes in the baptism of the washing of sin that Jesus received in the Jordan River and the sacrifice that He made by shedding His blood on the Cross as our own remission of sin. There is no other way. The only thing we need is the faith that believes in the gospel of the baptism and blood of Jesus. This is why for us to receive the remission of sin and enter Heaven, we must believe in the gospel of the water and the Spirit that Jesus has fulfilled.

Jesus, the Lord of love, has fulfilled our perfect salvation through the gospel of the water and the Spirit. Because Jesus has already completed the salvation of the remission of sin, if sinners were only to believe in this gospel truth wholeheartedly, they can be saved from all their sins. Our Lord has remitted all our sins, whether we have many or only a few sins, and He has enabled anyone to enter Heaven but only by faith.

That Jesus has opened the gate of Heaven, so that sinners may enter it by believing in the gospel of the water and the Spirit, is the grace of salvation that is truly special. "The Lord was baptized to bear all my sins and died on the Cross in my place! He has washed away my sins and opened the gate of Heaven for me! He loved me so much that He was baptized, shed His blood, and fulfilled my remission of sin like this!" In this way, when you thus believe in the truth of salvation, you will enter Heaven by this faith.

For people to believe in Jesus as their Savior is not that difficult, but it is, in fact, rather easy, for all that they have to do is just accept into their hearts the already accomplished facts that Jesus achieved when He came to this earth and believe in them. Because Jesus has blotted out all our sins and delivered us from them through His baptism in the Jordan River that He received from John the Baptist, and through the blood that He shed on the Cross and through the Spirit, when we believe in this Jesus in our hearts, we will all be saved.

"You shall know the truth, and the truth shall make you free" (John 8:32). Whether our sins are great or small, by being baptized and shedding His blood, Jesus has made them all disappear. It is by believing in this gospel of the water and the Spirit, the truth that sets us free from sin, that we can receive our eternal salvation and encounter the freedom of this true salvation.

By fulfilling the gospel of the water and the Spirit, our Lord has flung the gate of Heaven wide open. Our Lord came to this earth, was baptized, died on the Cross, and rose from the dead again in three days-this truth, the gospel of the water and the Spirit, has moved us close to God, and it has enabled us to make Heaven ours in the future. Now, if you want to enter Heaven, as well as to be freed from sin and become God's children, then you must receive your remission of sin by believing in the baptism of Jesus and the blood of the Cross. It is this faith that will enable you to receive the remission of sin and lead you into the gate of Heaven.

Our Lord knows everything about us. He knows when we were born, and He knows all about the sins that we have committed and are to commit. And He also knows very well that no matter how hard we try, we cannot make our sins disappear on our own. Because the Lord knows us so well, He Himself has blotted out all our sins with His baptism and the blood of the Cross.

Why Did Jesus Come to This Earth?

The name Jesus means the Savior. Jesus was born on this earth because our salvation from sin is accomplishable by no human being, but it falls only within the purview of divine power. Like this, the birth of Jesus entailed a clear purpose. This is why to save mankind from all sins, Jesus was born on this earth through the body of a virgin. In other words, Jesus was born through the body of a woman for the sake of sinners who inherited sin because of the transgression of Adam and Eve. To become the Savior who saves all the sinners of this world from all their iniquities, the Lord came to this world, conceived in the body of a virgin by the power of God.

Our Lord was born on this earth through the body of His own creation so that He Himself may become our unblemished offering. And when the time came, step-by-step He proceeded with His plan to bring salvation to us. When our Lord turned 30, he was baptized in the Jordan River. To achieve the purpose of His birth on this earth, Jesus had to accept the sins of the world by being baptized, and so it was to fulfill this task that He was baptized by John (Matthew 3:13-17).

When three years had passed since Jesus thus accepted the

Free book request www.bjnewlife.org

sins of the world through His baptism, He was crucified. It was because our Lord was baptized and had taken upon the sins of the world that He was vicariously condemned for our sins. Through the baptism given by John the Baptist and His blood of the Cross, the Lord has made all sins disappear, and He has thereby enabled those who believe to be saved from their sins.

No matter in what ignorance people find themselves, in what weaknesses they are trapped, and what kind of sinners they may be, God has enabled us believers in the gospel of the water and the Spirit to enter Heaven, the Kingdom of the Lord. It was to pay the wages of sin that Jesus was baptized in the Jordan River and shed His blood on the Cross. Because of the salvation that Jesus has fulfilled by paying the wages of our sins and sacrificing Himself, those of us who believe can now be washed of our sins only by our faith in the gospel of the water and the Spirit. This is the fundamental truth of Christianity and the core of the remission of sin.

The Lord came to this world to become the Savior of all the sinners of this world. And the Lord has actually saved all of us from sin. Our Lord has enabled all sinners, no matter who they may be, to enter Heaven by believing in His works.

This is the love of the Lord. It was because our Lord loved us so much that He was baptized and shed His blood to save us. To deliver us from sin, whom He loved as much as His own body, our Lord fulfilled salvation by being baptized and shedding His blood. We had been sinners who would continue to sin until the day we die. Tormented by our sins, we kept moving away from God only further. To save such people as us, the Lord had to accomplish the works of salvation that enable us to become united with Him.

Our Lord has saved us who were sinners with the love of God. To save us sinners from our iniquities, He has completed the righteousness and love of God by receiving His baptism and shedding His blood. We who believe in this gospel are so thankful for what the Lord has done for us that words simply fail us to express our thanks of faith as we bow down before Him. The truth of the remission of sin that our Lord has given us is such a noble and absolute love that no words of logic, no words of sweetness can ever describe it.

Over 2,000 years ago, none of us were even born at that time. It was about 2,000 years ago that the veil of the earthly Temple and the heavenly Temple of the Kingdom of God were opened. We were not even in the wombs of our mothers at that time, but our Lord already knew all about us. He knew that you would be born, and that you would all live your lives each according to your own unique way. And the Lord has loved me—not only me, but He has loved you and everyone else the same. The Lord has loved us so much that He has enabled all sinners to enter Heaven by believing in the gospel of the water, the blood, and the Spirit that Jesus has fulfilled for us. Through the water and the Spirit (the baptism of Jesus and His blood of the Cross), Jesus has completed our salvation from sin.

That the veil of the Temple was torn from top to bottom is a truly amazing event. How could this veil of the Most Holy be torn, just because Jesus died on the Cross? This veil was like today's carpets. It was woven very thick and sturdy. In Palestine, even now we can still come across such thick veils woven like carpets. They are woven so tightly that it is said that it takes four horses pulling in the opposite direction to tear them apart. How strong is a horse? Yet the veil that was so strong that it would have required four horses to tear was ripped from top to bottom when Jesus died on the Cross.

Why was the veil torn? It was torn because Jesus had washed away all the sins that were in the hearts of mankind. It was torn because Jesus had fulfilled all His righteous works by being baptized and crucified to death. By accepting the sins of the world through His baptism and being condemned on the Cross, Jesus opened the way for those who believe to enter Heaven. All that you have to do now is just believe. The Lord has opened the gate of Heaven so that you may all enter it just by believing.

Are Both Jesus' Baptism and Blood Essential to Our Salvation?

It was according to the method of salvation planned even before the time of the Old Testament that hands were laid on the head of Jesus, a ritual that was reserved only for sacrificial offerings. Because its was the law of salvation set by God for the sacrificial offering to accept all sins with the laying on of hands and to die, Jesus, coming as our own sacrificial offering to save us forever, could blot out all our sins only by receiving His baptism, a form of the laying on of hands. This is why to enter into the Most Holy, even the High Priest had to make sure to take with him the blood of the sacrificial offering which had taken upon sins with the laying on of hands.

Why, then, did the High Priest have to enter into this place with blood? For the life of the flesh is in the blood, God had given it to the High Priest to make atonement for his soul before he came into His presence (Leviticus 17:11). All people had to die for their sins, but because Jesus took upon all the sins of mankind by being baptized in the Jordan River (all sins were passed onto Jesus with His baptism) and shouldered them all, Jesus was crucified and has thereby saved us with the blood that He shed, with His own life. This tells us that when sinners come before God, they must for sure take with them the faith that believes in the water and the blood. Only when we wholeheartedly believe in the water of the baptism of Jesus and the blood that He shed can we escape from being condemned for our sins.

Now, Jesus has washed away all sins, so that no one would have to give prayers of repentance, or fast, or give offerings for his/her remission of sin. We do not have to give prayers of repentance, nor do we have be punished for our sins, for Jesus has already given the offering of the remission of sin and condemnation. All that we have to do is just believe with our hearts in the salvation manifested in the blue, purple, and scarlet thread.

All that anyone has to do is just believe in the baptism that Jesus received as the blue thread that was used for the Tabernacle of the Old Testament, and to believe in the blood that Jesus shed on the Cross as its scarlet thread. And the truth that Jesus is the King in His fundamental essence is manifested in the purple thread used for the door of the Tabernacle. As such, if we are washed of our sins by believing in the remission of sin manifested as the blue, purple, and scarlet thread, and believe that all our condemnation has already ended, then any of us can now enter the Kingdom of Heaven. This gospel is the very gospel of the water and the Spirit.

Why Was the Veil of the Temple Torn When Jesus Died on the Cross? Let Us Consider This One More Time

The blue, purple, and scarlet thread manifested in the Old Testament is the gospel that brings the blessings of receiving the remission of sin and entering the Kingdom of Heaven to those who believe. This is why the veil was torn when Jesus, having been baptized, died on the Cross. For those who believe in Jesus, this is the truth of the gospel of the water and the Spirit given by God Himself. "Ah, it was because Jesus was baptized by John in my place that He shed His blood and died on the Cross, and thereby paid the wages of death, the wages of sin." Dying on the Cross, Jesus said, *"It is finished,"* and it was at this moment that He opened the way for us to enter the Kingdom of Heaven.

Jesus came to this earth to save those who were separated from God by the wall of sins that they could not avoid but keep building. This was Jesus' own will, but at the same time it was also the command of God the Father and His love for us. Obeying the will of the Father, Jesus received the baptism that passed the sins of the world onto His own body. It was because Jesus shouldered the sins of the world through His baptism that He went to the Cross, was crucified, shed His blood and died, rose from the dead in three days, and thereby completed His works of salvation. These are the ministries manifested in the blue, purple, and scarlet thread, the remission of sin that delivers sinners from their iniquities, and the completion of the sacrificial system.

It is because Jesus has fulfilled salvation with His ministries that the gate of Heaven, which no man could enter so far, has now been opened. This demonstrates that the door of salvation is no longer opened with the laying on of hands and the blood of the animal that was used for the sacrificial offering of the Old Testament, but it is now opened with the faith that believes in the baptism that Jesus received and the blood that He shed on the Cross. That the veil was torn manifests the completion of salvation, that God has now enabled anyone who knows and truly believes in the gospel of the water and the Spirit fulfilled by the Lord to enter Heaven. This is why the veil of the Temple had to be torn.

You must enter the Kingdom of Heaven with the faith that believes in the baptism of Jesus and the blood of the Cross. Jesus who had no sin at all came to this earth incarnated in the flesh and was baptized by John to accept all our sins (Matthew 3:15). Moreover, our Lord gave up the life of His body as the wages of our sins and has become the everlasting offering of atonement that we must take with us when we come before God. Therefore, all of us must believe in this blood that Jesus shed after being baptized as our salvation. To deliver mankind from sin and make them God's own people, Jesus opened the gate of Heaven by tearing His own body.

When it comes to Jesus saving us, we must know that He did not just bleed on the Cross. Three years before dying on the Cross, He had already taken upon our sins by being baptized in the Jordan River. So Jesus was baptized by John for the sake of the entire mankind and then was crucified by Roman soldiers. Even before you and I were born in this world, Jesus had already cleansed away all our sins by being baptized and shedding His blood.

That Jesus was baptized by John was the method of salvation that He had to fulfill for sure in order to take upon our sins beforehand all at once. And the blood that He shed was the payment of the wages of all those sins. Because Jesus is God Himself, the baptism that He received and the blood that He shed on the Cross could certainly constitute our salvation from sin. This was our Lord's perfect sacrifice that He made for the salvation of the entire mankind. Do you believe that the gospel Word of the water and the Spirit has cleansed away our sins and delivered us from all our sins and condemnation?

Free book request www.bjnewlife.org

Through the Baptism of Jesus and the Blood of the Cross, All the Sins of Mankind Have Now Been Washed away

It was to wash away the sins of mankind that Jesus was baptized by John. If we look at Jesus' ministries of salvation by leaving out this baptism of Jesus from His public life, then the salvation of mankind planned in Jesus Christ from before the foundation of the world would all turn into lies. Even before the foundation of the world, Jesus was already preparing to be baptized to take upon the sins of mankind and to shed His blood.

This is why Jesus was baptized by John the Baptist, the representative of all mankind, and thereby accepted all sins (Matthew 11:11-12; Matthew 3:15). For Jesus to wash away the iniquities of sinners by being baptized was the method of salvation. Jesus accepted the iniquities of sinners and cleansed them away, and instead of us dying for our sins, He died vicariously in our place, and by doing so He has delivered those who believe in this from all their sins and condemnation. Through this method (the method of being baptized), Jesus could accept all the sins of mankind onto Himself and bear all the condemnation of sin by shedding His blood on the Cross. *"For thus it is fitting for us to fulfill all righteousness" (Matthew 3:15).* That Jesus was baptized in the Jordan River meant that He accepted all the sins of us sinners.

Brothers and sisters, are you unable to believe that Jesus came to this earth over 2,000 years ago, that He was baptized when He turned 30, and that He shed His blood for you, just because you did not see this with your own eyes? But knowing all about our insufficiencies, God had already planned our salvation with the water and the blood even before the foundation of the world, and by sending Jesus Christ and John the Baptist to this earth according to this plan, He has fulfilled the salvation of all of us. To enable us to realize and know all this truth, God made His servants write down His Word. Through His written Word, God has revealed everything about the plan of salvation and its fulfillment to the entire mankind. He has now enabled anyone to realize through the written Word of God the truth that Jesus was baptized by John in the Jordan River to take upon all our sins.

All of us must now believe in the baptism that Jesus received and the blood that He shed on the Cross as our own salvation. Though we have not seen it with our eyes of the flesh, we must believe in our hearts. True faith comes to us when our faith is based on His Word. The Lord said to Thomas, *"Blessed are those who have not seen and yet have believed" (John 20:29)*. Jesus has saved you and me with the baptism that He received and the blood that He shed. God has enabled anyone who believes in this to enter Heaven.

This is why God tore the veil of the Temple when Jesus died on the Cross. Jesus brought down the wall of sin that had blocked us mankind from God. What Jesus had done was more than sufficient to tear down all the wall of sin. He has made it possible for anyone to enter Heaven absolutely unimpeded just by believing in this gospel of the water and the Spirit in the heart. I thank our Lord for giving us this truth, so that we may all truly enter Heaven if we only believe in our hearts.

How great is this event, that Jesus was born on this earth in the body of a mere creature to save sinners? It is a truly remarkable event, even when compared to His creation of the world. It is only a matter of course that the Lord, the Creator who made all things, would create His creatures, but that the Creator became like a creature, took upon the sins of the world by being baptized, and was crucified, cannot be anything else but the great event of salvation.

How could the Creator Himself become like one of His creatures? Yet Jesus, God Himself, lowered Himself to such an extent that He was even baptized by John the Baptist, the representative of mankind, in the Jordan River. What an amazing event is this? But this is not the end of it, for Jesus lowered Himself all the way down, obeying to even His death, to endure countless cruel sufferings on the Cross, to shed His blood and die. All these things cannot be anything else but the love of God, His mercy and His great grace.

All the sins of mankind were completely cleansed away once for all with the baptism of the Lord and His blood of the Cross. And having torn the veil of the Temple, Jesus rose from the dead in three days, and He now wants to meet in the truth all those who believe in this truth. Like this, the works of the Lord that have saved sinners are a event that is greater and larger than even His works of the creation that made this universe and all things in it. The birth of Jesus, His baptism, His death on the Cross, His resurrection, ascension and return, and that He has made us His own children are the works of the love of God.

Our Lord has saved you and me from all sins. Our Lord has delivered you and me once for all from the sins of the world through the gospel of the water and the Spirit. We can therefore become righteous by faith and thank God. God has bestowed on us His blessing of salvation to its fullness. Do you believe?

Brothers and sisters, you and I had been someone who could not but be cast into Hell. We had been someone who could not but be destroyed for our sins and live our lives in sadness, but the Lord has saved us from sin with the salvation that He had planned even before the foundation of the world. We had no other choice but to live our lives sitting in the midst of our sins, wailing, resenting, and cursing our fate, but to enable such people like us to enter the Kingdom of Heaven, the Lord has delivered us from all our sins. Our Lord has thus become the Lord of our salvation.

Jesus has given us the gospel of the water and the Spirit, and He has also guaranteed our remission of sin. Jesus Himself has become the Lord of salvation. Jesus took upon the sins of the world in our place, died in our stead, and has thereby become our perfect Savior.

Do You Believe in the Baptism that Jesus Received and the Blood That He Shed?

Our deliverance from sin is fulfilled by believing in the baptism that Jesus received and the blood of the Cross. For sinners to be saved by believing in Jesus as the Savior, they must make sure to consider His baptism and Cross in order, and they must believe that it is by the union of these two that the perfect salvation is fulfilled.

By any chance, are you not believing that Jesus was baptized and died on the Cross? Are you not ignoring the baptism that Jesus received from John and refusing to believe in it? The righteousness of God was fulfilled because the baptism that Jesus received was the process through which He took upon all the iniquities of sinners, and the death that He suffered by shedding His precious blood was the condemnation of our sins. As such, when you and I profess to believe in Jesus, we must believe both in His baptism and His blood of the Cross as one salvation.

God wrote the necessity of the baptism and bloodshed of Jesus in His Word, and yet despite this many people still insist that they need to believe only in the blood of the Cross to be saved. If you are one of them, then you must seriously reconsider your belief, turn around, and believe in both these two essentials. If you do not do so but believe only in the blood of the Cross, you will then end up turning the holy ministries of the public life of the Lord all in vain. If you happen to have such faith, then you must turn around from this flawed faith and have the true faith that is spoken of throughout the Bible. Without His baptism, what relevance would His death on the Cross have for us? If Jesus had not been baptized by John the Baptist, His death would have had nothing to do with our sins.

Brothers and sisters, if you were to erase your names from a bill, would you not have to actually bring money and pay the creditor? Debtors must hand over money for the corresponding amount of their debts, and only then can they erase their names from the list. Like this, to pay the wages of our sins, Jesus accepted such sins and iniquities of ours through His baptism and blotted them out by shedding His blood.

Through the baptism that He received, the Lord actually took away all our sins, and this is why He could be condemned for all our sins by shedding His blood. To pay off a debt, common sense dictates that one should bring a value that corresponds to this debt. If debtors do not bring money but only claim to have paid off their debts and demand their names to be erased from the bill, would their names really be erased? No matter how seriously they believe that their names have been erased, the fact of the matter is that their names still remain recorded in the bill.

As debtors can be freed from their debts only when the debts are actually paid off, for us sinners to receive the remission of sin, we must have in our hearts the faith that believes that our sins were passed onto Jesus through the baptism that He received. We ourselves did not give this baptism that passed our sins onto the head of Jesus.

But through an intermediary named John the Baptist, we were able to pass our sins onto Jesus. Jesus who was baptized by John the Baptist shouldered the sins of the world, went to the Cross, shed His blood and died. By believing in His baptism, the antitype and receipt of salvation, through which Jesus took upon our sins and has saved us, we can receive the proof of our salvation. By believing in what our Lord has done for us in our hearts, we are now able to receive the remission of sin. Why? Because through His baptism and blood, our Lord has given us new life.

When Jesus died on the Cross, the veil of the Most Holy was torn into two pieces, the earth was shaken, rocks were rolled, tombs were opened, and many bodies of the saints who had fallen asleep were raised. Through these events, God showed that He would raise those who believed in His Word, that Jesus Christ would come and blot out all the sins of mankind. He showed that Jesus indeed rose from the dead, and that those who believe in Jesus would indeed be brought alive. Jesus has not only saved us from sin, but He has also given new life to us who were spiritually dead. It was to given us new life that Jesus was baptized, died on the Cross, and lived again. God has enabled us to enter His Holy City and live in it forever. I give my true thanks to Him with my faith.

The place where those who have received the remission will live is Heaven. So do believe that those who have received the remission of sin on this earth will all enter Heaven and live in it. Heaven belongs to those who have received the remission of sin. Believing in the gospel of the water and the Spirit and being born again are not two separate things, but they are both the same.

If anyone believes in the gospel Word of the water and the Spirit, then this person is born again the very moment he/she believes. When sinners receive the remission of sin, they become God's own children, and to His children, God gives Heaven as a gift. Even though in our flesh we have no work of our own, looking at just one thing, our faith that believes in the Savior, our Lord has given us the remission of sin and Heaven as His gifts for us.

The fact that our Lord came to this earth, that He was baptized, and that He shed His blood, is all true. When Jesus died on the Cross, He had already taken upon the sins of the world with His baptism. Before Jesus was crucified, having been baptized by John beforehand, He was already carrying the sins of the world. So it was because Jesus had shouldered all the sins of the world by being baptized that He had to bear the punishment of the law declaring the wages of sin to be death. For Jesus to save mankind from sin, He had to die on the Cross while He was carrying the sins of the world that He had taken upon with His baptism.

When Jesus was crucified, people who nailed Him were not Jews, but they were Roman soldiers. Jesus was crucified by Gentile soldiers. Shedding all His blood for the sake of our sins, Jesus cried out, "It is finished!" with His last breath. At the very moment, the veil of the Temple was torn in two from top to bottom. Moreover, the Bible also tells us that the earth quaked, the rocks were split, and the graves were opened; and that many bodies of the saints who had fallen asleep were raised as well (Matthew 27:51-52). When the centurion and the Roman soldiers saw what happened when Jesus died on the Cross, they testified, *"Truly this was the Son of God!"*

(Matthew 27:54). God had made the mouths of these Gentile soldiers to testify, "Jesus was the Son of the living God."

Now, those who must testify the true gospel throughout the world are none other that us, the believers of the gospel of the water and the Spirit. It is through the gospel of the water and the Spirit that everyone is changed. When people receive the remission of sin from Jesus, they are transformed spiritually without even trying, for the Holy Spirit comes to dwell in their hearts. And the hearts of the born-again righteous are renewed everyday, for in God's Church they can consistently hear the Word of the gospel of the water and the Spirit. They come to hear the Word, praise Jesus, and as they praise, they experience that the lyrics are engraved into their hearts, thereby renewing their hearts everyday. The righteous have their hearts continuously transformed, and they can feel such tangible changes in themselves.

And seeing our changed selves, who have become righteous, unbelievers come to testify, "They are truly saved. They are real Christians, the people of God." Like this, our remission of sin is not the kind of salvation that is proven by ourselves alone. The Roman centurion and soldiers also testified this truth, that Jesus as the Son of God had saved sinners from the sins of the world when He was crucified. Like this, God Himself bore witness to those who believe in the truth that Jesus has saved us from all our sins with the water and the blood.

The Gospel of the Water and the Spirit That Made Even the Devil Surrender

The gospel of the water and the Spirit is the salvation to

which even the Devil has surrendered. When Jesus said, *"It is finished"* on His death, the Devil might have said, "Ah! This is mortifying, but there is nothing I can do about it! He is right. There is no sin in this world anymore. Everyone is now completely sinless without any exception! It's eating up my heart, but I can't do anything about it!"

In other words, the Devil himself could not help but also acknowledge this salvation that Jesus fulfilled. But he still tries to hinder those who have received the remission of sin from living their lives of faith. As those who believe in the gospel of the water and the Spirit fulfilled by Jesus are God's children, they try to live for Him. But for the Devil, this can only mean that there would be fewer servants of his who are enslaved to sin, and so he tries to prevent God's servants from spreading this truth all over the world.

If those who have received the remission of sin continue to spread the gospel of the water and the Spirit, then there would be even more people who are remitted of sin. This is why Satan sinks his teeth into the weaknesses of people and wouldn't let go, hindering them so that even just one more person would be thwarted from following Jesus.

Inciting people's hearts by telling them, "Kill Jesus!", the Devil made them crucify Him to death. But just when the Devil thought that everything ended with this, Jesus, crucified and dying, shouted out loud, *"It is finished!"* Satan was shocked by this. Far from being thwarted, by taking upon all our sins through His baptism in the Jordan River and dying on the Cross, Jesus had righteously fulfilled the salvation that delivers mankind from sin and condemnation. The Devil had been oblivious of this wisdom of God. He had thought that everything would be over if he just kills Jesus on the Cross, but this was not the case. After taking upon the sins of the world through His baptism, Jesus completed sinners' remission of sin by giving up His body on the Cross and dying.

With the death of His body, Jesus has already paid off all the wages of sin. As such, sin can no longer be found in people. Why? Because according to the law declaring the wages of sin to be death, Jesus already died instead of sinners. We must believe that it was because Jesus had taken upon all the iniquities of sinners in the Jordan River that He could die vicariously instead of sinners.

"It is finished!" This is what Jesus shouted out on the Cross with His last breath. Because Jesus died, the Devil can no longer say to us, "You have sin, don't you?" Because of the birth of Jesus, His baptism, His death on the Cross, and His blood and resurrection, the Devil suffered a crushing defeat before Jesus. Though the Devil had estranged our relationship with God by making us sin all the time, in the end, because of the wisdom of Jesus the Son of God, His washing of sin and condemnation, he ultimately could not avoid but be totally defeated.

When you believe in the baptism of Jesus and the blood of the Cross, do you still have sin? Of course not! Saying that we have no sin is something that just cannot be said with the conscience of the flesh. Bu by believing in the baptism and blood of Jesus, we are now able to declare boldly that we are sinless. Do you believe the truth that Jesus took upon our sins by being baptized in the Jordan River, died on the Cross in our place, and has thereby saved us? By our faith in this truth, we can say now that we have no sin. And in fact, there can be no sin at all in our hearts, not even as small as a penny. This is why grateful hearts spring up in us before God, giving our thanks with faith.

"God, my faith may not be great, but even with a faith that

is as small as a mustard seed, I still give my thanks you. I was someone who could not even bear Your great love, but You still came into my heart, and so with my faith that believes in the gospel of the water and the Spirit, I now hold Your love in my heart. My heart is thankful to You everyday, for the Lord who dwells in my heart and is with me. For giving this heart, I give all my thanks to You." Like this, our Lord has given us thankful hearts. And our Lord blesses us everyday.

So not only I, but also everyone else who hears and believes in the truth of His perfect salvation also, we all clearly have no sin at all in our hearts. Because we believe in the truth of the water and the Spirit, we have received the blessing of salvation, of becoming God's own children. And God wholeheartedly wants all to realize that there is no way for them to be saved from all their sins without believing in the birth of Jesus and His baptism and blood, and to return to Him and believe in this truth.

Acts 4:12 declares, *"Nor is there salvation in any other, for there is no other name under heaven given among men by which we must be saved."* We believe in Jesus as our Savior. In those who believe in this, thankful hearts spring up. We therefore have hearts that are thankful to the Lord. Our Lord has given us salvation, and He has also given us thankful hearts. The Lord has given us eternal life. We cannot help but glorify the Lord with our thanks for giving us all these abundant blessings.

Even if our faith is as small as a mustard seed, if we still believe in what Jesus has done for us in our hearts, we can all be saved. I beseech you all to realize that there is nothing else we can do for our salvation but only believe, to know this salvation that God has given us freely, and to believe in it. It is because the remission of sin cannot be attained through our own efforts that God has unilaterally blotted out all our sins on His own and has given His salvation to those of us who believe. Now, all that remains for us to do is just receive this remission of sin by faith.

There is a saying in Korea that goes, "If you like freebies too much, you will go bald." In English parlance, its equivalent might be, "There is no such thing as a free lunch." That is certainly true; nothing in life comes to us for free. And we are apt to ridicule those who expect to receive gifts without giving anything in return. Nonetheless, being saved and going to Heaven are achieved by believing in the gospel of the water and the Spirit, all for free. Baldness from receiving too many freebies may be unsightly in the flesh, but spiritual baldness to receive God's gift is a blessing before God. I pray you would all realize that God is rejoiced to see our sinless hearts, and that seeing this, He embraces us in His arms.

We are fond of God's free grace. And we cannot but thank the Lord: Our Lord came to this earth, received His baptism by water, shed His blood on the Cross, and has thereby opened the gate of Heaven. By tearing the veil of the Most Holy from top to bottom, He has enabled anyone who is born again by believing in the gospel of the water and the Spirit to enter the Kingdom of Heaven. You, too, must also enter Heaven by believing in this gospel of the water and the Spirit in your hearts.

I thank our Lord for being baptized, shedding His blood, rising from the dead, and for the grace that has thereby opened the door of the remission of sin for us. ✉

You can download Rev. Paul C. Jong's Christian Books on
iPhone, iPad, or Blackberry by going to Amazon's Kindle
e-bookstore (www.amazon.com).

SERMON

5

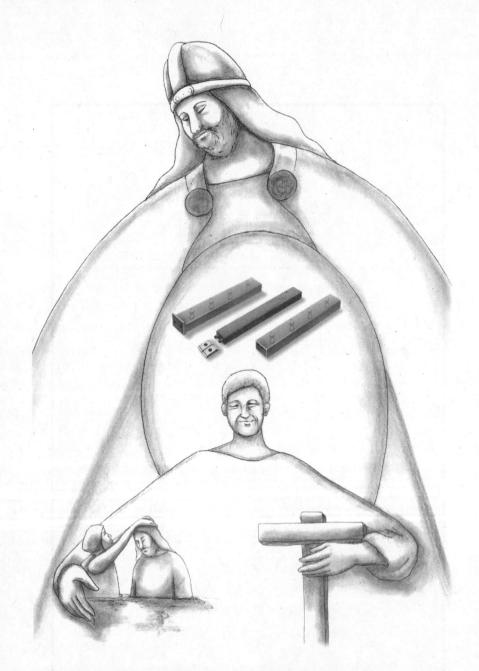

You can download Rev. Paul C. Jong's Christian Books on iPhone, iPad, or Blackberry by going to Amazon's Kindle e-bookstore (www.amazon.com).

Two Silver Sockets and Two Tenons for Each Board of the Tabernacle

< Exodus 26:15-37 >

"And for the tabernacle you shall make the boards of acacia wood, standing upright. Ten cubits shall be the length of a board, and a cubit and a half shall be the width of each board. Two tenons shall be in each board for binding one to another. Thus you shall make for all the boards of the tabernacle. And you shall make the boards for the tabernacle, twenty boards for the south side. You shall make forty sockets of silver under the twenty boards: two sockets under each of the boards for its two tenons. And for the second side of the tabernacle, the north side, there shall be twenty boards and their forty sockets of silver: two sockets under each of the boards. For the far side of the tabernacle, westward, you shall make six boards. And you shall also make two boards for the two back corners of the tabernacle. They shall be coupled together at the bottom and they shall be coupled together at the top by one ring. Thus it shall be for both of them. They shall be for the two corners. So there shall be eight boards with their sockets of silver—sixteen sockets—two sockets under each of the boards. And you shall make bars of acacia wood: five for the boards on one side of the tabernacle, five bars for the boards on the other side of the tabernacle, and five bars for the boards of the side of the tabernacle, for the far side westward. The middle bar shall pass through the midst of the boards from end to end. You shall overlay the boards with gold, make their rings of gold as holders for the bars, and overlay the bars with gold. And you shall raise up the tabernacle according to its pattern which you were shown on the mountain. You shall make a veil woven of blue, purple, and scarlet thread, and fine woven linen. It shall be woven with an artistic design of cherubim. You shall hang it upon the four pillars of acacia wood overlaid with gold. Their hooks shall be gold, upon four sockets of silver. And you shall hang the veil from the clasps. Then you shall bring the ark of the Testimony in there, behind the veil. The veil shall be a divider for you between the holy place and the Most Holy. You shall put the mercy seat upon the ark of the Testimony in the Most Holy. You shall set the table outside the veil, and the lampstand across from the table on the side of the tabernacle toward the south; and you shall put the table on the north side. You shall make a screen for the door of the tabernacle, woven of blue, purple, and scarlet thread, and fine woven linen, made by a weaver. And you shall make for the screen five pillars of acacia wood, and overlay them with gold; their hooks shall be gold, and you shall cast five sockets of bronze for them."

The Tabernacle itself was constructed with 48 boards; twenty boards each for the south and north sides, six boards of the west side, and two boards for the two back corners. Each board measured 4.5 m (15 feet) in length and about 67.5 cm (2.2 feet) in width. For each board to stand upright, there were two silver sockets and two tenons that fitted correctly together.

This shows us again that God's salvation is given only by His grace through faith in Christ.

Salvation by Grace through Faith in Christ

Most Christians know and even recite the famous passage of Ephesians 2:8-9, *"For by grace you have been saved through faith, and that not of yourselves; it is the gift of God, not of works, lest anyone should boast."* But unfortunately, they don't know what His grace exactly is and what kind of faith they should have to be saved. However, the mystery of the two silver sockets and two tenons that fitted correctly together shows us clearly the mystery of God's salvation.

For us to realize the truth of the "two tenons and two silver sockets" placed at the bottom of the boards, we need to first know the basic truth of the gospel. All the doors of the Tabernacle were woven of blue, purple, and scarlet thread and fine woven linen. These four colors show us that for us to be saved from our sins and destruction, the baptism and blood of Jesus were necessary. And they enable us to believe in the truth of Jesus' salvation, free from any doubt. We must have a clear knowledge of the truth that has saved us, manifested in the blue, purple, and scarlet thread and the fine woven linen, and believe in it.

Jesus said, *"You shall know the truth, and the truth shall make you free" (John 8:32).* As such, we must all receive the perfect remission of our sins by knowing the spiritual truth that is hidden in the four colors manifested in the screen door of the Tabernacle and the veil of the Most Holy. Blue, purple, and scarlet thread and fine woven linen are the materials of the door of the Tabernacle.

In other words, Jesus Christ is our Savior and the King of those who believe, He who has at once saved us from all the sins of the world by being baptized by John and taking upon all our sins onto His own body once for all, and by carrying the sins of the world and shedding His blood on the Cross. That Jesus Christ, who is the King, could have definitively saved us from our sins is because He was baptized and crucified. Therefore, the blue and scarlet threads tell us of the clear and certain truth which cannot be left out for us to be saved from our sins. To take upon our sins, Jesus was baptized by John, and by carrying the sins of the world and shedding His blood on the Cross, He has saved us once for all from all our sins, thus completing His works of salvation.

Here, we must believe that these four points of the blue thread (Jesus' baptism), the scarlet thread (His bloodshed), the purple thread (He is our King), and the fine woven linen (He is the God of the elaborate Word, and has made us righteous) are all the materials used for our salvation. We must realize that if we in spite of this try to be saved from all our sins by believing in only one of these, then such salvation will not be whole. Why? Because at the bottom of each board of the Tabernacle, there were two tenons coming out to be plugged into the silver sockets to support the board.

Silver in the Bible denotes God's grace, the gift of God. And it is written in Romans 5:1-2, *"Therefore, having been justified by faith, we have peace with God through our Lord Jesus Christ, through whom also we have access by faith into this grace in which we stand, and rejoice in hope of the glory of God."* Our salvation can be granted to us only when our faith meets God's grace correctly. Just as there were two tenons at the bottom of each board of the Tabernacle, and these tenons were fitted into the silver sockets to support the board,

God is telling us that our salvation is completed only when we likewise believe in both the baptism of Jesus and the blood of the Cross.

All of us had to believe in the reason and the actual substance as to why each board had two tenons protruding.

These two sockets and two tenons of the board are the shadow of the gospel of the water and the Spirit, that in the age of the New Testament Jesus Christ would come, be baptized by John the Baptist, be crucified, shed His blood and die on the Cross, and thereby fulfill our salvation completely.

The grace of the remission of sin, in other words, is bestowed on the hearts of only those who actually believe in their righteous salvation that Jesus fulfilled by being baptized by John and shedding His blood on the Cross to blot out their sins. As such, for us to be saved from our sins, we need the faith that believes in these two works of Jesus. As a matter of fact, everything of the Tabernacle provides a detailed portrait of Jesus who has saved us from our sins. It was not for no reason that the Lord made the Israelites to use two tenons and two silver sockets for each board of the Tabernacle.

We have been saved and delivered from all our sins and all the condemnation of sin entirely through the works of baptism and bloodshed that God has given us. In other words, it is by believing in the gospel of the water and the Spirit that we have received the right to become God's children. Our faith that is like pure gold has been built by receiving this gift of God.

Do You Still Not Know Who You Really Are Even as You Believe In Jesus?

Do you consider yourselves as good? Do you think by yourselves that you have a righteous character that cannot tolerate any unrighteousness at all, under any circumstances and in any forms? Do you think that you are somehow righteous before God, just because you keep God's commandments in your hearts everyday and try to obey and act them out in your lives? All that we are doing is just pretending to be righteous, while we are committing adultery and fornication in privacy.

Nowadays, hundreds of channels are available for viewing from cable or satellite TV. Running for 24 hours a day, these channels carry their own specialty-programs and feed them continuously. Among these channels, the most commercially successful specialty-channels are, above all, adult channels. There are many such adult channels where all kinds of pornographic materials are available for viewing by simply flipping through channels. How about pornographic web sites? Needlessly to say, a flood of pornographic spam-mails are now deluging the world. Everyone deplores the evils of these obscene websites, but when we think of "the law of supply and demand," their success can only mean that countless people actually enjoy such websites in their privacy.

This phenomenon shows us that we human beings are fundamentally corrupted and obscene. The Bible points out the sinful hearts of mankind by referring to fornications, adulteries, and lewdness. God said that these things come out from the hearts of people and defile them, and that they are clearly sins. Are we not, then, all filled with sin? God repeatedly said that the properties intrinsic to us are sinful.

But do we really admit this? How is it? Can we escape from the properties of sin that are intrinsic to us by closing our eyes and covering our ears? We cannot help but commit all kinds of sin with the imaginations of our minds and thoughts. No matter how much we tell ourselves that we have to move away from such sins, and no matter how hard we try to do so, they are all in vain. In fact, our flesh is such that not only can we never become perfect saints who commit no carnal sin, but we actually have affinity to sin with no desire to be distanced from it. The flesh and hearts of mankind are always far removed from the things that are holy, and it is a fact, moreover, that they not only want to be closer to sin, but they want to commit even greater sins.

In the East, many learn the teachings of Confucius from their birth, and so they try very hard to put these teachings into practice. In the West, on the other hand, Catholicism or legalistic Christian churches have dominated its religious landscape, and many Westerners have tried hard to keep the Law of God, thinking that they can be holier and holier as long as they keep trying harder. But no matter what their religious backgrounds may be, when they place themselves before God and are stripped to their true selves, they are all just masses of sin and seeds of evildoer alike.

Human beings are unrighteous, full of blemishes, and masses of sin made of dust and dirt. Even the seemingly good people whose good deeds are done not for recognition but out of their sincere hearts, and who are actually discomforted to receive any praise for their good deeds, cannot escape from the fact that when their fundamental essence is reflected before God, they are masses of sin and seeds of evildoers. Because advocating the righteous of mankind is a great evil before God, people cannot escape from the condemnation of sin unless they recognize their punishment and accept the gospel of the water and the Spirit, the love of God. Before God, the efforts of mankind cannot be translated into any goodness, not even as small as dust, and the will of mankind is only filthy before Him.

In the Bible, human beings are often implied as wood. A log of acacia wood itself cannot be raised as a pillar at the entrance of the Temple of God unless God first overlays them with gold. And without the grace of salvation given by God, people are nothing more than dust that cannot but face the judgment of fire.

However, God removed all our sins and transgressions by having Jesus Christ the Messiah receive baptism and bleed to death, even as we remained only as sinners. Such salvation was prophesied in detail by King David about a thousand years before the Messiah came: *"As far as the east is from the west, So far has He removed our transgressions from us. As a father pities his children, so the LORD pities those who fear Him. For He knows our frame; He remembers that we are dust"* (Psalm 103:12-14).

Before we knew the righteousness of God, the righteousness of mankind had been our standard of life. I, too, had been like that when I did not know God's gift of salvation and did not have faith in His Word. In fact, I had no righteousness of my own, but I still thought of myself as decent. So since my childhood, there had been many times when I could not tolerate injustice and got into a fight with even people for whom I was no match. "Live a righteous life" had been my motto. Like this, because I had failed to see myself before God, I was full of my own righteousness. So I thought of myself better than others and tried hard to live righteously.

But such a being as myself was no more than a mere mass of sin before the righteousness of God. I was not someone who could keep even one of the Ten Commandments or the 613 laws that God commanded to be kept. The fact that I had the will to keep them was itself an act of unrighteousness that rebelled against the Word of God declaring me to be completely incapable of doing nothing but sin, and that stood against Him. All the righteousness of mankind is only unrighteousness before God.

This generation, which has lost God and His Law amid a flood of lewdness and corruption, has also lost any sense of guilt. However, we have to recognize that we human beings cannot but sin everyday and therefore we are doomed to go to hell without exception.

We Had Been Unrighteous and Filled with Sin, But the Lord Has Now Made Us His Own People by Saving Us from Our Sins with the Gospel of the Water and the Spirit

We were all unrighteous, but through the gift of salvation, the Lord has saved such beings as us from all our sins. Each board of the Holy Place, measuring 4.5 m (15 feet) in height and 67.5 cm (2.2 feet) in width, were made of acacia wood overlaid with gold and raised as the walls of the Holy Place. Under each board, two silver sockets were placed to sustain the board. The silver sockets here manifest that God has saved you and me entirely on His own.

The truth that God has saved us from sin is His love, in that Jesus Christ came to this earth and was baptized to take upon our sins, bore the condemnation of our sins by dying on the Cross, has thereby saved us from all the sins of the world and all condemnation. By believing in the gift of salvation He has given us, we have been born again. This gift of salvation that the Lord has given us is incorruptible like gold, and so it is forever unchanging.

The salvation that the Lord has given us is made of the baptism and blood of Jesus, and it has entirely and cleanly blotted out all our sins. It is because the Lord has saved us from all our sins that you and I could have been wholly delivered from all the sins that we commit with our minds, with our thoughts, and with our actual deeds. By believing in the gift of salvation that God has given us in our hearts, we have become His precious saints. Through the two sockets that sustained each board of the Tabernacle, God is telling us of the salvation of the water and the Spirit. God is telling us that it is 100 percent His grace and gift that we have become His children.

If we take out our faith in the baptism and blood of Jesus from us, then there is nothing remaining in us. We had all been such beings that were bound to be condemned for sin. We had been mere mortals who were bound to tremble before our certain death in accordance to the law of God declaring the wages of sin to be death, who were to realize and morn over the righteous judgment of fire awaiting us. This is why we are nothing if we leave out our faith in the gospel of the water and the Spirit.

Living in an age that is permeated by sin now, we must never forget that our fate had been that of waiting only for the judgment of fire. We were such mortal beings. However, God's grace has been bestowed on us entirely because He has given us the salvation of the water and the Spirit. The Messiah came to this earth, was baptized by John, shed His blood and died on the Cross, rose from the dead again, and has thereby saved us from all our sins, all our unrighteousness, and all our condemnation. By believing in this perfect gospel of the water and the blood, we have now been saved from all sins, and we can only thank God with our faith.

Though we are insufficient in the flesh, our workers, ministers, and I are preaching this gospel of the water and the Spirit throughout the whole world. Though this age is such a corrupt one, because we believe in the gospel of the water and the Spirit, we have been able to serve the Lord purely, free of any wickedness. That we have come to have this mind is not because of our own power, but because the Lord has given us holiness by clothing us in His grace of salvation.

It is because the Lord has saved us perfectly from sin and condemnation that we have been clothed in the power of this salvation, and it is entirely because of this that we have been able to serve the Lord purely. Because the Lord has saved us from all our sins with the water and the Spirit, I believe that we can serve Him in spite of our insufficiencies, no longer bound by our sins, shortcomings, and condemnation.

That I Am What I Am Is Absolutely by the Grace of God

Truly, these are all impossible things to do had it not been for the grace of our Lord. Spreading the gospel of the water and the Spirit throughout the whole world and serving this gospel purely would not have been possible at all if it had not been for the grace of the Lord. It is 100 percent by the grace of salvation God has given us that you and I are able to live our lives defending and serving the gospel.

We have become the pillars of the Temple of God (Revelation 3:12) and the people of His Kingdom by faith. Because the Lord has given us faith like gold, we now live in the House of God. In this age when the world is flooded by and drowning in sin, in an era when most people are forgetting or even blaspheming God, we have been washed with clear water and become clean, and we have been able to drink clear water and serve the Lord purely—words cannot express just how profoundly grateful I am for this blessing.

This is indeed how our faith is. How could we have become righteous? How have we been able to call ourselves righteous when there is no goodness in us. How could such sinful beings as you and I become sinless? Could you have become sinless and righteous by the righteousness of your flesh? The thoughts of the flesh, your own efforts, and your own deeds—could any of these turn you into sinless, righteous ones? Could you have become righteous but by faith in the gospel of the water and the Spirit? Could you have become righteous but by your faith in God's salvation manifested in the blue, purple, and scarlet thread and the fine woven linen? Could you have become righteous without believing in your salvation through the gospel of the water and the Spirit fulfilled by the Messiah and revealed in the Word of God? You could never have become so! By believing in only the scarlet thread, we can never become righteous.

Because Jesus Christ, our Savior and Messiah, shouldered all the sins of the world, including all the sins of our entire lifetime, through the baptism that He received from John to blot out all our sins on our behalf, we have become righteous by faith. Just as the sacrificial offering of the Old Testament bore sin when sinners or the High Priest put their hands on its head, in the New Testament's time, Jesus accepted all the sins of the world passed onto Him by being baptized by John. Jesus actually took upon all our sins through His baptism (Matthew 3:15) And He was testified by John as *"the Lamb of God who takes away the sins of the world" (John 1:29).*

Having received His baptism, Jesus lived the next three years of His life for our salvation, ending all our sins and condemnation by going to the Cross and giving up His own body to God, as a silent sheep before its shearers, and has given us new life.

It is because Jesus Christ took upon our sins through the baptism that He received from John that He gave Himself up quietly and was nailed on both His hands and feet when He was crucified by Roman soldiers. Hung on the Cross, Jesus shed all the blood that was in His body. And He put the final period to our salvation, saying, *"It is finished"(John 19:30).*

Having thus died, He rose again from the dead in three days, ascended to the Kingdom of Heaven, and has become our Savior by giving us eternal life. By shouldering the sins of the world through the baptism that He received from John the Baptist, and by His Cross, resurrection, and ascension, Jesus has become our perfect Savior. So, the Bible declares, *"Now where there is remission of these, there is no longer an offering for sin" (Hebrews 10:18).*

Faith in Only the Blood of the Cross and the Doctrine of Incremental Sanctification Has Never Saved You Wholly from Your Sins

Christians should know that they cannot be saved perfectly from their sins by believing only in Jesus' blood of the Cross. Because people sin everyday with their eyes and acts, they cannot blot out their sins just by believing in the blood of the Cross alone. One of the most pervasive iniquities committed in people's lives nowadays is sexual immorality. As a culture of explicit and obscene sexuality pervades the world, this sin is ingrained in our flesh. The Bible commands not to commit adultery, but today's reality is that because of the circumstances that surround them, many people end up committing this sin even as they do not want to.

God declares that anyone who looks at a woman lustfully has already committed adultery with her in his heart (Matthew 5:28), and yet what our eyes see everyday is all obscene. So people are committing such lewd sins every minute and every second. When this is the case, how can they be sanctified by giving their prayers of repentance and enter the Kingdom of God? How can they become righteous? Do their hearts become righteous when they discipline themselves for a long time and somehow get sanctified when they get old? Do their character become meeker? Do they become more patient? Of course not! What happens is the exact opposite.

Among the prevailing Christian doctrines is the "doctrine of incremental sanctification." This doctrine holds that when Christians believe in the death of Jesus on the Cross for a long time, give prayers of repentance daily, and serve the Lord daily, then they gradually become holy and good-tempered. It claims that the more time goes by since we began to believe in Jesus, the more we are made into someone who has nothing to do with sin and whose deeds are virtuous, and that by the time death approaches us, we would have become completely sanctified and therefore completely sinless.

And it also teaches that because we would have given our prayers of repentance all the time, we would have been washed of our sins everyday, as our clothes are washed, and therefore when we die in the end, we would go to God as someone who has become perfectly righteous. There are many who believe like this. But this is only a hypothetical speculation conjured up by man-made thoughts.

Romans 5:19 says, *"For as by one man's disobedience many were made sinners, so also by one Man's obedience many will be made righteous."* The passage tells us that all of us are made sinless by one Man's obedience. What you and I could not do, Jesus Christ achieved when He personally came to this earth. Knowing well that you and I could not free ourselves from sin, Jesus remitted our sins on our half, something that neither you nor I could ever do. By coming to this earth, receiving baptism, being crucified, and rising from the dead again, He has saved you and me and cleansed us from all our sins once for all.

That Jesus Christ could give salvation to His people by the remission of their sins was because He obeyed the will of God. Obeying God's will as the Messiah, Jesus Christ has bestowed on us the grace of salvation through His baptism, Cross, and resurrection. By thus giving us the gift of salvation, Jesus fulfilled the remission of sin perfectly. And now, by faith, we have been clothed in the grace of this salvation, for the Lord has fulfilled our salvation from sin, which could never have been achieved by our own endeavors.

However, most Christians do not believe in the baptism that Jesus received, but instead believe only in the blood that He shed on the Cross and try to become sanctified through their own deeds. In other words, even as Jesus took upon all the sins of mankind when He was baptized by John, people still do not believe in this truth. Chapter 3 of Matthew tells us that the first thing that Jesus did in His public life was receiving baptism from John. This is the truth attested by all the four gospel-writers.

Jesus took upon our sins by being baptized by John the Baptist, the representative of mankind and the greatest of all who were born of women, and yet there are so many people who ignore this fact and do not believe in it. Such people believe in Jesus without believing in His baptism, and fervently praise only the precious blood of the Cross that He shed. Pained by the death of Jesus on the Cross, they rouse up their emotions, make all kinds of rackets in their praise, shouting out, "♫There's wonderful power in the blood. ♪There is power, wonder-working power in the precious blood of the Lamb!♫" They try to go to God, in other words, fueled by their own emotions, vigor and strength. But you must realize that the more they do so, the more hypocritical they become, pretending to be holy but actually accumulating sins in their hearts in secrecy.

How Could We Believe in Jesus as Our Savior without Even Knowing the Gospel of the Water and the Spirit?

When we hear people talking about the Tabernacle, we often see that they don't even the slightest clue as to what they are really talking about. When it comes to believing in the Tabernacle, how can we just believe in whatever way we deem convenient and fitting? Because the salvation from sin that the Lord has fulfilled is so elaborate, God has enabled us to realize how elaborately and how concretely our salvation has been fulfilled.

Through the Tabernacle, He has also made us realize that the Lord has saved us with the blue and purple threads, the water and the blood. We come to realize that to blot out our sins, the Lord came *"not only by water, but by water and blood" (1 John 5:6).* The water, the blood, and the Spirit in which we believe are one. It is by coming as a man, being baptized by John the Baptist, dying, and rising from the dead again that God has saved us.

Through the Tabernacle, we have been able to discover and believe in this detailed portrait of salvation. By studying the two tenons and two silver sockets of each board, we have come to realize the method by which Jesus has saved us from our sins. And we have thus found the truth that we must surely believe in the ministries of Jesus manifested in the blue, purple, and scarlet thread.

Apart from the Bible, nowhere else can this salvation find its origin. We need the gift of salvation that is made of these two elements of baptism and the Cross. Those who believe in this truth can then become the ones who are born of God. By delivering us from our sins with the water and the Spirit, God has fulfilled our salvation perfectly.

Two tenons, in other words, were made under each board and plugged into two silver sockets. This truth is absolutely necessary and tremendously important for us and our remission of sin. Most critically, we must believe in our salvation that God has completed for us, for if we do not believe in the truth of the blue, purple, and scarlet thread, we can never be saved.

As each board of the Holy Tabernacle needed two silver sockets to stand upright, when it comes to believing in Jesus Christ, two truths of His grace are absolutely necessary. What are they? They are that Jesus took upon our sins by being baptized, and that He bore all the condemnation and curses of our sins by carrying them to the Cross and being crucified. Whoever is made righteous can be made so only when he/she wholly believes in these two graces of perfect salvation. Our faith in both the baptism of Jesus and the blood of the Cross, the two pivots of His gift of salvation, makes us stand firmly in

Free book request www.bjnewlife.org

the House of God. As the two tenons were put into the two silver sockets, each board could stand upright.

Like this, it is by our correct faith that believes in the two pivots of His salvation that we are made His truly blameless people. By believing in the gospel of the water and the blood given by Jesus, we receive faith like gold that is forever unchanging. By believing in this gospel of the water and the Spirit manifested in the blue, purple, and scarlet thread and the fine woven linen, we become the saints who have received the salvation of the perfect remission of sin.

Theology Until Now and the Age of the Gospel of the Water and the Spirit

Excluding the Early Church period, since the Edict of Milan in 313 A.D., Christianity, including today's Christianity, has been spreading the gospel of the Cross that leaves out Jesus' baptism. From the Early Church period to 313 A.D., which legalized Christianity as the new Roman religion, Christianity had preached the gospel of the water and the Spirit, but afterward the Roman Catholic Church came to dominate the religious scene. Then from the early 14th century, a culture that centered everything on man-made thoughts and called for the restoration of humanity began to emerge, first in some prosperous city-states of northern Italy. This was Renaissance.

By the 16th century, the undercurrent of this culture that began in Italy started to spread throughout the western world, and scholars who studied humanistic, man-made philosophy began to study theology. Interpreting the Bible with their own heads, they began to build Christian doctrines. But because they did not know the truth, they could not understand the

Bible soundly and wholly. So what they could not understand with their heads, they overcame by incorporating their secular knowledge and thoughts, thus producing their own Christian doctrines.

As a result, a multitude of Christian doctrines and theologies arose in Christian history: Lutheranism, Calvinism, Arminianism, New Theology, Conservatism, Rationalism, Critical Theology, Mystical Theology, Liberation Theology, Feminist Theology, Black Theology, and even Atheistic Theology, etc.

The history of Christianity may seem very long, but it actually is not that long. For 300 years since the Early Church period, people could learn about the Bible, but this was soon followed by the Medieval Age, the dark age of Christianity. During this era, for laymen reading the Bible itself was a crime punishable to death by beheading. It was not until the 1700s when the wind of theology began to blow, and then Christianity seemed to blossom in the 1800s and 1900s as its theologies grew vibrant and active, but now, many people have fallen into mystical doctrines, believing in God based on their own personal experiences. But despite its theological diversities, all the branch streams of Christianity have one common denominator of faith, that is, believing in only the blood of Jesus.

But is this the truth? When you believed in this way, did your sins actually disappear? You sin everyday. You sin everyday with your hearts, thoughts, acts, and shortcomings. Can you then be remitted of these sins just by believing only in the blood that Jesus shed on the Cross? That Jesus shouldered our sins by being baptized and died on the Cross is the biblical truth. Yet there are so many people who say that their sins have been remitted by believing only in the blood of the Cross and giving their prayers of repentance everyday. Were the sins of your hearts and consciences cleansed away by giving such prayers repentance? This is impossible.

If you are Christians, then you must now know and believe in the salvation of this truth, that Jesus Christ came to this earth and took upon our sins of the world by being baptized by John. In spite of this, do you yet ignore this truth, not even trying to know it, nor to believe in it? If so, you are committing the sin of mocking Jesus, of lowering and despising His name, and you cannot say that you truly believe in Jesus as your Savior. By leaving out Jesus' baptism from this salvation fulfilled by Jesus Christ and believing in Him in whatever way that you want, you can never be clothed in the grace of salvation.

Yet many Christians do not believe in the truth as it is, that Jesus has blotted out our sins, but instead follow their own thoughts and believe in whatever twisted truths they want to believe. Nowadays, their hearts have been hardened more and more by their mistaken doctrinal faith, believing that their sins can be blotted out just by believing in the blood of the Cross alone.

But the answer of salvation planned by God is as the following: We can receive the everlasting remission of sin by believing in Jesus' baptism, His death on the Cross, and His resurrection. Yet there have risen a countless number of people who believe in Jesus by taking out His baptism from this truth of salvation, misunderstanding and misbelieving the following equation to be an immutable law: "Jesus (the Cross and His resurrection) + prayers of repentance + virtuous deeds = salvation received through incremental sanctification." Those who believe in this way are only saying with their lips that they have received their remission of sin. However, the truth is that their hearts are actually filled with heaps of sins that still remain unsolved.

Do you still have sin in your hearts? If you have sin in your hearts even as you now believe in Jesus, then clearly, there is a serious problem with your faith. It is because you believe in Jesus merely as a matter of religion that your consciences are not clean and you have sin. However, the very fact that you can realize you still have sin remaining in your hearts is extremely fortunate in itself. Why? Because those who truly realize that they have sin will recognize that they cannot avoid but be bound to hell for this sin, and when they do so they can finally become the poor in spirit and thereby be able to hear the Word of true salvation.

If you want to receive the remission of sin from God, then your hearts must be prepared. Those whose hearts are ready before God admit, "God, I want to receive the remission of sin. I have believed in Jesus for a long time, but I still have sin. Because the wages of sin is death, I cannot but be cast into hell." Like this, they recognize themselves as wholly sinful before God. Those who recognize the Word of God, those who believe that the Word of God is surely fulfilled exactly as it says—none other than these are the ones whose hearts are ready.

God meets such souls without exception. Such people hear His Word, see the Word with their own eyes and confirm it, and from doing so they come to realize, "Ah, I had believed mistakenly. And a countless number of people are believing mistakenly now." And by believing in the gospel of the water and the Spirit, regardless of what others might say, they then receive their remission of sin.

Those Who Have Been Saved from All Their Sins Must Defend Their Faith by Believing in the Gospel of the Water and the Spirit

However, this world is full of countless evil doctrines that can unsettle and defile even the hearts of the born-again. The Lord Jesus warned us, *"Take heed, beware of the leaven of the Pharisees and the leaven of Herod" (Mark 8:15).* But we cannot even count just how many such leavened teachings there are, defiling people's heart just by hearing only once. We must realize just how this world is waving in sexual immorality.

We who believe must know exactly in what kind of age we are now living and defend our faith. Yet even as we live in such a sinful world, in our hearts is the unassailable truth that the Lord has delivered us from sin. The Word of testimony that bears witness to our unchanging salvation is the gospel of the water and the Spirit. We must have faith in the truth that is neither shaken by the world nor dragged by it.

Everything from this world is not the truth. God told us that the righteous overcome the world. It is by their faith in the gospel of the unchanging truth that the righteous overcome the Devil and triumph over the world. Though we are insufficient, our hearts, our thoughts, and our bodies are still in the House of God and are standing firmly on the gospel of salvation with faith. We are standing steadfastly on the gospel of the water and the blood with which the Lord has saved us.

Because of this, we are so thankful to God. No matter how sin abounds in this world, at least we the righteous truly have spotless consciences and faith that shine like gold in our hearts. We the righteous will all live a life that overcomes the world by this faith. Until the day of the Lord's return, and even as we are in His Kingdom, all of us will praise this faith. We will forever praise the Lord who has saved us and praise our God who has given us this faith.

As this truthful faith that we have with us before God is raised on the rock, it is not shaken under any circumstances. As such, no matter what happens to us as we live on this earth until the day we stand before the Lord, we will defend our hearts by faith. Even if everything in this world is destroyed, even if this world is drowning in sin, and even if this world becomes worse than Sodom and Gomorrah of the old, we will not follow this world, but we will believe in God chastely, we will pursue His righteousness, and we will continue to do the works that spread these two graces (the baptism of Jesus and His death on the Cross) of salvation, the true graces of God.

Those Who Pretend to Believe in the True Gospel

Some people, even as they do not actually believe in the gospel of the water and the Spirit, still pretend to believe in the truth of the blue, purple, and scarlet thread. But we can see that such people have sin in their hearts from not believing in the gospel of the water and the Spirit sincerely. They are like the one who lost the iron ax head, which he had borrowed from his neighbor, into the water (2 Kings 6:5).

In a similar manner, it is possible, as needs arise, for some people to make use of the gospel of the water and the Spirit for a short while. But without believing that this gospel of the water and the Spirit is the truth, they are unable to speak with the true faith when preaching or having fellowship. And those without faith in the truth tragically end up renouncing their life of faith in midway. But the truth of the gospel of the water and the Spirit does not change, and this is why they must believe in this gospel of the water and the Spirit.

But quoting Hebrew 7:12, which says, *"For the priesthood being changed, of necessity there is also a change of the law,"* some people claim, "The Law has also changed. So the salvation that Jesus fulfilled was not really fulfilled according to the same method in the Old Testament. Jesus Christ came and has saved us just by dying on the Cross, a modified method." Some others claim, "It seems likely that it was when Jesus died on the Cross when God passed our sins onto His Son."

But such claims are all flawed and groundless. We can easily refute their claims by asking, "Does this then mean that God just crucified Jesus who was sinless and only then passed the sins of the world onto Him?" When we believe in the Word of God, we must believe as it is, not by insisting on our own thoughts. Even if we happen to have our own contentions, if the Bible tells us that these contentions are wrong, then we have to break off our own righteousness and believe in the Word of God.

The more time goes by, the more grateful and precious is the fact that the Lord has saved us with the gospel of the water and the Spirit. When we believed according to our own thoughts, there were times when our life of faith was at risk and we almost fell apart from the Church. But just as two tenons held up each board of the Tabernacle by being put into two silver sockets, our faith in the truth of Jesus, that He took upon our sins by being baptized and shed His blood, holds us steadfastly. By being baptized by John and bearing our condemnation by being crucified and shedding His blood, our Lord has saved us from all our sins. As such, our faith will not waver forever.

Proverbs 25:4 says, *"Take away the dross from silver,*

And it will go to the silversmith for jewelry." Like this passage, even as many vile, evil, and corrupted things emerge in our thoughts of the flesh, with His baptism and blood, Jesus has purified us of these filthy things, of the sins of mankind, and has made us the workers of the righteousness of God. The Lord has purified us of the sins of the world. By being baptized by John and thereby accepting all our sins once for all, and by being crucified and shedding His blood and thereby bearing all the condemnation of our sins, Jesus has cleanly saved us from the sins of the world.

As such, those who believe in the gospel of the water and the Spirit are guaranteed of their everlasting salvation. Our acts may seem worrisome for at times, but the gospel of the water and the Spirit holds our faith steadfastly, just as silver sockets sustained each board by grabbing its two tenons.

The Everlasting Grace of Salvation That Holds Us

Now, let us turn our attention to the bars that held the boards of the Tabernacle together. Exodus 26:26-27 says, *"And you shall make bars of acacia wood: five for the boards on one side of the tabernacle, five bars for the boards on the other side of the tabernacle, and five bars for the boards of the side of the tabernacle, for the far side westward."* The overall shape of the Tabernacle was rectangular. Pillars were placed at the door of the Tabernacle and for the veil of the Most Holy, and the rest was made of boards. These boards were wrapped around with five bars.

To hold these bars, five gold rings were placed on each board, and the bars themselves, made of acacia wood, were also overlaid with gold. The five bars were placed on the boards on all three sides of the Tabernacle, north, south, and west. As the boards were held by these bars passing through the rings of gold, they remained fixed. So supported at their bottom by silver sockets, and held together at their sides by five bars, the boards stood firm and fixed.

And as the 48 boards were wrapped around by five bars and supported one another, the people of God are also tied together with God with the gospel of the water and the Spirit. God's Church is the place where those who have received the gift of the salvation of the water and the Spirit gather together and live their lives of faith. Jesus told Peter that He would build His Church on the rock (Matthew 16:18-19). As such, the place where the Kingdom of God is formed by the gathering of those who have received the remission of sin is God's Church. God is showing us that He has saved us wholly from the sins of the world with the works of Jesus manifested in the blue, purple, and scarlet thread.

Exodus 26:28 says, *"The middle bar shall pass through the midst of the boards from end to end."* This middle bar was made long enough to bind all the boards of one side all at once. What, then, is the meaning of this middle bar passing through the midst of the boards from end to end? It means that the righteous unite with each other, and that their faith commune with each other. In other words, by believing in salvation fulfilled through the gospel of the water and the Spirit given by the Lord, they can commune with one another in faith. The righteous meet eye to eye by their faith. This is why when we meet our fellow saints or ministers and have fellowship with them, we can actually feel this communion of hearts.

"One Faith, One Baptism, and One God"

Let's turn to Ephesians 4:3-7: *"Endeavoring to keep the unity of the Spirit in the bond of peace. There is one body and one Spirit, just as you were called in one hope of your calling; one Lord, one faith, one baptism; one God and Father of all, who is above all, and through all, and in you all. But to each one of us grace was given according to the measure of Christ's gift."* The Apostle Paul told us to endeavor to keep the unity of the Spirit in the bond of peace. Jesus' baptism and the Cross—when we receive the gift of salvation made of these two, then peace comes into our hearts. When we receive the remission of sin into our hearts, then we become one family in Christ. We become, in short, one body.

"One Lord." Jesus Christ who has saved us is one. *"One faith."* What do you believe in? You believe in the salvation of the water and blood of Jesus and of the Spirit, manifested in the blue, purple, and scarlet thread and the fine woven linen. *"One baptism."* The Apostle Paul emphasized Jesus' baptism once again. He did not refer to the Cross here, but rather he stressed the baptism of Jesus that cleansed all believers unconditionally. For us to believe in His baptism is being baptized into Christ and thus having put on Christ (Galatians 3:27). *"One God."* God is one. This God has saved us by sending His own Son.

All these things refer to one faith in the water, the blood, and the Spirit (1 John 5:8). It is when we have faith in the gospel of the water and the Spirit that our hearts can commune with one another. Those who have received the remission of sin can meet each other eye to eye. There may be a few times when they cannot understand each other completely. But as the middle bar passed through the midst of the boards from end to end, if they have really received the remission of sin in the center of their heart, then they can all commune with one another. "This brother has also been saved from sin, but his flesh is weak and there are many carnal remnants in his heart. Like everyone else, he, too, a seed of evildoers, but the Lord has still remitted his sin with the gospel of the water and the Spirit." Like this, they come to understand one another and praise the Lord.

No matter how insufficient people may be, if they receive the remission of sin and stay in the Church, then their faces will light up, their thoughts will light up, their hearts will light up also, and they will be able to commune with one another. The righteous can see each another eye to eye. What makes this possible? Faith makes it possible. They see each other eye to eye not because of any other condition but because of faith. What, then, explains our inability to commune with some others? We cannot share our hearts with those who are not in Christ, because they do not, in their hearts, believe in the truth, in the gospel of the water and the Spirit. Those who do not believe in this gospel of the water and the Spirit cannot commune with us at all.

Brothers and sister, what exactly is God's Church? It is the gathering of those who are sanctified in Christ Jesus, called to be saints (1 Corinthians 1:2). It is the congregation of those who believe in the truth that Jesus Christ has washed away their sins by being baptized, that He has saved them by shouldering these sins and bearing all their condemnation on the Cross, and that He rose from the dead again and has become their own Savior. God's Church is none other than this gathering of those who have become one by believing in the gospel of the water and the Spirit.

It is because this faith is in both my heart and your hearts that we can see each other eye to eye when we are in His

Church. Just as God does not look at our outside appearances but at the center of our hearts when He sees us, we who have received the remission of sin do not look at outside appearances either, but we have fellowship by looking at the center of each other's faith. "Does this person really believe in the truth in the heart?"—this is what we look for. No matter what difference there may be in his/her personality, this does not matter at all as long as he/she believes in *"one Lord, one faith, one baptism; one God and Father of all."*

Because we believe, we have become the pillars and boards of the Tabernacle, and because we believe, we have become the family of God. Do you believe in the gospel of the water and the Spirit? It is because we believe that we are spreading the light of salvation throughout the whole world, just as pure gold (faith) shines in the House of God. We can share our hearts with those who have only recently received the remission of sin, for the Holy Spirit dwells in their hearts also. If only we have received the remission of sin, then we can all commune with each other, but if we have not received the remission of sin, then we cannot commune with one another. Sinners who discriminate people based on outside appearances treat each other differently based on such superficial aspects as looks, wealth, or fame, but we the righteous just do not do this in our hearts. There is no discrimination for the righteous.

When people first receive the remission of sin, I often ask them, "Have you really received the remission of sin? Do you still have sin, or have all your sins disappeared? By the way, you must have a lot of questions about the Bible, don't you? Ask them in time as you go along with your life of faith. Also, your shortcomings will be revealed and you will probably make some mistakes along the way. But the leaders and those who have gone before you in the Church will help you, so that everything will turn out just fine."

Brothers and sisters, we the righteous need the Church. The Tabernacle also means God's Church. Those who do not believe in the water and the blood cannot come into God's Church and dwell in it. Those who do not believe in the gospel of the water and the Spirit manifested in the blue, purple, and scarlet thread cannot come into and dwell in His Church. Only those who believe in the truth can dwell in the Church, become God's people and His workers, and see the glory of God also. It is not only by blood or some qualification of their flesh that people can become God's children. No matter how authoritative some pastors might be, if they do not believe in the gospel of the water and the Spirit, then they are not God's children.

Jesus Who Came by Water and Blood Has Saved Us Perfectly

What the Lord did when He came to this earth can be summarized by His birth, baptism, bloodshed, and resurrection. All these are His ministries of the remission of sin. Jesus has fulfilled His mission with His ministries of the blue, purple, and scarlet thread. The blue, purple, and scarlet thread manifested in the Tabernacle were for our own salvation from sin. God's salvation is so elaborate that we should not believe in Him in our own way. We have to believe in His salvation as it is.

Our faith should correctly accord with the two truths of His salvation: His baptism and His blood on the Cross. That's why the two tenons were correctly fit to the holes of the two silver sockets. We cannot regard the truth that Jesus has given us as just one of the knowledge of the world and believe it only as such. You and I are the ones who have been saved from sin before God by believing in Jesus' works of salvation manifested in the two silver sockets.

The Tabernacle tells us of Jesus' detailed method of salvation, and this salvation has actually been fulfilled for us already. Believe in the two gifts of salvation that God has given you. Gold that used in the Tabernacle implies faith. If you believe in the truth as it is, then salvation and the glory of the Lord can become yours, but not if you do not believe. Do you want to live inside the Tabernacle by faith, clothed in God's glory and protected by Him, or do you want be cursed forever by continuing to not believe? If you believe only in the blood of the Cross, then you cannot be saved. You must believe that the blood of the Cross and baptism are one. The gift of the Lord is made of these two.

The Spirit of God dwells in our hearts only when we believe in both of these two elements (Jesus' baptism and bloodshed). The Holy Spirit never dwells in the hearts of those who do not believe in them. If you confess your faith only with your lips but do not believe in your hearts, and if your knowledge is no more than a mere intellectual exercise, then you can never be saved. To be saved, you must first draw a clear line of demarcation setting the boundaries of your salvation: "Until now, I had not been saved. The salvation that I had believed in was not the real one. But by believing in Jesus who came by the water and the blood, I have now been saved." People can become righteous only when they first become sinners at least once. They must admit that as the unsaved, they are bound to be condemned for their sins, and then become the perfectly saved ones by believing in the gospel of the water and the Spirit.

With the blue and purple thread, the baptism and blood of

Jesus, we must receive our perfect salvation. With His baptism and blood, the Lord has given us the gift of perfect salvation. To prevent us from believing based on our own thoughts, the Lord revealed this salvation in detail through the Tabernacle also. Because this salvation is so precious and perfect, it is worthy for everyone to believe. Do not believe in just a single aspect of His salvation, the blood of the Cross, but believe in both the baptism and blood of Jesus all at once! If there is anyone among us who has not been saved yet, then it is my sincere hope that he/she would be saved by believing, even now, in this truth.

Is there anyone who still believes in the blood of Jesus alone? There are so many Christians who still believe such a half-baked gospel. But my hope is that such a wrong faith will never invade any of our hearts again. No matter what happens, I cannot belong to a crowd of the unsaved. We are the ones who have been saved perfectly by believing in these two things (blue and scarlet thread)—that is, in the baptism and blood of Jesus. I thank God for these two gifts of salvation through which the Lord has saved me. Because God has fulfilled my salvation perfectly, I have already been freed from curses and judgment also.

Truly, our salvation that has come of the blue and scarlet thread is precious beyond all words. Remember and believe that your salvation is made perfect not just by the blood of the Cross, nor by only the baptism of Jesus, but by both the baptism and the blood of the Cross, and that it is by believing in these two that you can become God's children. We have received eternal life by believing in the gospel Word of the water and the Spirit, the mystery hidden in the two tenons and the two silver sockets of the boards of the Tabernacle.

I give all my thanks to our Lord who has saved us from the sins of the world. Hallelujah! ⊠

SERMON

6

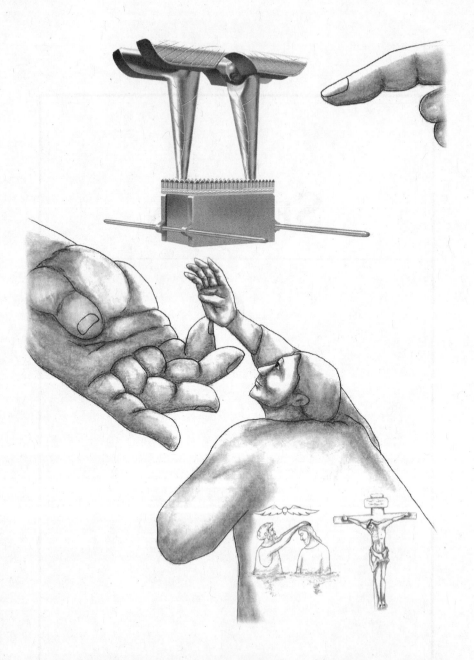

You can download Rev. Paul C. Jong's Christian Books on iPhone, iPad, or Blackberry by going to Amazon's Kindle e-bookstore (www.amazon.com).

The Spiritual Mysteries Hidden in the Ark of The Testimony

< Exodus 25:10-22 >

"And they shall make an ark of acacia wood; two and a half cubits shall be its length, a cubit and a half its width, and a cubit and a half its height. And you shall overlay it with pure gold, inside and out you shall overlay it, and shall make on it a molding of gold all around. You shall cast four rings of gold for it, and put them in its four corners; two rings shall be on one side, and two rings on the other side. And you shall make poles of acacia wood, and overlay them with gold. You shall put the poles into the rings on the sides of the ark, that the ark may be carried by them. The poles shall be in the rings of the ark; they shall not be taken from it. And you shall put into the ark the Testimony which I will give you. You shall make a mercy seat of pure gold; two and a half cubits shall be its length and a cubit and a half its width. And you shall make two cherubim of gold; of hammered work you shall make them at the two ends of the mercy seat. Make one cherub at one end, and the other cherub at the other end; you shall make the cherubim at the two ends of it of one piece with the mercy seat. And the cherubim shall stretch out their wings above, covering the mercy seat with their wings, and they shall face one another; the faces of the cherubim shall be toward the mercy seat. You shall put the mercy seat on top of the ark, and in the ark you shall put the Testimony that I will give you. And there I will meet with you, and I will speak with you from above the mercy seat, from between the two cherubim which are on the ark of the Testimony, about everything which I will give you in commandment to the children of Israel."

Today's topic is the Ark of the Testimony. The Ark of the Testimony, measuring 113 cm (3.7 feet) in its length, 68 cm (2.2 feet) in its width, and 68 cm (2.2 feet) in its height, was made of acacia wood and overlaid with pure gold. Inside this Ark, there were two stone tablets engraved with the Ten Commandments and a golden pot of manna, and later, Aaron's budded rod was added to them. What, then, are these three items placed inside the Ark of the Testimony telling us? Through these items, I would like to provide a thorough explanation of the three ministries of Jesus Christ. Let us now examine the spiritual truth manifested in these three items placed inside the Ark of the Testimony.

The Two Stone Tablets Engraved with the Law

The two stone tablets engraved with the Law that were placed inside the Ark of the Testimony tell us that God is the Lawmaker who has given us His laws. Romans 8:1-2 states, *"There is therefore now no condemnation to those who are in Christ Jesus, who do not walk according to the flesh, but according to the Spirit. For the law of the Spirit of life in Christ Jesus has made me free from the law of sin and death."*

Free book request www.nlmission.com

From this passage, we can see that God has established two laws in our hearts: the law of life and the law of condemnation.

With these two laws, the Lord has brought condemnation and salvation to all human beings. First of all, we can recognize through the Law that we are sinners inevitably destined to hell. However, to those who know their sinful nature and doomed fate, God has given His law of salvation, *"the law of the Spirit of life in Christ Jesus."* God has become the true Savior for all by giving them these two laws.

The Manna Contained in the Golden Pot

The golden pot that was also found in the Ark had manna. When the people of Israel spent 40 years in the wilderness, God brought them food from the heavens, and the Israelite lived on this manna cooking it in various ways. And it was like white coriander seed, and its taste was like wafers made with honey. This manna that God had given to the people of Israel sustained their lives until they entered into the land of Canaan. As such, it was to keep this food in remembrance that it was put in a pot.

This tells us that we, today's believers, also should eat the bread of life that the spiritual children of God must feed on while in this world until they enter Heaven. But there are times when we want to have the bread of the world, that is, the teachings of this world instead of the Word of God. Still, what the children of God must truly and actually live on before reaching the spiritual land of Canaan is the Word of God, which is the spiritual bread of true life that comes down from Heaven.

One never gets tired of always having the bread of true life. The more we have this spiritual bread, the more it become true life for our souls. But if we feed on the bread of the teachings of the world instead of the Word of God, our souls will ultimately end up dead.

God commanded the people of Israel to put the manna that came down from the heavens in a pot and keep it. As shown in Exodus 16:33, God said, "Take a pot and put an omer of manna in it, and lay it up before the LORD, to be kept for your generations." The manna that came down from the heavens was the bread of true life for the people's souls. *So He humbled you, allowed you to hunger, and fed you with manna which you did not know nor did your fathers know, that He might make you know that man shall not live by bread alone; but man lives by every word that proceeds from the mouth of the LORD" (Deuteronomy 8:3).*

Who Then Is the True Bread of Life for Us?

The baptism that Jesus Christ received to take our sins upon His body and His crucifixion and bloodshed are our bread of true life. By giving us His flesh and blood, Jesus Christ has become the bread of eternal life. As John 6:48-58 tells us: *"'I am the bread of life. Your fathers ate the manna in the wilderness, and are dead. This is the bread which comes down from heaven, that one may eat of it and not die. I am the living bread which came down from heaven. If anyone eats of this bread, he will live forever; and the bread that I shall give is My flesh, which I shall give for the life of the world.' The Jews therefore quarreled among themselves, saying, 'How can this Man give us His flesh to eat?' Then Jesus said to them, 'Most assuredly, I say to you, unless you eat the flesh of the Son of Man and drink His blood, you have no life in you. Whoever eats My flesh and drinks My blood has eternal life, and I will raise him up at the last day. For My flesh is food indeed, and My blood is drink indeed. He who eats My flesh and drinks My blood abides in Me, and I in him. As the living Father sent Me, and I live because of the Father, so he who feeds on Me will live because of Me. This is the bread which came down from heaven—not as your fathers ate the manna, and are dead. He who eats this bread will live forever.'"*

Our Lord said, *"This is the bread which came down from heaven—not as your fathers ate the manna, and are dead. He who eats this bread will live forever."* What was *"the bread which came down from heaven"*? It meant the flesh and blood of Jesus. In the Bible, the flesh of Jesus tells us that Jesus Christ took upon the sins of the world by being baptized by John in the Jordan River. And the blood of Jesus tells us that because Jesus was baptized, He carried the sins of the world and bore the condemnation of sin by being crucified.

The manna in the pot that was placed inside the Ark of the Testimony was the bread of life for the Israelites when they were in the wilderness, and in New Testament's time, its spiritual meaning refers to the flesh of Jesus Christ. This truth shows us the baptism through which Jesus Christ took upon the iniquities of all sinners and the blood that He shed on the Cross. Because Jesus Christ took all the sins of this world upon His body through His baptism and shed His blood and died on the Cross, His baptism and bloodshed have become the everlasting fountainhead of new life that enables believers to be born again.

The flesh that Jesus gave up to take upon the iniquities of sinners through His baptism and the blood that He shed on the Cross are the bread of life that enables all sinners to receive the remission of sin. We must therefore realize the reason why Jesus said, *"unless you eat the flesh of the Son of Man and drink His blood, you have no life in you" (John 6:53).*

Who Is Greater?

When we look at John 6, we can see that most Jews at the time considered Moses to be greater than Jesus. When Jesus came to this earth, they asked Him, "Are you greater than our father Moses?" In fact, they considered Moses to be the greatest of all. Because the Jews had failed to recognize Jesus as the Messiah, they saw Him as an eyesore. So they challenged Him by asking, *"Are you greater than Moses?"* The people of Israel believed in Jehovah God, and along came a young man of only 30 years of age claiming, *"Though your fathers ate the manna and died, those who eat the bread that I give will not die."* This is why they came to compare the power of the two, Moses and Jesus.

As Jesus declared later, *"Before Abraham was, I am,"* He is greater than any human being of the entire human history, for He is the Creator Himself. How could mere creatures even dare to challenge their should be Creator? Even so, some people still say that Jesus is only a great teacher, merely one of the great sages in human history. What a blasphemy! Jesus is God, the King of kings, and the Creator of the whole universe. He is the omnipotent and omniscient God. Yet He humbled Himself and came to this earth in the flesh of a man to save you and me from all our sins and eternal death, to become our true Savior.

Jesus Christ said, *"It is written in the prophets, 'And they shall all be taught by God.' Therefore everyone who has heard and learned from the Father comes to Me. Not that anyone has seen the Father, except He who is from God; He has seen the*

Father." In the end, Jesus was ultimately saying that He is the Christ that the Jews had been waiting for. But they failed to understand what Jesus was saying, neither able to believe nor to accept it, and this resulted into a serious misunderstanding, as they wondered, "How can you give us your flesh to eat? Are you saying that we would attain eternal life if we actually eat your flesh and drink your blood? Do you think we are some kind of cannibals here?"

But those who eat the flesh of Jesus and drink His blood will live forever. The flesh of Jesus is the bread of life. The real substance of the manna that was put in this pot, the bread of life, is the flesh and blood of Jesus Christ. By coming to this earth and giving up His flesh and blood, Jesus has enabled us to eat the bread of life and receive eternal life.

How, then, can everyone eat the flesh of Jesus and drink His blood? The only way to eat the flesh of Jesus and drink His blood is to believe in the baptism of Jesus and His blood of the Cross. We must eat the flesh of Jesus and drink His blood by faith. To give you and me the remission of sin and to enable us to live forever in the Kingdom of Heaven, our Lord has blotted out our sins once for all by being baptized and shedding His blood, and He has thereby become the food for our souls. Now, by believing in God's Word of the water and the Spirit, we must eat this spiritual food and receive eternal life.

Let me testify in more detail just how we can eat the flesh of Jesus and drink His blood. As you and I know very well, Jesus Christ came to this earth and took upon the sins of mankind by being baptized by John at the age of 30, and then, He bore all the condemnation of our sins by bleeding to death on the Cross. It is by believing in this very truth that we can eat His flesh and drink His blood. The washing of sin was fulfilled as the sins of mankind were passed onto the body of Jesus through the baptism that He received. Drinking His blood means that as Jesus was baptized and shed His blood on the Cross, this blood that He shed bore the condemnation of our sins.

As such, those who believe in the blood of Jesus in their hearts are quenched of their thirst, for the condemnation of all their sins ended completely with the punishment of the Cross that Jesus bore. We must realize this truth. And we must believe in it. Because Jesus Christ came to this earth and accepted our sins by being baptized by John, by believing in this truth we have been cleansed of all sins once for all.

God told us to eat the flesh of Jesus and drink His blood by faith. Because Jesus took upon all sins through the baptism that He received from John, leaving the iniquities of no one, and because He gave up His body to the punishment of the Cross and shed His precious blood, the hearts of those who believe are now clean and thirst-free, as they have washed away all their sins and bore all the condemnation of sin by faith. This is why Jesus said, *"My flesh is food indeed, and My blood is drink indeed" (John 6:55).*

Most assuredly, this Jesus is the Savior indeed, the Son of God who has washed away our sins and bore the condemnation of our sins. To free us from the law that declares the wages of sin to be death, to wash us from all our sins, and to deliver us from all our punishment, this One, the Savior and the Son of God, gave up His own body on the Cross, shed His blood, and thereby cleansed the hearts of those who believe and quenched their thirst. This is the effect of the flesh and blood of Jesus.

Jesus is the Savior who took care of the sins and condemnation of mankind. Jesus is the Savior who accepted the sins of mankind through the baptism that He received, who was crucified and shed His blood to bear the condemnation of these sins. It was because Jesus had accepted the sins of the world passed onto Him from us that the punishment of sin that He bore by being crucified could become the punishment of our own sins.

It is by believing in the truth of the water and the Spirit that we can receive the remission of sin. You must all believe in the baptism of Jesus and His bloodshed as your own remission of sin. It is by believing in this gospel of truth that we can eat and drink the flesh and blood of Jesus spiritually. It is by believing, in other words, that Jesus Christ the Son of God came to this earth, took upon our sins through His baptism, and bore all the condemnation of our sins on the Cross that we can become the ones who are able to eat His flesh, drink His blood, and thereby receive eternal life. By believing in the baptism and bloodshed of Jesus, we can now eat His flesh and drink His blood. By eat the baptism of Jesus and the blood that He shed on the Cross as our own food of the remission of sin, we can be remitted of all sins. It is through this faith that we have been able to receive the remission of our sins, become God's children, and live forever in the Kingdom of God.

Aaron's Rod That Budded

Among the items placed inside the Ark of the Testimony, Aaron's rod that budded refers to Jesus Christ as the everlasting High Priest of the Kingdom of Heaven. It also tells us that eternal life is found in Him. To facilitate our understanding of this, let us turn to Numbers 16:1-2: *"Now Korah the son of Izhar, the son of Kohath, the son of Levi, with Dathan and Abiram the sons of Eliab, and On the son of Peleth, sons of Reuben, took men; and they rose up before Moses with*

Free book request www.bjnewlife.org

some of the children of Israel, two hundred and fifty leaders of the congregation, representatives of the congregation, men of renown."

The passage here tells us that among the Levites, 250 famed leaders of the congregation drew together and rose up against Moses. They said, "What have you, Moses and Aaron, done for us by leading us out of the land of Egypt? Have you given us vineyards? Have you led us to an oasis? What have you done for us? Have you not brought us to the wilderness only to die on desert sand in the end? How can you call yourselves as the servants of God? Does God work only through you?" There arose, in other words, a rebellion against the leadership of Moses and Aaron.

At that time, God said to Korah, Dathan, On, and other leaders of the congregation who led the rebellion, *"Bring a rod from each father's house and write each man's name on his rod. Then place these rods in the Tabernacle of Meeting. Leave them there for a night and check them the next day."* God then said, *"It shall be that the rod of the man whom I choose will blossom; thus I will rid Myself of the complaints of the children of Israel, which they make against you"* (Numbers 17:5). In verse 8, we see that *"the rod of Aaron, of the house of Levi, had sprouted and put forth buds, had produced blossoms and yielded ripe almonds."*

Then in verse 10, we see, *"And the LORD said to Moses, 'Bring Aaron's rod back before the Testimony, to be kept as a sign against the rebels, that you may put their complaints away from Me, lest they die.'"* This is how Aaron's rod that budded came to be placed and kept inside the Ark of the Testimony.

This shows that Aaron, a descendant of Levi, was anointed as the High Priest of the people of Israel. Moses was God's prophet and Aaron and his descendents were the High

Priests of the people of Israel. God Himself had entrusted the duties of the earthly High Priest to Aaron. God had shown the sacrificial system to Moses, where the people of Israel brought sacrificial offerings and offered them to God whenever they sinned, and He had made Aaron oversee the giving of these offerings in accordance to the requirements of the sacrificial system.

Even as God had entrusted all priestly duties to Aaron the High Priest, there were still people who challenged against his priesthood, and this is why God brought Aaron's rod to bud, demonstrating that his priesthood came from God. He then made the people of Israel keep this rod inside the Ark of the Testimony in remembrance of this lesson. This is how the two stone tablets of the Law, the pot that had the manna, and Aaron's rod that budded were all placed inside the Ark of the Testimony. To what do these three items refer spiritually? They refer to the ministries of Jesus Christ our Savior.

What Ministries Did Jesus Christ Fulfill to Blot Out All Our sins?

First, He fulfilled the ministry of the Prophet. He is the Alpha and the Omega. He knows the beginning and the end, and He has taught us all about the first and the last. Our Lord knew what would happen to mankind, to you and me, if we had remained sinful.

Second, Jesus has become the everlasting High Priest of the Kingdom of Heaven. He came to this earth because He wanted to save us from sin by becoming our own Savior Himself, to save us wholly by becoming our true High Priest of the Kingdom of Heaven.

Third, Jesus Christ is our King. The Bible declares, *"And He has on His robe and on His thigh a name written: KING OF KINGS AND LORD OF LORDS" (Revelation 19:16).* He is the very Creator of the whole universe, and thus has the authority to rule over everything in it.

We should all realize that Jesus Christ, who is our true King, the Prophet who has taught us the truth of our salvation from sin, and the eternal High Priest of Heaven, has now become our true Savior.

Our Lord has delivered you and me from sin, made us God's people, His children and His workers, and He has enabled us to do good works. He has made our souls be born again so that we may live new lives even on this earth, and He has given us new life so that when the time comes, He may raise our bodies and enable us to live forever with Him in Heaven. Who is Jesus Christ for you and me? He is our true Savior. And Jesus Christ is our Prophet, our everlasting High Priest and our King.

Although we do not want to disobey the will of God, we are so insufficient and weak that we cannot help but sin all the time. If we continue to live like this, die like this and then stand before God, what would be the proper place for us to go? Would it be Heaven or hell? If all of us were to be judged according to the Law that declares, "The wages of sin is death," would we not all be destroyed? He who has saved such people as us from sin and destruction and become our Savior is Jesus Christ. He Himself came to this earth, loved us, and has become the Savior who has delivered us from sin, thereby becoming the Great Shepard of His flock.

John 3:16 states, *"For God so loved the world that He gave His only begotten Son, that whoever believes in Him should not perish but have everlasting life."* God loved you and me so much that He Himself came to this earth for us, was baptized to take upon the sins of the world, was crucified and died on the Cross, rose from the dead again, and has thereby truly become our Savior. Therefore, by believing in Jesus Christ who has become our Savior in our hearts, we have become the ones who are cleansed from sin, who have received the gift of salvation, which has enabled us to become God's children and attain eternal life.

There is one thing that we must absolutely make sure to believe before God. It is that because God loved us, and to blot out our sins, He came to this earth incarnated into the flesh of a man, was baptized, died on the Cross, rose from the dead, and has thereby become our true Savior. It is by eating the flesh of Jesus and drinking His blood by our faith in our hearts that eternal life can be added to us. Because nothing can be clearer than this fact, we cannot help but acknowledge this and believe in it.

We must eat the flesh of Jesus and drink His blood by faith. And anyone can have this one faith that recognizes and believes in the gospel of the water and the Spirit fulfilled by Jesus as it is. What else is there for us to do but believe? We cannot do anything else but stand against God. We are quick to disobey God and to sin. But God has still saved you and me from all our sins once for all, for He loves us all.

How Did God Speak of His Salvation in the Old Testament's Time?

Through what method, then, has the Lord saved us? In the Old Testament, He spoke of this salvation through the colors manifested in the door of the Tabernacle and the garments worn by the High Priest. The colors of the blue, purple, and scarlet thread and the fine woven linen manifested in the door of the Tabernacle are the revelation that shows us His perfect salvation. And on the garments of the High Priest, gold thread was added.

The blue thread tells us that Jesus Christ came to this earth as our Savior and took upon our sins by being baptized. The purple thread tells us that Jesus Christ is the King of kings and God the Creator who made the universe. The scarlet thread tells us that because Jesus Christ took upon our sins through His baptism, He carried the sins of the world and was condemned for them on the Cross by shedding His blood and dying, thereby giving us the salvation that has delivered us from the condemnation of all our sins.

The fine woven linen means the elaborate Word of the Old and New Testaments which tells us that our Lord came to this earth, was baptized, died on the Cross, rose from the dead again, and has thereby blotted out the sins of those who truly believe, cleansed their spirits as white as snow, and saved them. The gold thread signifies the faith that believes in what Jesus Christ has done for us. This is why the gold thread shines. You and I have nothing to boast of, but when we wholeheartedly believe in what Jesus Christ, God Himself and the Son of God, has done for us. We can truly be clothed in the love of God, receive His blessings, and be cherished by Him only by having faith in the righteous acts that He has done. This is what God is telling us through the Tabernacle.

We must realize what God is telling us through the Ark of the Testimony that was placed inside the Tabernacle. We must know and believe that Jesus Christ came to this earth, took upon the sins of mankind and all ours by being baptized by John the Baptist, bore our condemnation of sin by dying on the

Cross, and rose from the dead to live again. Through the Ark of the Testimony, God is making it manifest that we must truly believe in Jesus Christ as our own Savior, as our own God. Those who believe in the baptism of Jesus as the taking of their own sins, in Jesus' bloodshed of the Cross as the condemnation of their sins, in the death of Jesus Christ as their own death, in His resurrection as their own resurrection-these are the ones whom God has saved.

So, to whom does this Tabernacle refer then? It refers to Jesus Christ. It tells us of the method of salvation with which Jesus Christ has saved you and me from our sins. In the New Testament, it was Jesus Christ who was baptized and died on the Cross, thereby blotting out all our sins, washing them all away, being condemned for all our iniquities, and saving us from all sins once for all.

In the Old Testament, it was the offering of sacrifice that saved sinners by accepting their iniquities as their hands were laid on its head, and by shedding its blood and dying. The Old Testament describes the death of the sacrificial offering that took upon the sins of these sinners through the laying on of hands and died in their place as the death of atonement. The sacrificial system of atonement manifested in the Old Testament, when juxtaposed to the New Testament, refers to Jesus Christ, the accomplisher of the gospel of the water and the Spirit who came of baptism and blood.

Who, then, made and set this law of salvation? God our Savior set it. God established the law of salvation that delivers sinners from sin, and He has given this law to us. In the Ark of the Testimony were the two tablets of the Law, the pot of manna, and Aaron's rod that budded, and all these things speak to us about the attributes and ministries of Jesus Christ.

Aaron's rod that budded tells us that God saves us when

we believe in Jesus Christ who has spiritually become the High Priest of the Kingdom of Heaven and our Great Shepard. The pot of manna also tells us about the flesh and blood of Jesus Christ who has become our bread of life. The two stone tablets of the Law also tell us that God is the Lawmaker. The laws established by God are the law of sin and death and the law of the remission of sin and salvation. As our God, Jesus has established the law of life and the law of condemnation to us.

Like this, the Ark of the Testimony and everything in it all speak to us of Jesus Christ. It is by believing in Jesus Christ as our Savior that we can be cleansed from all our sins and received our salvation. No matter how insufficient and weak we may be, if we accept and follow the two laws that Jesus Christ has established, we can then become sinners once, and then become righteous by receiving the remission of all our sins once again and thereby become God's own people. Do you believe?

Now at this present time, almost all Christians throughout the world are prone to believe in Jesus in vain, for they do not know the truth manifested in the Tabernacle. They believe that they can receive the remission of sin just by believing in Jesus' blood of the Cross alone. They believe, in other words, that Jesus has saved them only with the blood of the Cross. But did Jesus in fact just die on the Cross for our salvation? Is it all that He did for our redemption? Did He not, on the contrary, take upon all the sins of the world once for all by being baptized by John (Matthew 3:13-15, 1 Peter 3:21,1 John 5:6)?

Yet today's Christians believe only in Jesus' blood of the Cross, receiving the remission of sin only by half. So having been remitted of their original sin by believing in Jesus Christ as the Savior, they give their prayers of repentance everyday trying to wash away their actual sins on their own. How contradictory is this salvation? It is like washing only half their sins by faith, and then trying to wash away the rest through their own efforts.

When this is the case, how can I not help but continue to preach by repeatedly bringing the baptism and blood of Jesus together? Until now, many Christians of this world, apart from the Christians of the Early Church period, have believed in half-empty salvation. Isn't this why people now believe in Christianity as if it were only a worldly religion?

Not too long ago, a woman named Valeria Jones from the United States received the remission of sin after reading the first volume of this Tabernacle series. Before she read this book, she had already read several of our other publications. Although she agreed with what our books were saying, she could not yet quite bring herself to be totally convinced of the gospel of the water and the Spirit. She told us that she still had some doubts, wondering, "This seems to be right, but then how come so many people are not preaching it?" But she confessed that when she finished reading the first volume of the Tabernacle series, she came to have the clear faith of salvation, believing that the gospel of the water is right, that it is the very truth manifested in the Tabernacle.

A reader of the same book from Benin also wrote to us, "You would be greatly surprised to know that after receiving the remission of sin by reading your book, I have now left my church. Why did I leave the church that I had been attending? Because they preached the doctrine of incremental sanctification, something that is not taught in the Bible. This doctrine of incremental sanctification was completely unbiblical. As they kept teaching that I must and can be sanctified when in fact my flesh can never be sanctified, it was unbearable for me to sit and hear such sermons.

That is why I came out of this church and separated myself from it. Because I have received the remission of my sins by reading your book, I had no choice but to leave the church that I had been attending and separate myself from it now. As we who have gone through all this have now become the people of faith and united ourselves with God's Church, all the people of this world can change also if they only know the truth, as the Word says, *'You shall know the truth and the truth shall set you free.'*"

The Tabernacle's Ark of the Testimony also manifests Jesus Christ. This Ark of the Testimony was placed in the deepest part of the Tabernacle. One could see it only by lifting the screen of the Tabernacle and entering into it, and then lifting the veil of the Most Holy and walking into it. In other words, the door of the Tabernacle was located at the east, and the Ark was placed at the far west end of the Tabernacle.

The Poles Shall Not Be Removed from the Ark

Exodus 25:14-15 says, *"You shall put the poles into the rings on the sides of the ark, that the ark may be carried by them. The poles shall be in the rings of the ark; they shall not be taken from it."* What do these verses mean? With these verses, God is telling us that we should serve the gospel of the water and the Spirit by dedicating ourselves to Him. The gospel is spread only when we devote ourselves to His work. To serve the Lord by devoting ourselves to the gospel is to follow the way of the Cross that our Lord had walked before us. That's why He said to His disciples, *"Whoever desires to come after Me, let him deny himself, and take up his cross, and follow Me" (Mark 8:34).*

To spread the true gospel all over the world, tremendous sacrifice, endeavor and suffering are asked. We can find this out from seeing just how much the Apostle Paul suffered for the gospel of the water and the Spirit: *"Are they ministers of Christ?—I speak as a fool—I am more: in labors more abundant, in stripes above measure, in prisons more frequently, in deaths often. From the Jews five times I received forty stripes minus one. Three times I was beaten with rods; once I was stoned; three times I was shipwrecked; a night and a day I have been in the deep; in journeys often, in perils of waters, in perils of robbers, in perils of my own countrymen, in perils of the Gentiles, in perils in the city, in perils in the wilderness, in perils in the sea, in perils among false brethren; in weariness and toil, in sleeplessness often, in hunger and thirst, in fastings often, in cold and nakedness—besides the other things, what comes upon me daily: my deep concern for all the churches" (2 Corinthians 11:23-28).*

However, those who love themselves more than the Lord who gave Himself up to deliver them from all condemnation cannot sacrifice themselves for the Kingdom of God. There is no easy way to serve the gospel of the water and the Spirit. How can a farmer expect to have a good harvest without any sweat?

Like this, the Ark of the Testimony should be carried by our sacrifices. King David once tried to bring the Ark on a new cart pulled by oxen, instead of carrying it with the poles by his men as it was supposed to be carried. On their way, the oxen stumbled, and a man named Uzzah reached out his hands to the Ark of God and grabbed it. The anger of the Lord was then aroused against Uzzah, and God struck him there for his error. Uzzah died there by His Ark (2 Samuel 6:1-7). So David, terrified by this and afraid of the Lord that day, took the Ark aside into the house of Obed-Edom the Gittite. It was only by bearing the Ark on his men's shoulders that he could bring it up to his castle three months later. As this account illustrates, we must carry the Ark of the Testimony exactly as God has told us, with our sweat and blood, with our sacrifices, with our unrelenting devotion to His gospel.

Those who have really received the remission of sin with great thankfulness are more than happy to dedicate themselves to the Lord who has dedicated Himself to us. We give our thanks over and over again to the Lord, our Savior and God. We thank Him for allowing us to serve the gospel on this earth.

We are all marveled and overjoyed by this dream-like fact, that the Lord has chosen us to make us serve this gospel of truth, to follow Him and live the kind of life that pleases Him. Allowing us to know the truth of salvation alone would have sufficed to overwhelm us with joy, and yet the Lord has permitted us to even serve this gospel. Given such great blessings, how could we possibly not thank Him? We give all our thanks to God. That is why we are willing to sacrifice ourselves to spread the true gospel, sparing no time, effort, or possession of ours to this holy task of world evangelism.

That we have received the remission of sin, in fact, is in itself something for which we are infinitely thankful. But God has not stopped at this, but He has moreover enabled us to encounter and spread the gospel of truth, the gospel of the water and the Spirit—what is this but a great blessing for us?

Who else can even dare to serve this gospel of the water and the Spirit? Not just anyone can serve this gospel. Can politicians serve it? Mayors? Presidents? Kings? No matter how high such people's social positions are, if they do not know and do not believe in the gospel of the water and the Spirit, they can never serve the true gospel. Yet God has given us such an undeserved opportunity and actually enabled us to serve this gospel. What a great blessing is this?

I thank God for the grace that has saved us, for He has loved us. Brothers and sisters, we believe that Jesus Christ is our God and Savior. We are the people of God who eat the flesh of Jesus and drink His blood through our spiritual faith. The Bible says that Jesus is not the God of the dead, but of the living (Luke 20:38), and the living here are none other than those who have received eternal life by believing in the gospel of the water and the Spirit. Whoever does not believe in the truth of this gospel is spiritually dead, and whoever believes in it is spiritually alive. God is indeed the God of those who believe in the gospel of the water and the Spirit.

Brothers and sisters, Jesus Himself has given us the remission of sin through His own flesh and blood. You must realize that if you do not believe in this truth, then you will have nothing to do with Jesus. Jesus Christ gives you heavenly blessings, eternal life, and the remission of your sins. Who is the One that has become the Shepard who bestows you with everlasting blessings, who leads and keeps you? It is Jesus Christ the Accomplisher of the gospel of the water and the Spirit. Jesus is this God. I hope and pray that each and every one of you would all believe in this Jesus as your God.

As for me, not only do I believe in this truth and serve God now, but I will always continue to do so in the future. But what about you? Do you believe in the gospel of the water and the Spirit? And do you believe that you must dwell in God's Church and the love of Christ by your faith? Let us all live our lives by believing in the gospel of the water and the Spirit until the day we meet our Lord. ✉

You can download Rev. Paul C. Jong's Christian Books on iPhone, iPad, or Blackberry by going to Amazon's Kindle e-bookstore (www.amazon.com).

SERMON

7

You can download Rev. Paul C. Jong's Christian Books on iPhone, iPad, or Blackberry by going to Amazon's Kindle e-bookstore (www.amazon.com).

The Offering of the Remission of Sin Given on the Mercy Seat

< Exodus 25:10-22 >

"And they shall make an ark of acacia wood; two and a half cubits shall be its length, a cubit and a half its width, and a cubit and a half its height. And you shall overlay it with pure gold, inside and out you shall overlay it, and shall make on it a molding of gold all around. You shall cast four rings of gold for it, and put them in its four corners; two rings shall be on one side, and two rings on the other side. And you shall make poles of acacia wood, and overlay them with gold. You shall put the poles into the rings on the sides of the ark, that the ark may be carried by them. The poles shall be in the rings of the ark; they shall not be taken from it. And you shall put into the ark the Testimony which I will give you. You shall make a mercy seat of pure gold; two and a half cubits shall be its length and a cubit and a half its width. And you shall make two cherubim of gold; of hammered work you shall make them at the two ends of the mercy seat. Make one cherub at one end, and the other cherub at the other end; you shall make the cherubim at the two ends of it of one piece with the mercy seat. And the cherubim shall stretch out their wings above, covering the mercy seat with their wings, and they shall face one another; the faces of the cherubim shall be toward the mercy seat. You shall put the mercy seat on top of the ark, and in the ark you shall put the Testimony that I will give you. And there I will meet with you, and I will speak with you from above the mercy seat, from between the two cherubim which are on the ark of the Testimony, about everything which I will give you in commandment to the children of Israel."

The Mercy Seat

A cubit is the length stretching from the tip of the hand to the elbow. In the Bible, a cubit is estimated at about 45 cm in today's measurement. The length of the mercy seat was two and a half cubits, and so when converted into the metric system, this length is about 113 cm (3.7 feet). And its width was one and a half cubits, measuring approximately 67.5 cm (2.2 feet). This provides us with a general sense of the size of the mercy seat.

The Ark of the Testimony was first made of acacia wood and overlaid with gold inside and out. But the mercy seat, which was placed on the Ark, was made solely of pure gold. And on its both ends, cherubim were placed to stretch out their wings above, covering the lid of the Ark—that is, the mercy seat—and the cherubim faced toward the mercy seat. The mercy seat is where God bestows His grace on those who come out to Him by faith.

Four gold rings were placed on each corner of the Ark. Two gold rings were cast for each side, and poles were put through the rings so that the Ark could be carried. These poles were made of acacia wood and overlaid with gold. By putting the poles through the two rings on one side and the other two rings on the other side, God made sure that two people could lift and carry it. And our Lord said, *"I will meet you on this mercy seat."*

God made the Israelites to carry the Ark of Testimony along with the mercy seat by putting poles through the Ark. This means that God wants us to spread the gospel throughout the whole world. The same was true of the altar of incense— that is, rings were also placed on both its sides, poles were put through these rings, and two people were made to carry the altar. This, too, means that we should ask for God's help whenever we face difficulties, and that we should also pray for the spreading of the gospel throughout the world wherever we may go.

In the Ark of the Testimony, three items were put in: the golden pot of the manna, Aaron's rod that budded, and the stone tablets of the Covenant. What do these mean? First, the golden pot of manna means that Jesus Christ gives new life to believers. He once proclaimed, *"I am the bread of life. He who comes to Me shall never hunger, and he who believes in Me shall never thirst" (John 6:35).*

Aaron's rod that budded tells us that Jesus Christ is the Lord of resurrection and that He gives us eternal life. The stone tablets of the Covenant tell us that we are inevitably to be condemned to death before the Law. However, the mercy of God is so great that it covers all the condemnations of our sins that the Law has accursed. The mercy seat was fit perfectly as the lit of the Ark lest the curse of the Law should come out. God has completed the mercy seat with the perfect sacrifice of His Son Jesus. Every believer in the gospel of the water and the Spirit can therefore come boldly to the throne of grace, the mercy seat.

The Precious Blood That Was Sprinkled on the Mercy Seat!

We must first find out what the mystery hidden in the mercy seat is. Once a year, the High Priest took the blood of a sacrificial offering and entered into the Most Holy. He then sprinkled this blood of the sacrificial offering on the mercy seat for exactly seven times. God said that He would meet the Israelites on this mercy seat then. God meets whoever has the same faith as that of the High Priest, that is, the faith in His remission of sin revealed in the sacrificial system.

The blood of sacrifice sprinkled on the mercy seat shows God's just judgment of sin and His mercy on mankind. On the Day of Atonement, the tenth day of the seventh month, Aaron the High Priest laid his hands on a sacrificial offering to pass over all the yearly sins of the people of Israel. He then cut its throat to draw its blood, and then he took this blood inside the veil and sprinkled it on the mercy seat (Leviticus 16:11-16).

Through the blood that was thus sprinkled, God met the Israelites and gave them the blessing of the remission of sin. It was God's grace on the Israelites that He had established the sacrificial system. With the laying on of hands on the sacrificial animal and its blood, God had justly blotted out their sins and given them His mercy, the remission of their sins by grace.

How, then, can we receive this grace? With what Word has God blotted out all our sins once for all? God has enabled us to realize that we must have the faith that knows and believes in the truth manifested in the sacrificial system for us to be able to receive the gift that He has bestowed on us. God made it possible for His righteousness to be fulfilled with these two factors; the laying on of hands on the head of the sacrifice and its blood. This sacrifice of the Old Testament refers to none other than the baptism that Jesus Christ received and the blood that He shed on the Cross.

For our own sins, Jesus Christ the Son of God was baptized by John to take upon the sins of the world, became the sacrificial offering on the Cross to pay the wages of these sins, died for us, and rose again from the dead to bring us alive. The baptism that Jesus Christ received and His bloodshed on the Cross were to give us the remission of sin, and they are the grace of true blessings that enables those who have such faith to meet God. This truth is a shadow of the gospel of the water and the Spirit. The gospel of the water and the Spirit is the truth that has established the foundation of the true faith that enables sinners to receive the remission of sin from God. Jesus Christ became the sacrificial offering for our sins. He became the bridge of truth that allows us to go to God the Holy Father.

Again, we can find the conclusive evidence for this truth in the colors of the four threads that were used for the door of the Tabernacle: the blue, purple, and scarlet thread, and the fine woven linen. The four threads of the Tabernacle's door, in other words, provide us with the clues of the true gospel.

The first clue is the mystery of the blue thread manifested in the door of the Tabernacle. This mystery is that Jesus Christ was baptized by John, meaning that He took upon our sins of the world. Our Lord, in other words, accepted our sins that John handed over to Him. That is why He urged John to baptize Him saying, *"Permit it to be so now, for thus it is fitting for us to fulfill all righteousness" (Matthew 3:15).*

The second clue is the purple thread manifested in the Tabernacle. The color "purple" is the color of king. Jesus Christ is the King of kings who came to this earth as the Savior of mankind to deliver them from sin. He forsook the glory of

Heaven and came to this earth to blot out our sins. Jesus Christ is God Himself in His essence, but to save us from all our sins, He came to this earth, and was baptized and crucified in obedience to the Father's will. To blot out all our sins, in other words, God forsook the throne of the glory of Heaven and was born of the body of the Virgin Mary unto this earth to save sinners. We must therefore believe that God Himself had to be born of the body of a virgin, be baptized, and shed His blood on the Cross, all according to the promise that He had made to the Prophet Isaiah over 700 years ago.

The third clue is the scarlet thread. It implies the blood of Jesus. This truth manifests that Jesus completed the mission of God's salvation by shedding His blood on the Cross. His bloodshed on the Cross was a punishment that was reserved for the evilest of all criminals. With the punishment of sins that Jesus bore through His baptism, all the sins of mankind were judged. By being crucified and shedding His blood, He bore the condemnation of all the sins of the world and has thereby delivered us from sin. By accepting our sins from John through His baptism and obeying the Father to death, God has saved all sinners from their iniquities.

Do you realize that Jesus ended all the condemnation of sin and has made believers God's children by vicariously bearing our own condemnation with His punishment of crucifixion? God did all these things so that we would believe in this truth and receive eternal life. That Jesus was baptized and then condemned on the Cross means that He has saved us from sin. This is why He cried out with His last breath, *"It is finished!" (John 19:30)* Jesus proclaimed with great joy and relief that He had completed our salvation from sin according to God the Father's will.

Lastly, the fine woven linen implies that Jesus is God of

the Word. He reveals God's will through His elaborate and righteous Word. Throughout the Old Testament, He had said in advance that He would come to this world and save all mankind with His baptism and crucifixion. He then fulfilled all His promises precisely in the New Testament. That is why the Bible states, *"In the beginning was the Word, and the Word was with God, and the Word was God… And the Word became flesh and dwelt among us, and we beheld His glory, the glory as of the only begotten of the Father, full of grace and truth"* *(John 1:1, 14).*

This truth has enabled us to be washed of all our sins as white as snow. The baptism that Jesus received and His bloodshed are none other than the laying on of hands and the atonement of judgment of the sacrificial system. It is because Jesus shouldered all the sins of the world on His own body that He shed His blood on the Cross. As Jesus was baptized to carry our sins on our behalf, and went to the Cross and shed His blood on it, this truth is what has become the atonement that has washed away our sins.

The baptism that our Lord received when He came to this earth as a man and the blood that He shed on the Cross are the truth manifested in the blue, purple, and scarlet thread. Jesus was born unto this earth 2,000 years ago, took upon the sins of the world by being baptized, died on the Cross, rose from the dead again in three days, bore witness for 40 days afterwards, and then ascended to the right hand of the throne of God—this is the truth manifested in the blue, purple, and scarlet thread. God is telling us to believe in this truth, that He has saved us from all sins by blotting out our sins.

When we believe in this truth, God says to us, "Now, you have become My children. You are not sinners. You are My people and no longer sinners. I have saved you from all your sins, condemnation, and curses. I have saved you with My unconditional love. Because you are so lovely to Me, I have saved you without any condition. Because I love you, I have saved you on My own. Not only have I loved you, but I have actually demonstrated My love to you in this way. Look at the blood of My sacrifice. This is the evidence of My love for you. I have shown you this evidence."

When we came out to the Lord as the poor in spirit, He showed us that He has saved us with the blue, purple, and scarlet thread. The Lord came to this earth, was baptized, was despised and condemned to death on the Cross, rose from the dead again, and ascended to Heaven. God meets whoever believes in His love of salvation.

God bestows the grace of salvation on those who believe. His salvation has turned mere creatures into God's own children. God is saying to us, "You are now My children. You are My sons and daughters. You are no longer the children of Satan, but My own children. You are no longer creatures, but My own people. I have atoned all your sins through My Son Jesus. I have now made you My people, and you have become My people by faith." God has not only saved sinners, but He has also bestowed on them the grace of making them His own children.

God called the lid of the Ark of the Testimony in the Tabernacle as the mercy seat. Two cherubim were placed facing down on it. Why did God say that He would meet the people of Israel above the mercy seat? The reason for this was because God remitted the sins of the people of Israel by accepting the blood of the sacrificial animal on which all their sins were passed over with the laying on of hands.

God said so, in other words, because He wanted to give the people of Israel the remission of their sins as a gift by having them pass their sins onto their sacrificial offering by laying their hands on its head, and by having this sacrificial offering pay the wages of these sins vicariously on their behalf, all in order to blot out the iniquities of His people. Because God could not meet sinners without the offering of atonement, it was through this sacrificial offering that He blotted out their sins and met them.

Everyone is born into this world with sin as a descendant of Adam. Everyone therefore has sin, and no one can meet God without the offering of sacrifice. This is why God said that He would accept the offering of sacrifice that atoned the sins of the Israelites and meet them above the mercy seat.

God made the people of Israel set the tenth day of the seventh month as the Day of Atonement. He made the High Priest to pass a year's worth of the sins of the Israelites onto the sacrificial offering and give this blood of sacrifice to Him. On the very day, the sins of the people of Israel were remitted for an entire year, and this was because on this day, the High Priest gave the sin offering on their behalf.

The Old Testament's Sacrificial System for the Deliverance of Sinners from Their Iniquities

As Leviticus 1:4 says, *"Then he shall put his hand on the head of the burnt offering, and it will be accepted on his behalf to make atonement for him,"* all the sins of a sinner were actually passed onto the scapegoat by laying his hands on the head of the sacrifice. God accepts with pleasure the kind of offerings that is given with the faith that truly believes in His Word. This was the essential and first step of sacrificial system that God had established for His people Israelites.

Free book request www.bjnewlife.org

Then the person cut its throat and drew its blood, and gave this blood to the priests. The priests then put this blood on the horns of the altar of burnt offering, placed its flesh on the altar and burn it, and thereby gave it to God as the sacrificial offering for the sins of the sinner. This was the law of salvation that God set to actually remit each sinner's sins.

However, on the Day of Atonement, the tenth day of the seventh month, God allowed His people to offer a sacrifice that could remit a year's worth of their sins. On that day, the High Priest, the representative of all Israelites, had to prepare two goats. *"Then Aaron shall cast lots for the two goats: one lot for the Lord and the other lot for the scapegoat. And Aaron shall bring the goat on which the Lord's lot fell, and offer it as a sin offering" (Leviticus 16:8-9).* He had to lay his hands on the head of the first goat so that a year's worth of the sins of all Israelites could pass onto the sacrifice. Then he drew its blood by actually killing it, went into the Most Holy, and sprinkled the blood with his finger on the mercy seat on the east side, and before the mercy seat he sprinkled it seven times. By accepting this blood of the sacrificial offering, God washed away their sins and approved them as His own people.

After this, the High Priest then came out of the Tabernacle, and gave the other goat before the presence of the people of Israel. To actually pass the sins of his people, he laid his hands again on the head of the sacrificial offering. He then confessed, "I pass all the sins that my people have committed during the last one year onto this offering." After this, he sent the offering away into the desert by the hand of a suitable man.

This goat had to be sent away into the arid wilderness to die (Leviticus 16:20-22). This tells us that the sins of the people of Israel were wholly remitted once for all with the sin offerings that were given on the Day of Atonement.

These scapegoats foreshadowed none other than Jesus. This sin offering manifests the truth of salvation that Jesus Christ completed by being baptized by John and being crucified to blot out the sins of everyone in this world. God promised to meet the people of Israel above the mercy seat when they offered the lawful sacrifice through the High Priest. The people of Israel considered the High Priest and the mercy seat precious, for it was the High Priest who gave the sin offering every year on their behalf, and it was the mercy seat where their iniquities were forgiven.

Likewise, Jesus reconciled us with God, having offered one sacrifice with His body for our sins forever through His baptism and bloodshed. That is why we cannot give enough thanks to the Lord Jesus, and why we have to believe in His baptism along with His crucifixion.

The Mercy Seat Sealed up the Two Stone Tablets of the Ten Commandments That Were Placed inside the Ark of the Testimony

On the Mountain Sinai, God commanded Moses to place the two stone tablets inscribed with the Ten Commandments inside the Ark of the Testimony and to seal up the Ark with the mercy seat. God did so because He wanted to bestow His love of mercy on the people of Israel, for they could not keep the Law. In other words, it was because God could not deal with the people of Israel who sinned everyday with His just Law that declared the wages of sin to be death. This, too, was to give the remission of sin to the people of Israel.

The people of Israel were, in other words, too insufficient before God to keep His Law with their deeds. So God gave

Free book request www.bjnewlife.org

them the sacrificial system with the Law. It was to make them be cleansed of all their sins through the offering of sacrifice. This shows us that to blot out the sins of the people of Israel, God demanded them to pass their sins onto the sacrificial offering by laying their hands on its head, and to kill it on their behalf by cutting its throat. God gave the law of His love of salvation along with the law of His just wrath to the people of Israel. As such, we also need to believe in the two pivotal truths of God's salvation; the baptism that the Messiah received from John and of the blood that He shed on the Cross.

The sacrificial animal for the sin offering in the Old Testament was the body of the Messiah in the New Testament. The sacrificial offerings that were given to us in the Scriptures were God's love of mercy that blots out all our sins. Now as before, to be remitted of our sins, we absolutely need the sacrificial offering of atonement. From long ago, to blot out the sins of mankind, there must have been the justice of God and His love of mercy.

Because the justice of God must judge us if we have sin, we had to wash away our sins by passing them onto the sin offering. As a saying in Korea goes, "Hate sin, but do not hate sinners," God hated our sins but He did not hate our souls. For God to blot out the sins of our souls, we needed to lay our hands on the offering of sacrifice, draw its blood and give it to Him. In the Old Testament, that God atoned the sins of the people of Israel means that God accepted their offering of sacrifice and thereby remitted their sins.

For the people of Israel, the only maker of the Law was God. Jehovah, who revealed Himself before the people of Israel, is He who exists by Himself. Just as we recognize God as the only legislator of the Law, we must recognize that He is the God of us all and accept the sacrificial system that He set to blot out our sins. Through the sacrificial system that God established, we are able to realize just how much God has loved us and how righteously He has delivered us from sin. And through the Law of God, we also are able to realize how we simply cannot keep His commandments. In our fundamentals, we had been idolaters before God, committing all kinds of iniquities and transgressions. Therefore, we cannot but admit that we were bound to hell for our sins at any time. That is why God Himself had to come to us as the Savior.

Jesus Christ gave His body as the sacrifice for the sins of the world forever. He offered Himself in the exactly same way as the sin offering of the Old Testament was given, especially the one shown in the passage on the Day of Atonement: by the laying on of hands on the sacrifice's head and its bloodshed. The two stone tablets in the Ark of the Testimony and the mercy seat were absolutely necessary for the people of Israel to receive the remission of their sins, for God enabled those who believed in the just Law of God and His promise of life to receive new life. Today, the Law that shows the justice of God and the Word of truth that brings eternal salvation from sin enables not only the people of Israel but also all of us to meet God and receive eternal life.

You and I who are living in this age must know and believe who our God is, what He is telling us, and through what He has made us receive the remission of our sins. Through the truth of the blue, purple, and scarlet thread and the fine woven linen manifested in the Old Testament's door of the Tabernacle, God has called you and me, accepted us, and given us the faith that believes in this.

Free book request www.bjnewlife.org

The Blue Thread Implies Exactly the Baptism That Jesus Received

Let us turn to Matthew 3:13-17: *"Then Jesus came from Galilee to John at the Jordan to be baptized by him. And John tried to prevent Him, saying, 'I need to be baptized by You, and are You coming to me?' But Jesus answered and said to him, 'Permit it to be so now, for thus it is fitting for us to fulfill all righteousness.' Then he allowed Him. When He had been baptized, Jesus came up immediately from the water; and behold, the heavens were opened to Him, and He saw the Spirit of God descending like a dove and alighting upon Him. And suddenly a voice came from heaven, saying, 'This is My beloved Son, in whom I am well pleased.'"*

Through the offerings given under the sacrificial system of the Old Testament, God the Father actually showed that He would pass all the sins of the world onto His only begotten Son Jesus Christ. John the Baptist did in fact baptized Jesus to fulfill all the righteousness of God. Because the sins of the world were indeed passed onto Jesus as He was baptized by John, those who believe in this could have been remitted of all the sins of their hearts.

This baptism that Jesus received has a completely different meaning from the water baptism that people usually receive as a ritual to become Christians. In other words, the water baptism that today's people receive is merely an outward sign of their conversion to the Christian religion. Jesus was baptized in the Jordan River to take upon all the sins of the world with the laying on of the hands of John the Baptist, the representative of mankind. The baptism that Jesus received was the baptism that fulfilled God's promise of everlasting salvation, of the remission of sin that God established through the sacrificial system in Leviticus. That Jesus took upon the sins of the world by personally being baptized and bled to death on the Cross to pay the wages of these sins is God's love for mankind and the perfect remission of sin.

It was to save us from all the sins of the world that God the Father made His Son be baptized by John. *"Permit it to be so now, for thus it is fitting for us to fulfill all righteousness" (Matthew 3:15).* *"Thus"* here means that Jesus would take upon the entire mankind's sins of the world by being baptized. Because John baptized Jesus Christ, our sins were passed onto Him. It was because Jesus Christ had taken upon our sins with His baptism that He shed His blood and died instead of us. The baptism that Jesus received is God's love of sacrifice and of the remission of sin. After He actually accepted all our sins passed onto Him, He submerged into water. That submersion implies His death. And that He came out of water testifies His resurrection in advance.

Jesus Is Our Creator and Savior

It is true that Jesus Christ who came to us is God Himself who created the universe and all things in it. Genesis 1:1 says, *"In the beginning God created the heavens and the earth,"* and Genesis 1:3 says, *"Then God said, 'Let there be light'; and there was light."* John 1:3 also states, *"All things were made through Him, and without Him nothing was made that was made."* Jesus Christ actually created the whole universe with the Father and the Holy Spirit.

Philippians 2:5-8 states, *"Let this mind be in you which was also in Christ Jesus, who, being in the form of God, did not consider it robbery to be equal with God, but made Himself of*

*no reputation, taking the form of a bondservant, and coming in
the likeness of men. And being found in appearance as a man,
He humbled Himself and became obedient to the point of death,
even the death of the cross."* He is the actual Creator who
made this world and created us mankind. To deliver us from
sin, this Lord Himself came to us as a man, took upon the sins
of the world by being baptized by John, shed His blood
because of this baptism, and has thereby saved us from all sins.

The Messiah actually made the Israelites to make all the
doors of the Tabernacle by weaving blue, purple, and scarlet
thread into white, fine woven linen. That He made them use
blue, purple, and scarlet thread for the doors of the Tabernacle
manifests His intention to save all mankind from their sins: to
take upon the sins of the world with the baptism that Jesus
would receive from John, and to pay their wages with His
blood on the Cross.

In the Old Testament, sinners brought their sacrificial
offering to the Tabernacle and passed their sins onto it by
laying their hands on its head before the altar of burnt offering.
He then drew its blood by cutting its throat, and gave this blood
to priests. The priests then gave this offering to God by putting
the blood on the four horns of the altar of burnt offering, as
well as pouring the rest of it on the ground.

On the Day of Atonement, when the High Priest took the
blood of the sacrificial offering on whose head he had laid his
hands into the Most Holy and sprinkled it on the mercy seat,
God accepted this blood of the sacrificial offering as the
vicarious judgment on His people. Why did the sacrificial
animal have to be killed? Because it had taken all the sins of
the Israelites through the laying on of the High Priest's hands
on its head. Its blood was, in other words, the result of this
laying on of hands. Thus, God accepted the blood of the

Free book request www.nlmission.com

sacrificial animal and smelt the sweet aroma of its flesh burnt on the altar, and thereby remitted all the sins of the people of Israel.

In the New Testament's time also, Jesus came to do exactly like this. To take upon our sins and bear the condemnation of sin, our Lord had to come to this earth through the body of the Virgin Mary, and He completed salvation by being baptized by John and shedding His blood on the Cross. The blue, purple, and scarlet thread is actually the gospel manifesting the truth that Jesus, God Himself, was baptized and crucified.

It is because Jesus took upon our sins with His baptism that He was crucified, shed all His blood, died, rose from the dead in three days, and has thereby become the Savior of us who believe, sitting at the right hand of the throne of God. Jesus Christ has enabled those who actually believe in Him as their Savior to call God as Abba, Father, by being remitted of all their sins once for all before God the Father. These are the mystery of the truth hidden in the blue, purple and scarlet thread.

Through His baptism and the blood of the Cross, the Messiah fulfilled the cleaning of our sins and bore the condemnation of our sins in our stead. Now, He has become the Savor of the world. As such, we must believe that the door of the Tabernacle in the Old Testament was made by weaving blue, purple, and scarlet thread on fine woven linen, and we must also believe that in the New Testament, the Messiah our Savior actually came to this earth, took upon the sins of the world with His baptism, and bore the condemnation of all sins on the Cross—thereby, we must receive the remission of our sins.

As Christians, How Much Attention Are You Paying to His Word?

Exodus 25:22 states, *"And there I will meet with you, and I will speak with you from above the mercy seat, from between the two cherubim which are on the ark of the Testimony, about everything which I will give you in commandment to the children of Israel."* How near are you, then, to the gospel of the water and the Spirit, the gospel of atonement? From where did the Lord say that He would speak to those of you who believe in Jesus as the Savior? In Exodus 25:22, He said that He would give you all His commandments from above the cover of the Ark of the Testimony. To the people of Israel in the Old Testament, God said that He would speak to them of everything from the mercy seat.

You must realize that this is God's promise that He would lead your lives after giving you the remission of sin through the lawful sacrificial offering and making you His people. God is telling us that no matter how much those of you who believe in Christianity try to be led by the Lord, if you believe in Jesus while remaining ignorant of the truth of the gospel of the water and the Spirit, then He cannot lead you. As such, if you really want to be led by the Lord, you must first know and accept the truth of the remission of sin that has remitted your sins all at once, and then wait for His guidance.

There is one thing that I want to tell you, and it is that if you want to become God's children, and if you want to become part of His Church, you must first be remitted of your sins by believing in the gospel of the water and the Spirit, the mystery of the blue, purple, and scarlet thread. Only after this can you also receive the Lord's commandments spoken to you from above the Ark of the Testimony.

We must remember and believe that the Lord has always commanded and led our lives when we have faith in the gospel of the water and the Spirit that has enabled us to receive the remission of sin. Are you now receiving the Lord's commandments given to you from above the mercy seat? Or are you following the Lord based on your own feelings?

Your own feelings and emotions cannot build your faith, but only lead you to confusion. If you seek to follow the commandments of God spoken to you from above the Ark of the Testimony, you must then realize and believe that the blue, purple, and scarlet thread and the fine woven line spoken of in the Tabernacle are the remission of sin that God has given us.

Hallelujah! I thank God for the baptism of the Lord, the blood of the Cross, and His power and love that have saved us from all the sins of the world. ✉

You can download Rev. Paul C. Jong's Christian Books on iPhone, iPad, or Blackberry by going to Amazon's Kindle e-bookstore (www.amazon.com).

SERMON

8

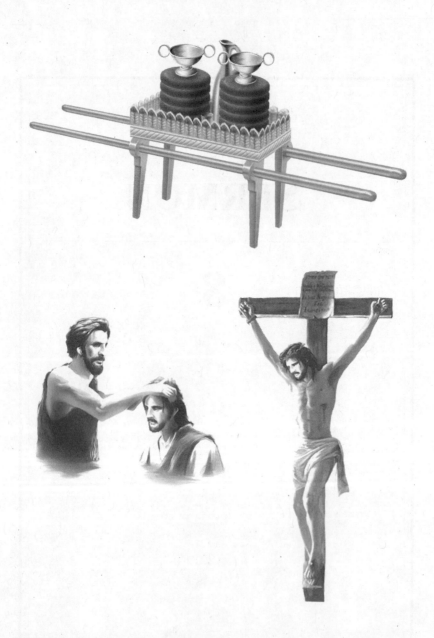

You can download Rev. Paul C. Jong's Christian Books on iPhone, iPad, or Blackberry by going to Amazon's Kindle e-bookstore (www.amazon.com).

The Table of Showbread

< Exodus 37:10-16 >
"He made the table of acacia wood; two cubits was its length, a cubit its width, and a cubit and a half its height. And he overlaid it with pure gold, and made a molding of gold all around it. Also he made a frame of a handbreadth all around it, and made a molding of gold for the frame all around it. And he cast for it four rings of gold, and put the rings on the four corners that were at its four legs. The rings were close to the frame, as holders for the poles to bear the table. And he made the poles of acacia wood to bear the table, and overlaid them with gold. He made of pure gold the utensils which were on the table: its dishes, its cups, its bowls, and its pitchers for pouring."

By Placing a Frame in Our Hearts, We Must Become the Ones Who Eat the Bread of Life

The table of showbread, one of the instruments found inside the Tabernacle, was made of acacia wood, and was overlaid with pure gold. Measuring two cubits (90 cm: 3 feet)) in length, a cubit and a half (67.5 cm: 2.2 feet) in height, and a cubit (45 cm: 1.5 feet) in width. On the table of showbread 12 loaves of bread were always placed, and this bread could be eaten only by priests (Leviticus 24:5-9).

Among the characteristics of the table of showbread are: it had a frame of a handbreadth all around it; a molding of gold was placed all around this frame; four rings of gold were put on the four corners; and the rings held the poles of acacia wood overlaid with gold that were used to transport the table. The utensils on the table—its dishes, cups, bowls, and pitchers for pouring—were also made of gold.

Exodus 37:11-12 records, *"And he overlaid it with pure gold, and made a molding of gold all around it. Also he made a frame of a handbreadth all around it, and made a molding of gold for the frame all around it."* The table of showbread in the Holy Place of the House of God had a frame that was as high as a handbreadth, and around the frame a gold molding was placed. Why did God command Moses to place such a frame? This frame of a handbreadth, protruding by about 10 cm, was to prevent the bread on the table from falling.

As only priests could eat the bread that was placed on the table of showbread, so must we become the ones who can eat this bread spiritually. Only those who have been saved from sin and received eternal life by believing in the baptism of Jesus Christ and the blood of the Cross—in other words, only those who believe in the gospel of the water and the Spirit as their salvation—can eat this bread.

Because a frame as high as a handbreadth was especially placed all around the Tabernacle's table of showbread, it made sure that the bread would not slip and fall down. And on every Sabbath, hot, fresh-made bread was placed on the table. We have to pay particular attention to the fact that a frame of a handbreadth was made around the table of showbread, and that the frame was wrapped all around with a molding of gold.

The frame of the table of showbread is teaching us that we must hold in our hearts the Word of truth that brings us salvation and thereby receive eternal life. This tells us that we can have the spiritual faith of the blue, purple, and scarlet thread and the fine woven linen used for the door of the

Tabernacle only when we believe in the baptism of Jesus Christ and the blood of the Cross. And we came to realize by this revelation that only those who believe in this truth manifested in these blue, purple, and scarlet thread and fine woven linen are made to be God's children.

Because we would have nothing to do with the Lord unless we believe in this way, those of us who seek to have the bread of life must have the faith that believes in the gospel of the water and the Spirit manifested in the blue, purple, and scarlet thread and the fine woven linen. We must believe that only the gospel of the water and the Spirit is the real truth of salvation. God is telling us, in short, to raise the frame of faith in our hearts so that the Word of salvation would not slip away from us.

This gospel of the water and the Spirit has been handed down to us from the age of the Early Church. From this age of the Early Church to the present day, God has cleansed away the sins of those who believe in this gospel. We can see that now as before, God saves the souls of those who believe in the truth of this gospel of the water and the Spirit. We have been saved by believing in the truth manifested in the door of the Tabernacle, and God has enabled us to live spiritually by raising a frame in our hearts.

From our faith in the gospel of the water and the Spirit given by the Lord, we have received eternal life, and by this gospel of truth we have been able to share the bread of life with others. And we have also come to serve the righteous works of God. Even when we believe in the gospel of the water and the Sprit, if we fail to hold steadfastly onto the truth of this gospel with passing time and lose it, then this will mean none other than the loss of our very life. As such, we must raise the frame of faith in our hearts by always ruminating on the gospel of the water and the Spirit with faith.

In Our Hearts Must Be the Faith That Believes in the Gospel Contained in the Blue, Purple, and Scarlet Thread

If people do not have faith in this truth, then they cannot be saved from their sins. They may insist on their own that they have been definitely saved, but right now, because their hearts are not holding onto and believing in the gospel of the water and the Spirit manifested in the blue, purple, and scarlet thread, this salvation that they have is merely an imperfect one.

Not believing in the gospel of the water and the Spirit as the truth is the same sin as abandoning the Lord on our own. The bread of life is not just something that we need to be in possession of, but it is something that we must put into our mouths, chew on it and eat it, and thereby make its truth ours. When we go on without believing in the Word of God and holding onto it in our hearts, then the truth of salvation will disappear from our hearts in no time.

You may wonder how it is possible for you to lose such precious salvation when you have already been saved from sin. But unfortunately, many who do not hold onto the Word of God, though they had received the truth in joy at first, will end up dying, for they do not have the root of faith grounded in the true gospel.

Regarding this matter, Jesus spoke of four different grounds of the heart in 'the parable of the sower' (Matthew 13:3-9, 18-23). In this parable, the seeds of the truth of God were sowed on four different grounds of the heart of mankind. The first ground was the wayside, the second was stony place, the third was thorny ground, and the fourth was the good ground. Of these, the seeds that fell on the first three grounds failed to bear any fruit, and only those that fell on the fourth ground, that good ground, bore fruits. This means that many people can lose their salvation midway even though they once heard and accepted the gospel of the water and the Spirit, the true gospel of salvation. As such, we must remember that if the soil of our hearts is not good, it is possible for us to lose our salvation that the Lord has given us.

If in our hearts we believe in the salvation that has come of the blue, purple, and scarlet thread, then the soil of our hearts can be good. But at times we see that some people lose their salvation from their inability to defend their faith as a result of not having their faith in the Word of God deeply rooted. This is why we must stay in God's Church, have the bread of life everyday, and grow in faith. With the truth manifested in the blue, purple, and scarlet thread, God is nurturing us everyday so that our faith would grow.

We must affirm in our hearts everyday the remission of sin that we have received. The truth that must be found in our hearts is the salvation of the gospel of the water and the Spirit manifested in the blue, purple, and scarlet thread and the fine woven linen. This truth of salvation is in the hearts of those who have received the remission of sin. By renewing our faith in this true gospel of the water and the Spirit, we can live on day by day as God's children.

As such, even those who believe in the gospel of the water and the Spirit must also ruminate everyday on the gospel of the righteousness of God manifested in the blue, purple, and scarlet thread and the fine woven linen, and affirm their faith everyday. Why? Because if we do not always hold onto the gospel of the water and the Spirit steadfastly and affirm it, then we may lose it at any time. We must always remember what the writer of Hebrews said to the Jewish Diaspora: *"Therefore we must give the more earnest heed to the things we have heard, lest we drift away" (Hebrew 2:1).*

Today, even among those who know the gospel of the water and the Spirit, we see that there are many whose faith in the gospel fades away as time goes by. This is because they, even though they had already believed in the gospel of the water and the Spirit, have failed to eat the bread of life continually in the Holy Place, and, as a result, their hearts have not been refined with the true faith.

There are also many servants of Satan in this world who are trying to kill the righteous by feeding them with the leavened bread, that is to say, the teachings of their own flesh. If the false gospel is introduced into God's Church, then the truth gets mixed with the lies, turning believers into someone who cannot be accepted by the Lord. Such people know the truth but do not believe because of their failure to raise the frame of faith, and so they end up as someone who is no longer wholly saved from sin. Proverbs 22:28 says, *"Do not remove the ancient landmark Which your fathers have set."*

It is therefore critically important for us not to remove the landmark of our faith. We must clearly have the boundary of our true faith and defend it until the day our Lord returns. Only then can we always feed on the bread of life, only then can the Lord dwell in the center of our hearts, and only then can we have eternal life. No matter how much bread God gives us, if we do not appreciate its preciousness and fail to hold onto it with our hearts, or if we remove the frame of our hearts and let the bread of life slip away from the table, we will then end up turning into the children of destruction.

Some of us have just recently received their remission of

sin, while for others, it's been decades since they first heard the gospel of the water and the Spirit and were remitted of their sins. Since what we hear everyday is about the Word of the gospel of the water and the Spirit, it may very well be possible that some of us may get tired as soon as the word "water" of the gospel of the water and the Spirit is mentioned. But still, we must continue to eat the bread of the true gospel. For how long must we do this? Until the day the Lord returns.

Some of you may complain that I am always and repetitively preaching the gospel of the water and the Spirit, but you need to realize why I have had to preach in this way. It is because our faith must be strengthened more and more by ruminating on the gospel of the water and the Spirit so that we may become the workers of God. We must fulfill the role of the faithful and trusty watchman for the souls of this age. For the born-again souls also, this true gospel of the water and the Spirit is the bread of life and the true food of faith. As such, we must have this bread everyday, and not only this—that is, we should not have it just for ourselves—but we must also share it with others everyday so that they may also come to receive their remission of sin.

The bread of the righteous is to spread the gospel Word of the water and the Spirit and thereby delivered people from the power of darkness and conveyed them into the Kingdom of the Son of His love (John 4:34, Colossians 1:13). If we neglect to have the bread of the gospel of the water and the Spirit, then we will inevitably fall ill or die. At times, because of the weakness of our flesh, our faith in the gospel of the water and the Spirit may be weakened. But if we hold onto the gospel of the water and the Sprit in times of trouble, then it can actually turn into a window of opportunity for our souls to become even stronger.

When we hear and ruminate on this gospel of truth, the more we hear it, the more our souls are strengthened, the stronger our faith is made, and the more renewed strength we see arising in our hearts. We need to hear the gospel of the water and the Spirit everyday, and affirm and refine our faith in this gospel. As God says, *"Take away the dross from silver, and it will go to the silversmith for jewelry" (Proverbs 25:4),* we need the refinement of faith—that is, we need to continue to hear the gospel of the water and the Spirit, acknowledge it in our hearts, and ruminate on it time after time—for the gospel of the water and the Spirit is the bread of life that makes us live! As Jesus said in the Lord's Prayer, "give us our daily bread," our Lord has indeed given us the Word of the gospel of the water and the Spirit. This is why He told us to pray in this way.

When it comes to the salvation of the remission of sin that God has given us, we must make it clear how our faith had been before we were saved from sin. "Before I knew this truth, I had not been saved from sin." We must clearly admit that at the time, though we believed in Jesus, we had not been saved from sin. "I had not been wholly saved from sin at that time, but when I continued to hear this gospel of the water and the Spirit, I came to believe it in my heart in time.

Though I had believed Jesus to be my Savior before, my salvation had not been perfect until then, but now, by hearing the true gospel of the water and the Spirit, I have been truly saved. Now I can really believe in the gospel of the water and the Spirit, and I do believe in it truly." It is only when you realize and believe that the Lord has wholly saved you from sin with His baptism and the blood of the Cross that the gift of true salvation descends on your hearts from Heaven. This faith that believes in the truth is the true faith that saves you.

The gospel of the water and the Spirit revealed in the

Bible is different from the faith that we had before. We, at that time, believed in the gospel of only the blood of the Cross, instead of this perfect gospel of the water and the Spirit. Faith only in the Cross and faith in the gospel of the water and the Spirit may appear similar at first, but the two are completely different in the end. Before you came to know this gospel of the water and the Spirit, had you not believed only in the blood of the Cross? Were all your sins remitted back then? Of course not! When you believe only in Jesus' blood of the Cross, you still had actual sins in your hearts. This is the difference between the faith that believes in the gospel of the water and the Spirit and the faith that believes only in the Cross.

The clear difference is that those who believe only in the blood of the Cross are not saved while those who believe in the gospel of the water and the Spirit are saved from all their sins. As such, their spirits are unmistakably different. But ordinary people do not realize this. Though the two gospels may seem similar, there is a great gap of faith between the two that cannot be abridged. When the small difference between whether or not we believe in the baptism of Jesus is what makes us receive or lose eternal life, then we can only acknowledge that there is a difference between these two faiths that can never be skirted off.

We must know exactly what faith constitutes the boundary of our salvation from sin. To be saved from sin, we must believe in the gospel of the water and the Spirit. This gospel of the water and the Spirit is the truth of the remission of sin. The clear-cut status of salvation will be yours when you admit that you were surely not saved before you believed in the gospel of the water and the Spirit, and that now you truly believe in the true gospel with all your hearts.

If you believe in the gospel of the water and the Spirit in

the center of your hearts, then you must clearly admit this before God, that you have received the remission of your sins by hearing and believing in the gospel of the water and the Spirit. If you have now believed in the truth of the gospel of the water and the Spirit, then you can unmistakably find its evidence in your hearts.

We must examine our faith carefully before God. There is absolutely no shame in examining our faith. If it took you five years since you first believed in Jesus to come to believe in the gospel of the water and the Spirit in the center of your hearts, there is no shame at all. If it took you 10 years to be saved, there is no shame in this, and if it took you even 20 years to be saved, there is still absolutely no shame in this. On the contrary, it is a blessing.

However, the reality is that there are many who pretend to be saved from sin. But the Holy Spirit, who searches all things, cannot approve their faith, because they don't draw a clear-cut line of salvation honestly. It is much wiser, even now, to set the boundary line of our salvation clearly—not to know the exact day we were saved, but what is important here is to clearly distinguish between before and after we have been saved—and to confess your perfect faith distinctly.

Our Fathers of Faith Also Believed in the Same Gospel that We Now Believe

Having crossed the Red Sea, when the people of Israel sought to cross the Jordan River to enter into the land of Canaan, they could safely make the crossing only when they actually followed their priests who first carried God's Ark of the Testimony. If we only think to ourselves, "Oh, so that's how I can cross the Jordan River," and do not actually make the crossing, then we cannot enter into the land of Canaan, for we would still be remaining on the other side of the river. To enter into the land of Canaan, we absolutely must cross the Red Sea and the Jordan River by our faith in the Lord.

Spiritually speaking, the Jordan River is the river of death and resurrection. The faith that has saved us from sin is the faith that believes, "I must be cast into hell, but the Lord came to this earth and has saved me with His baptism and the blood of the Cross." To save us perfectly, our Lord was baptized in the Jordan River and shed His blood on the Cross. In this way He took upon our sins and paid the wages of sin by giving up His own life on our behalf. Now, we must believe in this truth and draw the line of faith and the line of salvation clearly in our hearts.

As I preach the Word of God, I can see there are many in His Church who still have not clearly drawn the line of salvation in the center of their hearts and are therefore not able to follow the Lord. They wonder how they can draw this line between before and after their salvation. They excuse themselves by saying, "Has there ever been anyone on this earth who drew this line? Did the Apostle Paul do? Did Peter do? No one has ever done this." But the Apostles of faith such as Paul and Peter all drew the line of salvation.

In the case of Paul, he drew it while on his way to Damascus. So, he mentioned frequently the words "once, in times past, or before" in contrast with the word "now." As for Peter, he also uttered the same words above (1 Peter 2:10, 25). We can see that he also drew this line when we look at his confessions: *"You are the Christ, the Son of the living God" (Matthew 16:16)*, and, *"There is also an antitype which now saves us—baptism (not the removal of the filth of the flesh, but the answer of a good conscience toward God), through the resurrection of Jesus Christ" (1 Peter 3:21).* Both Paul and Peter clearly drew the line of faith between before and after their salvation.

Thus, this question of whether or not you believe in the gospel of the water and the Spirit is not someone else's problem, but it is very much a problem of your own soul. The servants of God in the Bible all tackle with the problem of sin. Because this is a critically important problem for all of us, we ourselves must solve it by faith. When we believe in the gospel of the water and the Spirit and thereby solve away the problem of sin from the center of our hearts, God is greatly pleased. Do you want to please God? Then all that you have to do is recognize your sinfulness and solve this problem by believing in the gospel of the water and the Spirit. If all this time you had not been saved yet, then you must confess, "God, I have not yet been saved."

Jesus said, *"Whatever you bind on earth will be bound in heaven, and whatever you loose on earth will be loosed in heaven" (Matthew 16:19).* On our side, we must first admit, "God has saved me with the water and the Spirit. Right now, in the center of my heart, I believe in the truth of the gospel of the water and the Spirit. There is no doubt at all that the Lord has saved me through the gospel of the water and the Spirit."

We must all accept the gospel of the water and the Spirit into our hearts. "I trust in this gospel. Because it is the truth, because the Lord has blotted out my sins more than enough, I believe in this gospel now. I have not been saved by faith until now." When we thus recognize and believe in the gospel given by the Lord, then God tells us, "I approve your faith."

When God has already given us the truth of the water and the Spirit that can save us perfectly, if we, for our part, do not draw the line of salvation and accept this salvation by believing in this truth, then God, for His part, cannot recognize us as the saved either. Because God treats us with personality and not compulsorily, if you do not believe in the gospel of the water and the Spirit in the center of your hearts, then He cannot give you the remission of sin. If you do not acknowledge the gospel of the water and the Spirit in your hearts, in other words, the Holy Spirit cannot dwell in your hearts.

Do we reject all other gospels but the gospel of the water and the Spirit as false? Or do we think that even such false gospels are still useful, and that there is no need to throw them away? We need to examine ourselves and see how exactly we believe. Let us assume for a moment that we came upon a pile of used appliances and electronics. Let us further assume that we brought some of them home, thinking that we could still salvage, but found out later that none of them worked and that they were all useless. Should we then still keep them or throw them away? Once we decide that they are all useless, of course we should throw them all away. When you reach a conclusion that something is never useful to you and is not authentic at all, then you must also know how to cast it away decidedly.

If this is how we should act on earthly affairs, how should we then act when it comes to our spiritual affairs? We must be even more decisive in our rejection of lies in our spiritual affairs. We must draw a clear line that distinguishes our faith in the gospel of the water and the Spirit from the false faith that believes only in the blood of the Cross; we must recognize that faith in only the blood of the Cross can never bring us salvation; and we must decidedly throw away this flawed doctrine. Which one is the biblically sound gospel? Is it the gospel of only the blood of the Cross? Or is it the gospel of the water and the Spirit? Your faith that believes in the gospel of the water and the Spirit and that has saved you from your sins is what pleases God.

In short, there are two kinds of Christians: Those who know and believe in the gospel of the water and the Spirit and those who do not. It may appear as though both lead a similar life of faith, but the truth of the matter is that the two are totally different. Do you, by any chance, think that the imperfect gospel you had believed before still has some use? Have you still kept it all this time, thinking that it could come handy sometime later?

Such a faith is a false faith, something that has come out of man-made thoughts, and so you must cast away all the old baggage of your past. It is because you have not still thrown away what are untrue and lies that you are having problems in the center of your hearts. I advise you to remember His Word: *"You shall keep My statutes. You shall not let your livestock breed with another kind. You shall not sow your field with mixed seed. Nor shall a garment of mixed linen and wool come upon you" (Leviticus 19:19).*

To Enter into the Holy Place, We Must Enter Only through Its Door

With what material was the door of the Tabernacle made? It was woven of blue, purple, and scarlet thread and fine woven linen. Those who have been born again of water and the Spirit must open this door of the Tabernacle and enter into the Holy Place. Under the pillars of the door of the Tabernacle, bronze sockets were placed. These bronze sockets make us acknowledge that the gospel of the water and the Spirit is the truth of salvation.

They teach us that though we had no choice but to be condemned by God and to die for our sins, by receiving the blessing of being born again of water and the Spirit through the gospel of the water and the Spirit, we have become God's own people. We can enter into the Tabernacle only when we cast away the mistaken notion that, of the colors of the four threads used for its door, we can be saved by believing just in the ministry of Jesus manifested in the scarlet thread alone.

Unless we throw away our self-centered thoughts and faith, we can never believe in salvation manifested in the blue, purple, and scarlet thread. We must recognize that the truth manifested in the blue, purple, and scarlet thread and the fine woven linen is the gospel of the water and the Sprit, and we must acknowledge the fallacy of our self-centered thoughts when we had believed only in the blood of the Cross before.

If God is willing, then He will lead you to the truth of the gospel of the water and the Spirit. Only those who believe in this truth of the gospel of the water and the Spirit can be remitted of all their sins and receive eternal life. Only then can we open the door of salvation by believing in this truth in the center of their hearts and enter into the Holy Place.

If you fail to discern the fallacy of our old faith that you had before you came to know the gospel of the water and the Spirit, then you will suffer the punishment of sin, for you would not be able to be saved. If this happens, you cannot even enter into the Holy Place and have the bread of life. Only when you enter into the Holy Place by believing in the gospel of the water and the Spirit can you have the steaming bread of life.

You must realize that the Lord has made you God's children by washing away your sins with His baptism, the blue thread, and by bearing the condemnation of your sins with the bloodshed of the Cross, the scarlet thread. And you must clearly realize and believe that the gospel of the water and the Spirit is the truth that is absolutely necessary for you. You can come into God's Church and share the bread of life with the righteous only when you know that God is the One who has given you the gospel of the water and the Spirit, and only when you believe in this gospel.

The Flesh of the Lord Is the Bread of Life and of the Remission of Sin

Let us turn to John 6:49-53: *"'Your fathers ate the manna in the wilderness, and are dead. This is the bread which comes down from heaven, that one may eat of it and not die. I am the living bread which came down from heaven. If anyone eats of this bread, he will live forever; and the bread that I shall give is My flesh, which I shall give for the life of the world.' The Jews therefore quarreled among themselves, saying, 'How can this Man give us His flesh to eat?' Then Jesus said to them, 'Most assuredly, I say to you, unless you eat the flesh of the Son of Man and drink His blood, you have no life in you.'"* Jesus said that those who eat His flesh and drink His blood have eternal life. This passage means that all of us must eat the flesh of Jesus and drink His blood.

How, then, can we eat the flesh of Jesus and drink His blood? It is by believing in the gospel of the water and the Spirit that we can eat the flesh of Jesus and drink His blood. By believing that Jesus took upon all our sins with His baptism, we can eat His flesh, and by believing that Jesus shouldered our sins and was condemned on the Cross for them, we can drink His blood.

We must also believe that through the works of salvation

manifested in the blue, purple, and scarlet thread and the fine woven linen, Jesus has blotted out our sins and made us God's own children. Regardless of how you might have believed before believing in the gospel of the water and the Spirit, you must acknowledge that this old faith of yours had been wrong, and you must now raise the frame of faith by having the flesh and blood of Jesus and eat the bread of Word.

John 6:53 states, *"Most assuredly, I say to you, unless you eat the flesh of the Son of Man and drink His blood, you have no life in you."* Even now, some people use this passage to argue for the doctrine of transubstantiation. This doctrine holds that the bread and wine used in the Holy Communion are turned into the actual flesh and blood of Jesus when they are performing the ritual by faith. But we must realize and believe that this passage of John 6:53, far from speaking of transubstantiation, in fact speaks of the gospel of the water of the Spirit.

During the Holy Communion, if you wait in a line and the priest puts a piece of bread into your mouth, would this bread then transform into the body of Jesus? It would not! We can eat the flesh of Jesus and drink His blood by believing that Jesus came to this earth, took upon the sins of the world and cleansed them away by being baptized, carried these sins to the Cross and died on it, and has thereby saved us from death.

Those who eat the flesh of Jesus and drink His blood by faith are those who believe in the truth that Jesus, with the blue and scarlet thread, has saved us from sin by taking upon our sins and bearing the condemnation of sin on His own body. We must eat the flesh of Jesus and drink His blood with our faith in the baptism and blood of Jesus Christ.

To accept our sins passed onto Him, Jesus was baptized by John the Baptist in the Jordan River. Let us turn to Matthew

3:15-17: *"But Jesus answered and said to him, 'Permit it to be so now, for thus it is fitting for us to fulfill all righteousness.' Then he allowed Him. When He had been baptized, Jesus came up immediately from the water; and behold, the heavens were opened to Him, and He saw the Spirit of God descending like a dove and alighting upon Him. And suddenly a voice came from heaven, saying, 'This is My beloved Son, in whom I am well pleased.'"*

It is because Jesus took upon all sins when He was baptized by John and died on the Cross that He has fulfilled all the righteousness of God. Our faith that believes in the truth of the gospel, that all the sins of the world were passed onto Jesus Christ when He was baptized by John, is the true faith with which we can eat the flesh of Jesus and drink His blood.

If you recognize this truth, then you have already eaten the flesh of Jesus by faith. That your sins of the world were passed onto Jesus Christ once for all is the truth, and therefore it is critically important for you to believe this in the center of your hearts. This faith is the faith that enables you to eat the flesh of Jesus. Were your sins passed onto Jesus through His baptism? Only when you believe this can you eat the flesh of Jesus. After baptizing Jesus, John the Baptist shouted out, *"Behold! The Lamb of God who takes away the sin of the world!" (John 1:29)*

And because Jesus had accepted the sins of the world through His baptism, He carried them all on His own body, was crucified, and shed His blood and died. Having thus been crucified, nailed on both His feet and hands, and shedding His blood, Jesus shouted out as He died, "It is finished!" He then rose from the dead in three days, bore witness for 40 days, ascended to Heaven exactly as He looked, and He now sits at the right hand of God the Father. And He also promised that

He would return just as He had ascended to Heaven. Do you believe in this truth in the center of your hearts? It is by believing in this truth that you can eat the flesh of Jesus and drink His blood. It is when we truly believe in the center of our hearts that we can eat the flesh of Jesus and drink His blood. It is with this faith that we can eat the bread of the Holy Place.

Our Lord commanded us to always remember His flesh and blood whenever we gather together (1 Corinthians 11:26). As such, every time we gather together, we must commemorate the flesh and blood of Jesus all the time. When it is by faith that we are supposed to eat the flesh of Jesus and drink His blood whenever we gather together, how could we just hold the Holy Communion only as a formalistic ritual?

Because we believe in the baptism through which Jesus took our sins upon His own body and in His sacrificial blood of the Cross, it is by faith that we are remembering His flesh and blood everyday. It is because we believe in the truth of the water and the Spirit that everyday we eat the flesh of Jesus and drink His blood. As Jesus said, *"Whoever eats My flesh and drinks My blood has eternal life (John 6:54),"* He will raise up those who eat His flesh and drink His blood on the last day.

We must admit that if our faith does not enable us to eat the flesh of Jesus and drink His blood, then it is a flawed faith. Our Lord said, *"Whoever eats My flesh and drinks My blood has eternal life, and I will raise him up at the last day. For My flesh is food indeed, and My blood is drink indeed. He who eats My flesh and drinks My blood abides in Me, and I in him. As the living Father sent Me, and I live because of the Father, so he who feeds on Me will live because of Me"* (John 6:54-57).

Those who eat the flesh of the Lord and drink His blood by faith will live because of Him. On the other hand, those who do not eat the Lord's flesh and drink His blood will die, because they had not believed. But it is not difficult for us to eat the flesh of Jesus and drink His blood by faith.

Let's assume for a moment here that there is an exam of salvation that we must take in order to enter the Kingdom of God. One of its questions asks, "What is the faith that enables you to eat the flesh of Jesus and drink His blood?" How should we answer this question? When both the flesh and blood of Jesus constitute the truth, could we say that we ate His flesh when in fact we only drank His blood? We must write down both the baptism and the Cross of Jesus as our answer. We can enter the Kingdom of Heaven only when we eat the flesh of Jesus and drink His blood. Even if we had misbelieved and misunderstood before, if we turn our hearts around, eat the flesh of Jesus and drink His blood, we can then pass the test. If we believe in the flesh and blood of Jesus right now, at this very moment, we can pass the exam sufficiently.

People look at the outside appearances, but God looks at the center of the heart, and so when we believe in both the baptism of Jesus and the blood of the Cross, we are then eating the flesh of Jesus and drinking His blood. God looks at the center of our hearts to see if we really have faith in the flesh and blood of Jesus in our hearts. Therefore, if we do not believe in the flesh and blood of Jesus in the center of our hearts, then we have not been saved from sin. No matter how you might have believed before, if you now have the faith that believes in both the flesh and blood of Jesus, you can then enter the Kingdom of Heaven.

Many religionists of this world are endlessly debating over the veracity of the doctrine of transubstantiation. What really need in fact is the faith that enables us to eat the flesh of Jesus and drink His blood. But this is possible only when we believe in the gospel of the water and the Spirit in our hearts.

Believing in Jesus in the center of our hearts through the gospel of the water and the Spirit is eating the true bread and drinking the true drink.

We Must Believe in the Baptism and Blood of Jesus as Our Remission of Sin

Our Lord said, *"My blood is drink indeed" (John 6:55)*. Our Lord bore the condemnation of sin on the Cross. The faith that believes that Jesus took upon our sins by being baptized and shed His blood on the Cross is the faith that enables us to drink the blood of Jesus. Through the baptism that He received from John, Jesus took upon all our sins, including those of your children, your parents, and each and every one of us, and by shedding His blood on the Cross He bore the condemnation of all these sins. With His baptism and blood, Jesus has solved away all our problems of sin absolutely for everyone in this entire world. Believing that Jesus thus took upon our sins with His baptism and was condemned for our sins with His blood of the Cross is drinking the blood of Jesus by faith.

In today's world, there are many who say that they believe in the gospel of the water and the Spirit only with their words. But they do not wholly believe in the flesh and blood of Jesus. Anyone who does not have the whole faith that believes in the flesh and blood of Jesus cannot be remitted of sin. You might have believed before that the blood of the Cross was the only truth, but now that you have found the real truth, you must have the faith that clearly believes in the flesh and blood of Jesus. Only then will God recognize you as the saved. But if, on the other hand, you do not draw the clear line of salvation on this issue—that is, on the remission of sin received by the faith that believes in the flesh and blood of Jesus in the center of the heart—then you cannot have your faith approved by God.

Our Lord said, *"He who eats My flesh and drinks My blood abides in Me, and I in him" (John 6:56).* But unless we eat the flesh of Jesus and drink His blood by faith, we cannot enter into the presence of God. And anyone who does not have this faith that believes in the flesh and blood of Jesus cannot abide in the Lord. It is my sincere hope that no one among the saints, the workers and servants of God in our Church will tragically fall away from this faith that believes in the flesh and blood of Jesus.

When Sodom and Gomorrah were destroyed by fire, Lot's sons-in-law regarded God's Word of life that Lot told them only as a joke. For those who do not take the Word of God seriously, the judgment of God will be brought upon them just as it is written. Unbelievers will be condemned for their sin of unbelief. They will be destroyed for their sins. This is no laughing matter that can be skirted over with a few chuckles.

The gospel of the water and the Spirit refers to faith in the flesh and blood of Jesus. It is by believing in this truth that we have been remitted of our sins and received eternal life. Because the faith of the flesh and blood of Jesus in which we believe is the true gospel and the real truth, we must keep this faith in our hearts. By first raising the frame of faith high in our hearts, we must hold tightly all the Word of God and never allow it to slip away from us. By believing in our hearts, we must accept the truth that God has blotted out all the iniquities of sinners with the flesh and blood of Jesus.

I hope and pray that you would all believe in the gospel of the water and the Spirit fulfilled by the Lord, eat the bread of salvation that saves you from your sins, and thereby receive eternal life. ✉

SERMON

9

You can download Rev. Paul C. Jong's Christian Books on iPhone, iPad, or Blackberry by going to Amazon's Kindle e-bookstore (www.amazon.com).

The Gold Lampstand

< Exodus 25:31-40 >

"You shall also make a lampstand of pure gold; the lampstand shall be of hammered work. Its shaft, its branches, its bowls, its ornamental knobs, and flowers shall be of one piece. And six branches shall come out of its sides: three branches of the lampstand out of one side, and three branches of the lampstand out of the other side. Three bowls shall be made like almond blossoms on one branch, with an ornamental knob and a flower, and three bowls made like almond blossoms on the other branch, with an ornamental knob and a flower—and so for the six branches that come out of the lampstand. On the lampstand itself four bowls shall be made like almond blossoms, each with its ornamental knob and flower. And there shall be a knob under the first two branches of the same, a knob under the second two branches of the same, and a knob under the third two branches of the same, according to the six branches that extend from the lampstand. Their knobs and their branches shall be of one piece; all of it shall be one hammered piece of pure gold. You shall make seven lamps for it, and they shall arrange its lamps so that they give light in front of it. And its wick-trimmers and their trays shall be of pure gold. It shall be made of a talent of pure gold, with all these utensils. And see to it that you make them according to the pattern which was shown you on the mountain."

The gold lampstand was made of a talent of pure gold. Its shaft was hammered out of a single piece of a talent of pure gold, with three branches coming out of each of its two sides, and seven lamps placed on top of the shaft and its six branches. As the gold lampstand was made of a talent of pure gold, it was a captivatingly splendid and beautiful sight to hold.

On top of the gold lampstand, there were seven lamps to hold oil, which was lit to illuminate the Holy Place at all times. One can enter into the Holy Place only by lifting and opening the Tabernacle's door woven of blue, purple, and scarlet thread and fine woven linen. Those who can enter this place are only the ones who believe in the works of salvation manifested in the blue, purple, and scarlet thread. As such, no one can enter into the Holy Place without this faith, for it is a place that is permitted only to those who know the mystery of the blue, purple, and scarlet thread and the fine woven linen manifested in the screen door of the Tabernacle.

Therefore, only those who believe in the marvelous salvation made of the blue, purple, and scarlet thread and the fine woven linen can become the members of God's Church. The four colors of the screen door of the Tabernacle are the shadow of the gospel of the water and the Spirit, prefiguring the coming of Jesus, who took upon our sins of the world by being baptized and bore the condemnation of our sins by being crucified and shedding His blood.

None other than this very gospel of the water and the Spirit is the gospel of the true remission of sin that the Lord has given us. The gospel of the water and the Spirit is made of the baptism that Jesus Christ received and the judgment of the Cross that He bore to give us the blessing of the remission of sin. As such, only those who wholeheartedly believe in this truth can be remitted of all their sins. God, in other words,

Free book request www.nlmission.com

allows only those who believe in the truth of the blue, purple, and scarlet thread and the fine woven linen to enter into the Holy Place.

As the gold lampstand inside the Holy Place always shone its bright light, so can those who become God's children by believing in the gospel of the water and the Spirit also illuminate this world with the light of salvation that saves people from their sins. In other words, only those who have received the remission of sin through the gospel of the water and the Spirit can fulfill the role of the lampstand that gives out the light of salvation, so that others may know also this truth and receive the remission of their sins.

The gold lampstand had flowers, ornamental knobs, and bowls. As God commanded that seven lamps should be placed on the lampstand, when the lampstand was lit, darkness gave way in the Holy Place at all times. This means that the righteous who have been cleansed of their sins by believing in the gospel of the water and the Spirit would gather together, build God's Church, and illuminate this world. The light of the lampstand that shone in the Holy Place is the gospel of the water and the Spirit, which drives away the darkness of this world.

To save us from sin, Jesus Christ came to this earth, incarnated in the flesh of a man. And take upon our sins, He was baptized by John, and to bear the condemnation of our sins, He was crucified. Jesus has thereby become the light of salvation. In the court of the Tabernacle, sinners passed their sins onto their sacrificial offering by laying their hands on its head and letting it bear the condemnation of their sins by killing this sacrifice.

Likewise, Jesus Christ has completed our salvation by being baptized and dying on the Cross according to the law of

Free book request www.bjnewlife.org

God, and He has become the light of salvation for all mankind. With the ministries manifested in the blue, purple, and scarlet thread and the fine woven linen, Jesus Christ has fulfilled the salvation of mankind. We have thus been saved from our sins by believing in the gospel of the baptism and the blood that Jesus Christ has given us. All who believe in Jesus must also discover this light of truth.

Jesus Christ has shone the light of salvation unto this world so that only those who are born again of water and the Spirit can enter the Kingdom of God. As such, only those who are born again of water and the Spirit can become part of God's Church and be qualified to shine and spread the light of the water and the Spirit throughout the whole world. Because only they believe in the gospel of the water and the Spirit and spread it, God has entrusted this gospel of the water and the Spirit especially to them and permitted them to shine the light of the true gospel.

As such, we should realize that this work of spreading the light of the gospel throughout the world can be done only by those who believe in the gospel of the water and the Spirit as the real truth. Sinners cannot enter into the Holy Place. Only those who believe in the gospel manifested in the blue, purple, and scarlet thread of the door of the Tabernacle can enter. Therefore, only those who know the truth of the blue, purple, and scarlet thread and believe in it in their hearts can come into the Tabernacle and carry out the task of illuminating the bright light of salvation.

At the gate of the court of the Tabernacle, a screen made of blue, purple, and scarlet thread also illuminated the way. For those who are looking for the Tabernacle to give their offerings in it, God made the gate of its court with the same four colors. But the people of the Old Testament's time could not become whole forever through their daily offerings. They had to therefore continue to wait for the Messiah. However, when Jesus Christ the Messiah actually came, they failed to realize that He became the true Messiah by giving one everlasting offering according to the revelation made in the colors of the screen door of the Tabernacle.

This is just like those Christians of today who, even as they call on the name of Jesus, do not know that He came of the blue, purple, and scarlet thread and the fine woven linen and has saved us perfectly. When the people of the Old Testament gave their sacrificial offerings everyday with the laying on of hands and the blood of the offerings, they had to believe that the Savior would appear in this way, just like their sacrificial offering.

Likewise, the people of this world must also believe that Jesus Christ the Savior came to this earth, took upon the sins of the world by being baptized according to the Old Testament's sacrificial system of the laying on of hands and blood, was crucified and shed His blood, and has thereby saved His people from sin. But because they do not even know the sacrificial system of the Old Testament, they have no idea whether Jesus came by His baptism and blood, or by the blood of the Cross alone, or just as a plain Savior.

In God's eyes, the faith that today's Christians place in the sacrificial system of the Old Testament is as flawed as that of the people of Israel. Because they do not have true faith in the Messiah who is manifested in the sacrificial system, they cannot believe that the Messiah came, was baptized, and shed His blood. But all the peoples of this world, including the people of Israel, must believe in the gospel of the water and the Spirit, that Jesus has saved them from their sins through the ministries of His baptism and His crucifixion.

To save you and me from all our sins and condemnation, Jesus Christ was baptized and shed His blood. Through the truth held in the blue, purple, and scarlet thread manifested in the door of the Tabernacle, the shadow of the gospel of the water and the Spirit, we are therefore able to know Jesus Christ. This truth of salvation is that people can receive the remission of their sins by believing in the true gospel in their hearts. By believing in the gospel of the water and the Spirit that Jesus Christ has given us by actually coming to this world, being baptized, and dying on the Cross, you must have the faith that saves you in your hearts. This truth has saved you from all your sins.

In the holy House of God, there were three screen doors. All these doors were woven of blue, purple, and scarlet thread and fine woven linen. As I have told you again and again, these four colors reveal exactly God's salvation: To save us from our sins, God has set the law of the remission of sin completed through the blue, purple, and scarlet thread and the fine woven linen. Therefore, if we believe according to this law of the remission of sin, then God will accept our faith and forever save us from our sins.

It is by believing in the gospel of the water and the Spirit manifested in the blue, purple, and scarlet thread that any of us can be saved from all sins forever. By knowing and believing in the true significance of the sacrificial system given by God, anyone can go to Him. At the entrance of the Holy Place, the House of God, there were five pillars, and a screen woven of blue, purple, and scarlet thread and fine woven linen was hung on these pillars. For us to go to God, we must have four faiths manifested in the four-colored screen door.

The faith shown in the blue thread is that Jesus Christ accepted our sins by being baptized, and the faith manifested in the scarlet thread is that Jesus bore the condemnation of sin by being crucified and shedding His blood. The faith revealed in the purple color is to believe that Jesus is God Himself, and the faith manifested in the fine woven linen is to believe in His elaborate Word that God has made us sinless by blotting out our sins with the aforementioned thread—that is, with the blue, purple, and scarlet thread. This truth is called the gospel of the water and the Spirit. As such, by believing that Jesus has saved us through the water and the Spirit, we can enter the Kingdom of God. This is the faith of those who can open the door of the Tabernacle and enter into the Holy Place.

The gate of the court of the Tabernacle woven of blue, purple, and scarlet thread enables us to realize God's plan for how He would save us, showing us that our salvation, coming from the remission of sin set by God, is not achieved through our own man-made efforts. Even if we ask for the forgiveness of our sins everyday, without the sacrificial offering for the atonement of sin, the passing of sin through the laying on of hands, and the bloodshed, we cannot be saved from our everlasting sins. Only when the sacrificial offering who came to save us from our sins takes upon our eternal sins of the world can we be wholly saved by believing in this truth and thereby receiving the remission of sin.

If we have in our hearts the faith that believes in this gospel of truth, then we will be able to spread the gospel of salvation that brings eternal life to every lost soul. By believing in the ministries of Jesus manifested in the blue, purple, and scarlet thread, we can illuminate this world with the truth of the remission of sin. The lampstand in the Holy Place had seven lamps, and so when these lamps were lit, their light was reflected by the walls of the Tabernacle made of boards overlaid with gold, thereby illuminating the whole inside of the

Holy Place brightly. If there had been no lampstand in the Holy Place, then it would only have been dark. This is the reason why God has placed, here in this darkening world, the saints and His servants who believe in the gospel of the water and the Spirit.

What Is the Role of the Gold Lampstand?

The gold lampstand shows us that God has given us the faith that believes in the truth, which becomes the light of the world. Our faith is to believe that Jesus Christ was born unto this earth, was baptized, and shed His blood on the Cross. God is telling us, in other words, to shine the light of salvation with this faith. When we hold the gospel of salvation in our hearts and spread this faith, it is this very moment when the light of truth shines. People would then see and come to this bright light, realizing that the Lord has saved them with the blue, purple, and scarlet thread and the fine woven linen, and becoming God's own people. This light of truth is the gospel of the water and the Spirit planned and fulfilled by God the Father, the Son, and the Holy Spirit.

With our faith in the truth that Jesus came to this earth, was baptized and crucified, shed His blood and died, and rose from the dead again to give us the remission of all sins, we are spreading the gospel to those who yearn to be saved. Had Jesus Christ not been baptized and sacrificed for us, you and I could never, ever have been saved from our sins.

Because Jesus was baptized, shed His blood, and was sacrificed for us, He could give to all sinners the faith that saves them. We are not just spreading some illusive doctrine here. Throughout the whole world, we are spreading the light of salvation manifested in the blue, purple, and scarlet thread and the fine woven linen. Because we have the faith that knows and believes in the baptism of Jesus and His sacrifice of the Cross, we are spreading the light of life to those whose hearts are in darkness. All those who have thus been illuminated by this light then bear witness to the marvelous wonder of all their sins disappearing from their hearts. All the people of the world will also come to know the baptism that Jesus received and the sacrifice of the Cross that He offered to blot out all the sins of the world, and by believing that these are their own remission of sin, they will come to discover the light of truth.

Why did Jesus Christ have to come to this earth? Why did He have to be baptized? Why did He have to die on the Cross? Why did He have to rise from the dead again in three days? The reason for all these is because Jesus Christ is the Messiah. To fulfill all the works of salvation as the Messiah, Jesus was baptized and shed His blood, and He has thereby shone the light of salvation to sinners. Therefore, by spreading the light of salvation throughout the whole world, we can enable many to know this truth, believe in it, and thereby receive eternal life.

You and I are the lampstand that illuminates this world with the light of the gospel of the water and the Spirit. Through the gospel that we are spreading, people will come to know the light of truth that saves them. Those who are looking for the light in this dark world will see this brilliant light that we are spreading, come to the light of truth, and be saved from all their sins. By coming to the faith that believes in this truth, all human beings can be saved.

This gospel is not a theoretical matter. As such, we must believe with our true hearts. We can work to spread the gospel only when we truly believe in the ministries of Jesus manifested in the blue, purple, and scarlet thread and the fine woven linen. But even if we have received the remission of sin, without the lamp where oil can be put in, we cannot give out light forever, and so God has given us God's Church, our lampstand. On each branch of the lampstand, there were bowls, and below these bowls were ornamental knobs. This means none other than the Church built by faith.

The place where only those who have truly received the remission of sin by believing in their hearts are gathered is God's true Church. The head of the Church is Jesus Christ, and the Church is His body. Just like the body moves exactly as the head commands, the Church therefore moves its arms and legs as commanded by Jesus Christ. This is how the gospel is served. What, then, does God's Church look at? Imbued in dark sins, the whole world is dying, and the Church looks at the souls in its midst that cannot avoid but be bound to hell. God's Church is illuminating them with the light of salvation. This is what you and I are doing in His Church with our faith in the gospel.

In countries where there is a long history of Christianity, there are many who are highly learnt and knowledgeable of the Bible. I believe that when those among such people who have been constantly looking for the real truth come to encounter this truth, they will at once receive the remission of their sins. So to spread the gospel of the water and the Spirit to such people, I work by uniting with all the born-again saints in faith.

Because Christianity, unlike other religions, has laid its foundation of faith on the Word, people will receive the remission of sin if we would only spread the Word correctly. But there are also those who ferociously stand against this truth, only deriding it and not believing in it, no matter how much it is preached at them. In particular, there are some stubborn religionists who do not believe in the Word of God, and such people will never believe in this truth of the water and the Spirit. But what about those who accept the Bible as the Word of God? A countless number of them will receive the remission of sin by hearing and believing in this gospel.

It is because I have this faith that I have been serving God, together with you, to this very day. In the days to come, this gospel will be spread to a myriad of people and great works of the gospel will arise. It may even be the case that God is working where we cannot see and thousands of people are actually receiving their remission of sin everyday. And like you and me, a multitude of people will become the lamps and spread to the people of the whole world the faith of their hearts that believes in the salvation manifested in the blue, purple, and scarlet thread and the fine woven linen. I believe that as they illuminate the whole world, new believers will continue to rise, and they, too, will be nurtured and spread this gospel in turn.

We who have now become the lamps of God are illuminating the light of salvation with our faith that believes in the truth manifested in the blue, purple, and scarlet thread and the fine woven linen. The blue thread is giving out the light of the truth of Jesus' baptism—that is, Jesus bore the sins of the whole world by being baptized by John; the purple thread is illuminating the light of truth that Jesus Christ is the King of kings; the scarlet thread is radiating the light of truth that Jesus carried the sins of the world to the Cross and shed His blood on it; and the fine woven linen is glowing with the light of truth that the Word of God has made sinners righteous. The gospel Word of the water and the Spirit given by God is the light of truth manifested in the blue, purple, and scarlet thread and the fine woven linen.

This gospel also tells us that He will return to this earth as the Lord of the Second Coming, bring us alive again, make us reign with Him for a thousand years in the Millennial Kingdom, and enable us to enter the everlasting Kingdom of God and live forever. Can you imagine what eternal life is?

This universe is so expansive and wide that scientists say that there are star systems upon star systems in other countless galaxies beyond our own solar system and the Milky Way. The domains of the universe that God created are stupendously colossal. Beyond our known universe, countless realms that we do not even know are lying throughout galaxies. The shooting stars that fall now are actually pieces of planets that fell apart far away in deep galaxies billions of years ago, only now reaching the earth's atmosphere and burning.

We are, in other words, confirming what had happened billions of years ago only now. Like this, the vast domains of the universe created by God still remain unknown. But even as the universe is unknown for us, for God, it is as small as the palm of a hand. God is the omniscient and omnipotent One who created all things and established the order of the universe.

We illuminate the world with the light of truth, that by believing in the gospel of the water and the Spirit all can receive the everlasting remission of sin and enjoy eternal life. The children of God have the bright light of life allowing them to live forever with Jesus Christ. God lives with us forever, allowing us to enjoy His pleasures and clothing us in His glory. Why? Because we believe in the light of the gospel of His power. Once we discovered this light that enabled us to know the truth, we could not but spread this light to others.

And when we saw the providence of God that works in the whole universe, our faith in His works could not but spring up. Some stars disappeared billions of years ago, and yet our eyes are still seeing them because they were billions of light-years away from this planet! We can merely imagine the concept of "eternity" when we speculate on the infinity of the universe.

We who have become part of God's Church now live our lives by spreading the light of the true gospel, for we believe in the truth manifested in the blue, purple, and scarlet thread. We believe that this salvation guarantees us eternal and blessed life in our Father's Kingdom. And we know that God desires all men to be saved and to come to the knowledge of the truth (1 Timothy 2:4). Therefore, those who know the light of salvation must carry out the spreading of the gospel of the water and the Spirit, a task that God has entrusted to them.

God has blessed us so that we would be able to do this work. Realizing just how great a blessing this fact is, the right for us to do is to carry out our assigned tasks by faith. I hope you would all fill your hearts with the light that knows the truth of God. By the grace of God, you and I have come to believe in the ministries of salvation manifested in the blue, purple, and scarlet thread and the fine woven linen, and we have become the light of salvation for the whole world, the ones who illuminate the entire world. Hallelujah! I give all my thanks to God. ✉

You can download Rev. Paul C. Jong's Christian Books on iPhone, iPad, or Blackberry by going to Amazon's Kindle e-bookstore (www.amazon.com).

SERMON

10

You can download Rev. Paul C. Jong's Christian Books on iPhone, iPad, or Blackberry by going to Amazon's Kindle e-bookstore (www.amazon.com).

The Altar of Incense

< Exodus 30:1-10 >

"You shall make an altar to burn incense on; you shall make it of acacia wood. A cubit shall be its length and a cubit its width—it shall be square—and two cubits shall be its height. Its horns shall be of one piece with it. And you shall overlay its top, its sides all around, and its horns with pure gold; and you shall make for it a molding of gold all around. Two gold rings you shall make for it, under the molding on both its sides. You shall place them on its two sides, and they will be holders for the poles with which to bear it. You shall make the poles of acacia wood, and overlay them with gold. And you shall put it before the veil that is before the ark of the Testimony, before the mercy seat that is over the Testimony, where I will meet with you. Aaron shall burn on it sweet incense every morning; when he tends the lamps, he shall burn incense on it. And when Aaron lights the lamps at twilight, he shall burn incense on it, a perpetual incense before the LORD throughout your generations. You shall not offer strange incense on it, or a burnt offering, or a grain offering; nor shall you pour a drink offering on it. And Aaron shall make atonement upon its horns once a year with the blood of the sin offering of atonement; once a year he shall make atonement upon it throughout your generations. It is most holy to the LORD."

The Altar of Incense Was a Place of Prayer

The altar of incense was made of acacia wood, and it was square, measuring a cubit (45 cm: 1.5 feet) in both its length and width, and 2 cubits in its height. Placed inside the Holy Place, the altar of incense was overlaid with gold in its entirety, with a molding of gold all around it. Four rings of gold were placed under its molding to hold the poles used to carry it. On this altar of incense, nothing else but only the holy anointing oil and the sweet incense were to be used (Exodus 30:22-25).

The altar of incense was where the incense of prayer was offered to God. But before we pray at the altar of incense, we must first find out whether we are qualified to pray to God at this altar or not. Whoever seeks to be qualified to pray to the holy God must first become sinless by washing away his/her sins by faith. To do so, one must be cleansed of all his/her sins by the faith of the burnt offering and of the laver.

God does not hear the prayers of sinners (Isaiah 59:1-3). Why? Because God accepts only those who have been washed of all their sins by believing in the gospel of the water and the Spirit. Because God has washed away all our sins by the truth manifested in the blue, purple, and scarlet thread and the fine woven linen. God, in other words, is pleased to hear only the prayers of the righteous (Psalms 34:15, 1 Peter 3:12).

The Nature and Reality of All Human Beings

When we look closely, we see that all human beings, including you and me, were fundamentally born as a sinful seed, and therefore they all sin. Each and every one is a seed of evildoer. Because people were originally born with sin, they cannot help but live their lives doing evil deeds. Think about yourself, whoever you may be. We can admit before God that we had been evil ones who could not avoid but be cast into hell. Above all, when we judge our acts before God, we come to recognize that in accordance to the law of God declaring the wages of sin to be death, we simply cannot escape from His righteous judgment of sin.

Because what comes out of the hearts of human beings is just evil thoughts, murders, adulteries, pride and foolishness, and so on, they do these things whenever they are given a chance (Mark 7:21-27). How can the hearts of human beings, who were fundamentally born as a seed of evildoers and cannot help but sin whenever circumstances allow and opportunities arise, ever be shameless before God? It is impossible through man-made efforts. But there is one and only faith that allows us to have no shame before God, and it is here. We must all know and believe in the truth made of the blue, purple, and scarlet thread and the fine woven linen, the truth that enables us to be washed of all our sins and therefore stand before God with no shame. As such, all of us absolutely need the gospel of the water and the Spirit.

None of us could deny the fact that we were all bound to hell for our sins but only admit this fate. And for those who recognize before God that they are bound to hell, it is not so difficult to believe in their hearts in the salvation that God has given them. When we face God with truthfulness and sincerity, we cannot deceptively hide our hearts from Him, and so we come to acknowledge the justice of the righteousness of God. Everyone is positioned in such a place that they cannot avoid but be punished for their sins by the righteous judgment of God.

The righteous law of God that declares the wages of sin to be death is not a law that all sinners can skirt around with their own thoughts or religious faith. Because the Law of God is detailed, exact, and just, it forces whoever stands before it to admit that he/she is bound to hell for his/her sins. All sinners come to realize that they cannot escape from God's judgment even for the smallest of their sins.

Therefore, we are in need of a Savior who delivers all of us from sin, and we have to find out who this Savior is. This is Jesus Christ, the Savior of the entire mankind. He is the Savior who came to this earth, who was baptized by John to take upon the sins of the world, who bore the punishment of the iniquities of all sinners by being crucified and shedding His blood, and who has thereby saved us from all our sins.

All of us had misunderstood that receiving the remission of sin would be extremely difficult. In fact, we had thought that we could be saved only if we know the Bible in its entirety, or that our salvation required some kind of good deeds. But the truth of salvation given by God was different. This truth of salvation opened and showed the way for us to be saved from all our sins by examining our consciences before the Law of God, recognizing all the sins that are found in our hearts, and believing in the gospel of the water and the Spirit. This truth was foreshadowed in the door of the Tabernacle.

Mankind's remission of sin comes from the truth of precious salvation fulfilled through the blue, purple, and scarlet thread and the fine woven linen. It is by believing in this truth that all can receive the eternal remission of sin once for all. To do so, everyone must recognize that they are all bound to hell for their sins and believe in the gospel manifested in the blue, purple, and scarlet thread, thereby receiving the remission of their sins all at once. The gospel that God has given us is the gospel that is found in the gospel of truth held in the blue, purple, and scarlet thread and the fine woven linen.

All must believe in this gospel of truth, for if they do not believe in the truth held in this gospel, then they cannot be freed from their sins. But those who believe in this truth of salvation that God has fulfilled with the gospel of the water and the Spirit are worthy enough to be saved from all their sins and become God's own children. As such, to become the ones who can go before God and pray to Him, we must first believe in the truth of the water and the Spirit, the gospel of the remission of sin. When we are saved from all sins by knowing the true gospel and believing in it in our true hearts, we then become qualified to pray to God. The faith that enables us to pray to God is attained by believing in our hearts the gospel of the water and the Spirit, the gospel from God.

It is wrong to try to pray to God without the faith that knows and believes in the truth of the blue, purple, and scarlet thread manifested in the screen door of the Tabernacle. Such faith is akin to committing the sins of blasphemy and mockery against God. How could we become God's enemy by refusing to believe in the truth manifested in the Tabernacle in our hearts?

When you refuse to believe in Jesus Christ who came by the truth of the blue, purple, and scarlet thread, it is a shortcut for you to garner the enmity of God. This is an act of horrendous unbelief that stands against God. The souls that continue to commit the sin of despising the holiness of God are those who do not believe in the salvation that God has fulfilled for them but believe according to their own thoughts and on their own accord. Such souls are the ones who, covering themselves in the garments of fig leaves called "hypocrisy," despise God's love and mercy.

But you must realize that though these people may be able to deceive their own hearts, they cannot escape from the judgment of God. Those with such unbelief will be condemned to suffer the terrifying punishment of sin by the righteous law of God. Why? Because they sought neither to know the gospel of the water and the Spirit with which the Lord has blotted out their sins, nor to believe in this gospel.

When our consciences are filthy even in our own eyes, how can we hide our sins from the holy God? This is simply impossible! Anyone who seeks to hide his/her sins will be left out of God's love and mercy. Those who deceive their own hearts will end up as the devil's evil servants who deceive God and their fellow human beings. The very notion that they can somehow deceive God just by blindfolding their own eyes is a reflection of their arrogance coming out of their conceited thoughts. In fact, those who rely on their own thoughts are the ones who challenge the gospel of the water and the Spirit, and who seek to become Satan's servants out of their own volition.

People must realize that though they may be able to deceive their own hearts, they can never deceive God. And they must change their minds to believe according to the Word of God. How could everyone wash away their sins without believing in the gospel of the water and the Spirit? As it is written that the wages of sin is death, no sinner who deceives his/her heart before God can ever escape from the judgment of God. If we acknowledge the Law of God, then it is clear that we are all bound to hell for our sins. As such, all those who seek to come out to God must be saved by believing in the truth of the gospel manifested in the door of the Tabernacle.

However, because many have failed to realize the fact that they are to be condemned for their sins, they have also failed to accept into their hearts the gospel of salvation that has come by the truth of the blue, purple, and scarlet thread, and, as a result, they are all heading to hell. Regardless of whether they are already Christians or not, those who do not believe in the gospel of the water and the Spirit will face the same punishment. As such, we must not deceive our own consciences before our God, but yield in our hearts to the gospel of the water and the Spirit, and acknowledge and believe in this gospel of truth.

We Must Cleanse away Our Sins by Believing in the Word of Truth

People have two consciences: one is the conscience of the flesh, and the other is the conscience of faith with respect to the gospel of truth. We must be honest to these two realms, but of these two, we cannot fail to have, in particular, the conscience of faith that recognizes the gospel of truth. We must examine the conscience of our faith before the Word of God; believe that Jesus accepted our sins by being baptized, was condemned on the Cross, and has thereby saved us; and wash away, by this faith, the sins of our consciences. It angers me that even when this is the truth that cannot possibly be any more definitive, there are still people who do not believe in the gospel of truth.

There is an order of faith to cleanse our consciences. First, we must recognize and confirm the fact that we are bound to hell, and second, we must believe in our hearts that our Savior came to this earth, was baptized by John for our sins, died on the Cross, rose from the dead, and has thereby saved us from all sins. Sinners must be saved from their iniquities and receive eternal life by their faith in the gospel of the water and the Spirit that is thus manifested in the blue, purple, and scarlet thread.

Despite the fact that we must be save from our sins, some

people still do not believe, even as they know about the remission of sin fulfilled through the blue, purple, and scarlet thread. How can they do this? Surely, they must be responsible for all the consequences of their own unbelief. If we had just known the truth manifested in the blue, purple, and scarlet thread but had not believed, then we would still be sinful, and if we are still sinful, then would we not have to be judged for our sins according to the law of God? Each and every one of us, male or female, all had to be saved from sin by believing in the heart in the truth of salvation that God has fulfilled through the blue, purple, and scarlet thread.

People must have the kind of faith that saves them from their sins. They must have the faith that only believes in the gospel of the water and the Spirit. Do you believe in the gospel manifested in the blue, purple, and scarlet thread, that the Lord bore all our sins by being baptized and has saved us with His bloodshed on the Cross? When you think of yourselves first, do you admit the fact that you were indeed destined to hell? Do you realize that even as we were bound to hell, the Lord has nonetheless saved us from our sins with the truth manifested in the blue, purple, and scarlet thread?

You must realize that it was to take care of all our sins that the Lord came to this earth, was baptized, and shed His blood. To blot out your and my sins, our Lord came to this earth incarnated into the flesh of man, accepted at once all the sins of the whole humanity onto His own body by being baptized by John in the Jordan River at the age of 30, and bore the condemnation of sin once for all by being crucified and shedding His blood. All at once, God has remitted all the sins of those who believe.

We can be saved from all our sins by believing in the truth manifested in the blue, purple, and scarlet thread. We must examine and confirm whether or not we have truly been saved from all our sins by this truth. We must have the faith that believes in Jesus Christ who came of the blue, purple, and scarlet thread as the Savior. As the Bible says, *"With the heart one believes unto righteousness, and with the mouth confession is made unto salvation" (Romans 10:10).* Romans 10:17 also declares, *"So then faith comes by hearing, and hearing by the word of God."*

This Word of Christ tells us that we are saved by believing in the salvation fulfilled with the blue, purple, and scarlet thread. The remission of sin is not something that is attained by believing with our own thoughts, but it is something that is taken by believing in our hearts in the salvation that has come of the blue, purple, and scarlet thread. The faith that can truly deliver us from sin is the faith that believes in the gospel of the water and the Spirit.

Must we then pray to God by placing our faith in this truth? Of course! We have to always give all prayers and supplications in the Spirit, having girded our waists with the truth (Ephesians 6:14,18). But what, then, is this truth?

It is the gospel that tells us that our Lord came to this earth to save us, was baptized by John the Baptist at the age of 30, carried all the sins of the world, was crucified on both his hands and feet, was spit at, shed His blood, and has thereby washed away our sins. We must confess that it is by our faith in this truth that our remission of sin has been fulfilled. Our Lord has saved us from our sins by being condemned for the sins of the world through His baptism and the blood of the Cross.

"Lord, You loved me so much that You have made me God's own child." This is how we must confess our faith. When all that we had was just sin, our Lord has still given us the qualification to enter the Kingdom of Heaven by blotting out all our sins through His baptism and crucifixion. We must all believe in this truth and receive eternal life.

What reason is there for you not to believe in this truth? As for me, I would have had nothing to say even if the Lord was not thus baptized to save me from my sins, and yet for my own sake, He was in fact baptized, shed His blood, and has thereby saved me from my sins. And so I believe! There is no reason why all of us should not believe in this gospel. It is clear that if sinners do not believe in the truth of the gospel of the water and the Spirit, then they will surely be cast into hell. But I want each and every one of you to be saved now from sin by believing in the gospel of the blue, purple, and scarlet thread.

There was a time when I myself had remained a sinner even as I professed to believe in Jesus. Wanting to be a good Christian, I tried very hard to have no shame under Heaven. But contrary to my wishes, I kept on sinning time after time; the only consolation was that when I compared myself to others, I thought I was at least somewhat better than them. However, my conscience kept telling me that I still had sin, and since the wages of sin is death according to the law of God, I was someone who was bound to hell for my iniquities.

After a decade of my weary and legalistic life, I was almost dead spiritually. However, God awakened me by grace that Jesus Christ was baptized for me and took upon my own sins. He took upon not only my sins, but also all the sins of everyone in the whole world. He then bore the condemnation of these sins by carrying them to the Cross and being crucified and dying on it, rose from the dead again, and has thereby become my true Savior who lives even now. When I came to know this gospel of truth, I could not but believe in it. And by believing that Jesus Christ has become my God of salvation through His baptism and His bloodshed on the Cross, all my sins have been washed away. I have received the remission of sin into my heart by faith.

It is not because I knew well about all the Word of God that I received the remission of my sins, but I was remitted of my sins because I knew the sins of my own conscience, passed these sins onto Jesus Christ through His baptism, and believed in my heart that Jesus was condemned on the Cross to pay the wages of my sins. It is because I have received this remission of sin that I am now living my life preaching the gospel. You and I are the same; there is no difference between us in reality.

Just like you, I had also been heading to hell, and just like you, I have also received the remission of sin by believing in the same gospel of the water and the Spirit. By believing in the gospel with which the Lord has blotted out our sins, you and I alike have both been saved by faith. So I give my thanks to the Lord. It is because in this way we now have the conscience of faith by receiving the perfect remission of sin through the water and the Spirit that we are now able to go to God and pray to Him as His own children have received the remission of sin.

As the Bible tells us that the fragrance for the altar of incense was made of the holy anointing oil and the sweet incense, Jesus has made us clean by washing away all our sins with the holy gospel of truth. In the ancient age of the Old Testament, the people of Israel had to make this incense and burn it on the altar exactly as God had commanded. So inside the Holy Place, incense was burnt and its aroma rose up everyday. This incense means praying to God.

In the age of the New Testament, for you to burn this incense in the Holy Place, you must first believe in the gospel of the truth and receive the remission of sin into your hearts. In other words, it is by believing in the gospel of truth that one can burn the incense of prayer. How else could we burn incense in the same way as it was burnt during the Old Testament's time? When such utensils of the Tabernacle as the altar of burnt offering and the altar of incense are not lying around before us now, how could you and I make incense and burn it on the altar? We can burn the incense of prayer by faith, for Jesus Christ has blotted out our sins and saved us. Because our hearts have been cleansed by faith when we received the remission of sin, we can now burn incense rising up to God with our fervent prayers.

We believe that by our wholehearted faith in the gospel of the water and the Spirit all our sins were passed onto Jesus Christ, and that Jesus Christ vicariously bore the condemnation of our sins in our stead. Your and my hearts have thereby become all clean. Since all the sins in our hearts were passed onto Jesus, our hearts have become, by faith, completely clean all at once. If all your sins were passed onto Jesus through the baptism that He received from John, then all your sins were washed away and blotted out once for all There is no longer any sin left in your hearts. Because our sins were blotted out and cleansed away by believing in the gospel, we can now go to the holy God and ask for His help. That we are able to pray to God is premised on our faith, that we have received the remission of sin by definitively believing in the gospel, which is now at the background of our sincere hearts.

Brothers and sisters, go to the altar of incense and pray incessantly. "Father, please help me. This is the situation that I am in, and this is what I need. I want to spread the true gospel and live righteously, Father. I want to live virtuous life fitting for someone who has truly been remitted of sin. And I want to bear the fruits of righteousness. Give me faith in You. I want to live my life according to Your will." Like this, asking for one's needs is what prayer is about. It is about asking for God's help according to His righteousness.

You probably have various passions and desires as well. Because we have been made righteous by our faith in the gospel of the water and the Spirit that has justified us, it has now been made possible for us to ask God for all things with our prayer. Those who are able to pray to God for His help are the happy. Now that all of us have received the remission of our sins by believing in the gospel of the water and the Spirit, there is no doubt that we can all pray to God.

Those who, by their faith in God and the gospel of the water and the Spirit, have received the remission of sin into their hearts have at least become qualified to go to the holy God and ask for His help. And all the born-again believers inevitably and instinctively come to pray for the Father's help in their lives, as a child makes a cry for help to his/her parents when he/she is in trouble. Their faith that has brought them the remission of sin is not only the faith that enables them to call God as their Father, but it is also the faith that enables them to pray for the Father's help at all times as His own sons and daughters. Because God has indeed become our own Father by our faith, we are now fit to ask for His help through our prayer according to our needs.

I do not know, of course, what your personal prayers have been or how they have been met by God after you've received your remission of sin. But what I do know is that when we pray to God to enable us to unite with His Church and spread the gospel, He surely answers our prayer. It is in this process that we come to pray for others. At first, everyone prays only for the needs of his/her flesh. But by the works of the Holy Spirit, we come to realize that we are in urgent need of prayers for others, and thus we come to devote ourselves to pray for the salvation of other souls and the spreading of the gospel of the water and the Spirit throughout the whole world. Why? Because the prayers of the born-again saints are led by the Holy Spirit. The Lord has told us, *"Seek first the kingdom of God and His righteousness" (Matthew 6:33).*

But among the born-again, those who are still spiritually immature do not know how to pray for the right things, for they have not yet experienced God's answer to their prayers. This is because they still do not know how powerful is faith in God's righteousness. Those of little faith not only do not know whether their prayers will be answered or not, but moreover, they are haunted by doubts.

As such, they must pray together with those who believed prior to them. Those whose faith is young are hesitant to pray to God. And when they do pray, they only ask for what they want—"give me, give me, give me." But if the young in faith unite with the Church even without any great faith in God, they can still learn what the true prayer is, for their predecessors of faith in the Church are praying for the righteousness of God. Also, because the Holy Spirit gives the faith of prayer to those who are united with the Church, they gradually come to pray for the righteousness of God. *"The effective, fervent prayer of a righteous man avails much" (James 5:16).*

The faithful prayers of the born-again who have the right to pray to God avail much. The prayers of those who have faith in God are actually answered by Him. When people pray to God, for their prayers to be answer by the Father, they must first believe that God is their own Father, and that He answers their prayers exactly according to their faith. As such, when the predecessors of faith unite together and pray for those who are following in their footsteps and for the righteous works of the spreading of the gospel, they come to experience great works. If you stand next to your predecessors of faith who believe in

God, you will be greatly helped in your faith. Because God knows that we are in need of much help not only with the grace of salvation but also in other aspects of life, He answers our prayers. This is why we all need the faith that is united with God's Church.

When we pray for the things that please God, our faith is greatly emboldened. As spiritual children emulating to pray eventually come to take such prayers as their own and mature, we can also come to pray to God the Father for our own problems later on. Those who by doing so truly believe in God then come to walk by faith on the path following the real truth. As the Bible tells us that the righteous shall live only by faith, they come to live not for themselves alone, but for the salvation of other souls.

How did we earn the qualification to pray to God? We earned it by being born again through our faith in the gospel of the water and the Spirit given by God. It is only to those who have received the remission of sin by believing in the gospel of the water and the Spirit that the boldness of faith enabling one to pray to God the Father is given. Faith is a gift from God. To earn the qualification to pray is to receive the great blessing of faith from God.

Among the many Christian believers on this planet, how many of them do you think are qualified to pray with such faith? Not many! One of the most blessed gifts from God is, first of all, that we have come to have the faith that has saved us from our sins with the truth manifested in the blue, purple, and scarlet thread. And the second is that we have received the power and qualification to pray to God as His own children; and third, that we have come to have the faith that allows us to live as God's workers.

God Does Not Answer the Prayers of Sinners

Some sinners, even as they profess to believe in Jesus, pray to God to blot out their sins by climbing some mountain and shouting out the name of the Lord incessantly. Even in cold and windy nights, they still climb the mountain, covering their bodies with plastic sheets, and though they are often fearful, they still pray fervently with all their devotion. But their prayers only ring hollow into the empty space.

Though they pray all night long, they have no faith whatsoever that God would really answer their prayers. The reason why they pray so devotedly in spite of this lack of faith is because they pray to show off to others, merely as an exhibition. Their prayers are unanswerable prayers. In fact, they know in their conscience that their prayers are not reaching God, for they still have sin in their hearts. Because they are yet to receive the remission of their sins, there is no answer to their many prayers, no matter how much they pray, cry and wail, scream on top of their lungs, and do all kinds of things to ask God for what they want.

What they need to realize is that the prerequisite to pray to God is met only when they first receive the remission of sin. But because many sinners have no alternative until they come to know the gospel of the water and the Spirit, they cannot help but continue to live their lives of faith as sinners. When people are not cleansed once for all by believing in their hearts in the gospel of the water and the Spirit given by the Lord, then their prayers are in fact all in vain. Whenever sinners try to pray to God, their consciences shout, "You think your prayers will reach God? Dream on! They're all in vain!" So even as they keep praying to God, "Give me this, give me that," their prayers are actually futile.

"Before you pray to Me, first receive the remission of your sins." This is God's will. When those who have not received the remission of sin pray to God, they realize out of their experience that their consciences do not consent to their reason. When sinners pray, they keep saying, "Give me this, Lord, and give me that also," but there is no answer to their prayers. Far from it, their consciences only tell them, "No way! Your prayers will go unanswered, because you are sinful!" When even in their own consciences sinners cannot tolerate their faith, how could they possibly deceive God, how could they be approved by Him, and how could their prayers be answered? Sinners are simply not qualified to pray to God. Far from it, even their own hearts distrust their prayers.

Our Prayers Begin to Be Answered When We Become Righteous by Faith

But the prayers of many who had been sinners before begin to be answered once they receive the remission of their sins by believing in the gospel of the water and the Spirit manifested in the blue, purple, and scarlet thread of the Tabernacle. Those who believe in the gospel of the water and the Spirit in the center of their hearts may be insufficient on their own, but they can go to God by faith, and by faith they can boldly pray to Him, asking Him for their needs. When those who have received the remission of sin by faith pray to God according to His will, then they come to pray in boldness.

But when they are praying for their own flesh, they at times feel unsuitable. We the righteous are the happiest when we pray for the spreading of the gospel of the water and the Spirit, for the souls of others. When we pray for the dynamic spreading of the gospel, snared by no hindrance of the flesh, then we can overcome the obstacles of our limitations through prayers of faith. But at times, we feel frustrated when we are unable to overcome such obstacles by faith. In times like these, all that we can do is pray, and believe that God will eventually answer. And sure enough, in time we witness that this prayer is indeed answered by God.

What we must do is pray and then wait, not wonder in impatience why our prayers are not answered right away. God wants us to pray by faith, and we believe that if our prayers are in harmony to God's will, then He will answer them when the time comes. And when we receive the remission of sin by faith, and when we pray by faith in our lives, then we will see at first-hand experience that many of our prayers are indeed answered.

But have you lived by faith like this? If so, then you can truly pray to God. When we examine ourselves once more, we realize that we are bound to hell, and we also realize once more that we can be qualified to pray only by receiving the remission of sin through our faith in the gospel of the water and the Spirit. As such, we must remember for sure that those who can pray are those who have received the remission of sin by believing that the Lord has blotted out all the sins of their entire lifetime with the gospel of the water and the Spirit.

Among those who have not yet been born again, there are many people who are so proud of themselves. What about you? Do you have anything to be proud of? Are your arms strong? Are your legs strong? No matter how strong our bodies may be, they cannot even withstand common cold viruses, nor can they resist for long any marginally strong physical force, belying their true weakness. Do you realize just how weak human beings are? We can die from a single mosquito bite, or drop

Free book request www.nlmission.com

dead hit by a falling stone while walking. We are nothing. If someone utters a single phrase that wounds our pride, our hearts can be hurt so much that we become half-dead. Is this not the case? Of course it is!

How many people die before even turning 60? There are countless people who die even before reaching 30. Such weak beings are none other than human beings. The everlasting strength of human beings can be found nowhere. Should such weak beings, then, be hardened only in their hearts and not believe in the Word of God in the center of their hearts? Having nothing to be proud of, nor pretend to be strong at— this is what human beings are.

As such, we must realize our own weaknesses, recognize our insufficiencies and sins, believe in the gospel of truth fulfilled through the blue, purple, and scarlet thread in our hearts, and thereby earn the qualification to pray to God. We must have faith in God. To have this faith that pleases God in the center of the heart, people must believe in the gospel of the water and the Spirit, but there are many who still do not believe in it. Could you have earned the right to pray to God from another gospel other than this gospel of the water and the Spirit? Could your sins have been blotted out had Jesus, coming to this earth, not taken upon your sins by being baptized for your sake? Could you have passed your sins of the heart onto Jesus and washed them away without believing in the baptism that Jesus received?

The answers are no, no, and absolutely not! It is because Jesus shouldered the sins of the world with the baptism received from John that He was crucified and bore the condemnation of all sins with His own blood. Could you then have been saved without the baptism of Jesus and the Cross? Of course not! That Jesus was baptized was to take upon our sins once for all and wash them away, to cleanse away our sins. And that He was crucified was to bear the punishment of our sins. It is by believing in this truth of the gospel of the water and the Spirit that we have been remitted of all our sins.

Thus, we can go to God at any time and boldly confess, "Lord, I am this insufficient, but because You have saved me with Your water and blood, I am now sinless. You came to this earth, at once took upon all sins by being baptized, carried these sins of the world to the Cross, was punished for them, and rose from the dead again. And by doing so, Lord, You have truly become my God of salvation. It is with my faith in this truth that I believe in You." When we keep our faith, in other words, we can always go to God and pray to Him despite our insufficiencies. We can pray for the expansion of His Kingdom, we can pray for our brothers and sisters, and we can pray for the other souls that are yet to receive the remission of sin.

It is only when people believe in the gospel of the water and the Spirit that they can always be without any shame under the heavens. But not having this faith in the gospel of the water and the Spirit, some people might try to fill the void with something else—you should realize that such efforts are completely futile. This is why their hearts are distressed and tormented, turning their lives unbearable. Whether in the truth or lies, everyone wants to believe in something. Consider yourselves.

Examine yourselves to see whether you really believe in the Lord with the faith that believes the gospel of the water and the Spirit, or whether you do not believe in this gospel of the water and the Spirit. The Lord has blotted out your sins with the water and the blood—if you believe in this, then, would there still be sin in your hearts? If you truly believe, in the

Free book request www.nlmission.com

bottom of your hearts and spirits, in this gospel of the water and the Spirit, then there is surely no sin at all. With your wholehearted faith in this truth, receive the true remission of your sins now.

Because God has given us our remission of sin through the truth manifested in the blue, purple, and scarlet thread and the fine woven linen, we have now received this everlasting remission of sin. And because of this, those who believe in this truth have become God's own children, clothed in the grace that enables them to come forth to Him. Therefore, we have to love one another, understand each other's insufficiencies, serve the works of God until the end, and then go to Him and stand before His presence.

Those who have received the remission of sin love all sinners. The hearts of the righteous desire every sinner to know the truth manifested in the blue, purple, and scarlet thread and be born again. But there is a certain kind of people who cannot actually love people. These are the obstinate sinner—Christians who deceive their own consciences of faith and delude themselves into thinking that they believe in God even as they still remain sinful.

By believing in the gospel of the water and the Spirit and receiving the remission of sin into our hearts, we must all defend our consciences of faith. Let us run our race well until the end, keeping our consciences of faith and not losing our faith. And when someone seems to be going through a hard time spiritually, then help each other and hold one another steadfast. No matter what happens, the righteous must not leave the Church. If the righteous leave God's Church, they will die immediately. Leaving God's Church is like losing your own home. Losing your home is losing your refuge, and so your hearts will find neither rest nor comfort anywhere, and you will die in the end.

God's Church is a place where His sheep are fed and given rest and relief. As such, when the sheep lose their strength and become too weary, God's Church helps their hearts to be strengthened by hearing the Word. When you accept the Word by believing in your hearts, then the Holy Spirit in you will rejoice, your hearts will also be strengthened, and, as the final result, you will receive eternal life.

All of us the righteous give our thanks to God. We thank the Lord, for in order to qualify us to pray, He has given us the gospel of the water and the Spirit. Hallelujah! I pray to the living God that He would enable us to trust in Him and live by faith. ⊠

SERMON

11

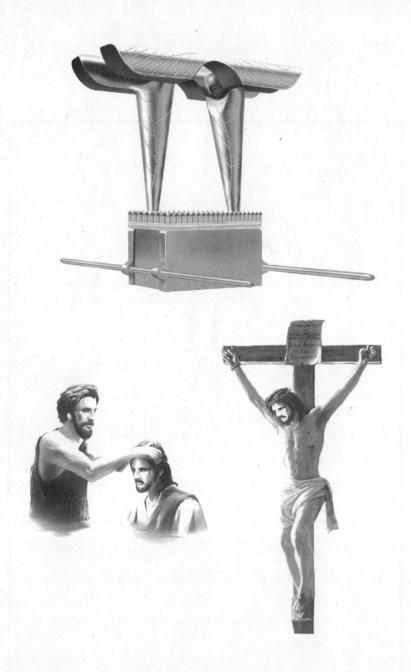

You can download Rev. Paul C. Jong's Christian Books on iPhone, iPad, or Blackberry by going to Amazon's Kindle e-bookstore (www.amazon.com).

The High Priest Who Gave the Offering of The Day of Atonement

< Leviticus 16:1-34 >

"Now the LORD spoke to Moses after the death of the two sons of Aaron, when they offered profane fire before the LORD, and died; and the LORD said to Moses: 'Tell Aaron your brother not to come at just any time into the Holy Place inside the veil, before the mercy seat which is on the ark, lest he die; for I will appear in the cloud above the mercy seat. Thus Aaron shall come into the Holy Place: with the blood of a young bull as a sin offering, and of a ram as a burnt offering. He shall put the holy linen tunic and the linen trousers on his body; he shall be girded with a linen sash, and with the linen turban he shall be attired. These are holy garments. Therefore he shall wash his body in water, and put them on. And he shall take from the congregation of the children of Israel two kids of the goats as a sin offering, and one ram as a burnt offering. Aaron shall offer the bull as a sin offering, which is for himself, and make atonement for himself and for his house. He shall take the two goats and present them before the LORD at the door of the tabernacle of meeting. Then Aaron shall cast lots for the two goats: one lot for the LORD and the other lot for the scapegoat. And Aaron shall bring the goat on which the LORD's lot fell, and offer it as a sin offering. But the goat on which the lot fell to be the scapegoat shall be presented alive before the LORD, to make atonement upon it, and to let it go as the scapegoat into the wilderness. And Aaron shall bring the bull of the sin offering, which is for himself, and make atonement for himself and for his house, and shall kill the bull as the sin offering which is for himself. Then he shall take a censer full of burning coals of fire from the altar before the LORD, with his hands full of sweet incense beaten fine, and bring it inside the veil. And he shall put the incense on the fire before the LORD, that the cloud of incense may cover the mercy seat that is on the Testimony, lest he die. He shall take some of the blood of the bull and sprinkle it with his finger on the mercy seat on the east side; and before the mercy seat he shall sprinkle some of the blood with his finger seven times. Then he shall kill the goat of the sin offering, which is for the people, bring its blood inside the veil, do with that blood as he did with the blood of the bull, and sprinkle it on the mercy seat and before the mercy seat. So he shall make atonement for the Holy Place, because of the uncleanness of the children of Israel, and because of their transgressions, for all their sins; and so he shall do for the tabernacle of meeting which remains among them in the midst of their uncleanness. There shall be no man in the tabernacle of meeting when he goes in to make atonement in the Holy Place, until he comes out, that he may make atonement for himself, for his household, and for all the assembly of Israel. And he shall go out to the altar that is before the LORD, and make atonement for it, and shall take some of the blood of the bull and some of the blood of the goat, and put it on the horns of the altar all around. Then he shall sprinkle some of the blood on it with his finger seven times, cleanse it, and consecrate it from the uncleanness of the children of Israel. And when he has made an end of atoning for the Holy Place, the tabernacle of meeting, and the altar, he shall bring the live goat. Aaron shall lay both his hands on the head of the live goat, confess over it all the iniquities of the children of Israel, and all their transgressions, concerning all their sins, putting them on the head of the goat, and shall send it away into the wilderness by the hand of a suitable man. The goat shall bear on itself all their iniquities to an uninhabited land; and he shall release the goat in the wilderness. Then Aaron shall come into the tabernacle of meeting, shall take off the linen garments which he put on when he went into the Holy Place, and shall leave them there. And he shall wash his body with water in a holy place, put on his garments, come out and offer his burnt offering and the burnt offering of the people, and make atonement for himself and for the people. The fat of the sin offering he shall burn on the altar. And he who released the goat as the scapegoat shall wash his clothes and bathe his body in water, and afterward he may come into the camp. The bull for the sin offering and the goat for the sin offering, whose blood was brought in to make atonement in the Holy Place, shall be carried outside the camp. And they shall burn in the fire their skins, their flesh, and their offal. Then he who burns them shall wash his clothes and bathe his body in water, and afterward he may come into the camp. This shall be a statute forever for you: In the seventh month, on the tenth day of the month, you shall afflict your souls, and do no work at all, whether a native of your own country or a stranger who dwells among you. For on that day the priest shall make atonement for you, to cleanse you, that you may be clean from all your sins before the LORD. It is

a sabbath of solemn rest for you, and you shall afflict your souls. It is a statute forever. And the priest, who is anointed and consecrated to minister as priest in his father's place, shall make atonement, and put on the linen clothes, the holy garments; then he shall make atonement for the Holy Sanctuary, and he shall make atonement for the tabernacle of meeting and for the altar, and he shall make atonement for the priests and for all the people of the assembly. This shall be an everlasting statute for you, to make atonement for the children of Israel, for all their sins, once a year.' And he did as the LORD commanded Moses."

The High Priest was the one who gave the offering of the Day of Atonement for the people of Israel. This offering was given once a year on the tenth day of the seventh month in the Israeli calendar. On this day, as the High Priest Aaron gave the offering on behalf of the people of Israel for their sake, all their iniquities were actually passed on to this offering of sacrifice and cleansed away. The Day of Atonement therefore became a great festival for the people of Israel.

Like other offerings, the offering of the Day of Atonement also had to be accompanied by three fixed standards: unblemished sacrificial animals, the laying on of hands, and the bloodshed of the sacrificial animals. God then accepted with pleasure the offering that was given in this way. What was different of this offering from the other offerings was that the High Priest had to take the blood of the sacrificial offering into the Most Holy.

After giving an offering for himself and his household, Aaron the High Priest offered two goats to God for the people of Israel. First, he offered one of them for the Lord God according to the same manner of the sin offering he had offered with a bull. And then he offered the second goat for the scapegoat. He passed the sins of the people of Israel onto the scapegoat by laying his hands on its head before the presence of the Israelites, and this goat that had accepted their sins was then sent out into the wilderness by the hand of a suitable man.

The Offering of the Day of Atonement Cleansed away All the Sins of the People of Israel

On the Day of Atonement, the High Priest, representing the people of Israel, passed their sins onto the head of the sacrificial offering by laying his hands on it. He brought two live goats, cast lots for them—one for God and the other for the people of Israel.

The laying on of hands here means passing all sins onto the sacrificial offering by putting hands on its head. This laying on of hands were the method of the washing of sin set by God, and in the New Testament' time also, the same method in a form of the laying of hands had to be applied equally for Jesus to wash away all the sins of mankind as well. To remit the High Priest's own sins, the sins of his household, and a year's worth of the sins of the people of Israel, he absolutely had to lay his hands on the head of the goat and pass all these sins onto it. Because the High Priest passed the sins of the people of Israel to the sacrificial offering by thus laying his hands on its head, a year's worth of the sins of the Israelites were all blotted out. Like this, through the offering of the Day of Atonement, the people of Israel could thank God for saving them from all their sins.

Everyone who has sin is to be condemned unavoidably.

For a sacrificial offering to be vicariously condemned for people's sins, it first had to accept their sins. Were the High Priest to give an offering to God without laying his hands on its head, this offering then would have been a blasphemy to God, and so he had to refrain from doing so. To save the entire mankind that had turned into sinners, God had to establish His plan of salvation fulfilled through the method of the laying on of hands. To blot out the sins of the people of Israel, God raised the High Priest and made him pass the sins of all his people once for all by laying his hands on the head of the sacrificial offering as their representative. As such, all the sacrificial animals that were offered to God in the Tabernacle accepted the sins of the Israelites with the laying on of hands, and they bore the condemnation of sin on their behalf, shedding its blood and dying.

To fulfill the righteousness and love of God wholly, the Israelites had to offer the sacrifice of the Day of Atonement by laying the High Priest's hands on the head of the sacrificial animals and cutting the throats to shed their blood vicariously once a year. Through this offering, in other words, God wanted to wash away a year's worth of all the sins of the people of Israel once for all. This was the law of God's love that satisfied both His mercifulness and His justness. Because God is just, to blot out people's sins all at once in accordance to His just law, God prepared Jesus Christ the Lamb, had Him take upon sins through the laying on of hands, and made Him bleed on the Cross.

Jesus, who had offered Himself as the eternal sacrifice, took upon everyone's sins once for all through this method, shed His blood once, and has thereby completed their salvation from sin. As such, we, too, must come before God with the faith that believes in the truth of salvation manifested in the blue, purple, and scarlet thread and the fine woven linen. It is by this faith that all sins can be remitted once for all. Therefore, whoever wants to receive the remission of sin all at once must come to God with the faith that truly believes in the gospel of the water and the Spirit.

The Meaning of the Laying on of Hands

The laying on of hands means, "to be passed, to be transferred, or to be buried" (Leviticus 1:3-4). When any of the common people of Israel sinned unintentionally and then became aware of it, he had to give a burnt offering to God (Leviticus 4:27-29). He first had to bring a sacrificial animal without blemish, and then had to pass his sins onto it by laying his hands on its head. And he had to cut its throat, draw its blood, and then give this blood to a priest (Leviticus 4:27-31). Then the priest had to take some of its blood with his finger, put it on the horns of the altar of burnt offering, and pour all the remaining blood at the base of the altar. He also had to burn its fat on the altar, and God then smelt the soothing aroma of the burning fat that was given in this offering.

We have already learned that to blot out the sins of the people of Israel, God prepared the offering of the Day of Atonement where hands were laid on the sacrificial animal and its blood was drawn. In this case also, God could not wash away the sins of the Israelites without the laying of hands on the sacrificial offering. Like this, the offering of the Day of Atonement that was given in the Old Testament is closely connected with the baptism and blood of Jesus in the New Testament's time.

Just as the sacrificial offering of the Old Testament had to be an unblemished animal, in the New Testament's time also, Jesus came as the unblemished Lamb of God, and was baptized and shed His blood on the Cross to wash away the iniquities of all sinners. As the sacrificial animal had to accept the iniquities of sinners with the laying on of hands in the Old Testament, all the sins of the world were passed onto Jesus when John the Baptist laid his hands on the head of Jesus to baptize Him in the Jordan River (Matthew 3:15). The Old Testament's sacrificial offering and the New Testament's Jesus alike had to receive the laying on of hands and bleed to die in the same way. The offering of the laying on of hands and bloodshed was the same offering that was prepared for sinners in both the Old and New Testaments alike.

The Sins of Mankind Are Infallibly Followed by the Wrath of God

Before God, we had been sinners who could not but die for our sins, just like the sin offering that was to be killed on account of the sins it had taken. When we picture this sacrificial offering being cut into pieces and burnt with fire on the altar of burnt offering, we can realize that like it, we had also been bound to be destroyed before God, and yet the Lord has saved us by being baptized by John and shedding His blood.

As such, those who have not been born again must acknowledge themselves as sinners facing fiery condemnation for their sins before God and believe in the baptism and blood of the Lord as their salvation. To save us from our sins instead of punishing us for them, God prepared the offering of salvation, passed our sins onto this offering of everlasting sacrifice, made Him bleed, and has thereby remitted all our sins

(Leviticus 16:1-34; Romans 8:3-4, Hebrews 10:10-12). Do you still have sin in your hearts? Then, you must first admit before God that you are sinners facing the condemnation of God, and you must believe that through Jesus Christ God has fulfilled the plan of your salvation that He had designed even before the foundation of the world.

Sin cannot be atoned without paying a proper ransom. That's why God had given the people of Israel the sacrificial system. In this sacrificial system, only the offering that was accompanied by the laying on of hands and bloodshed was the true offering of faith that could wash away the sins of the Israelites.

By faith, we must also give to God this offering that has the laying on of hands and bloodshed, all in accordance to the sacrificial system written in the Scriptures. The Lord shed His blood because He had taken our sins through His baptism, vicariously bore the condemnation of sin in our place, and thereby blotted out these sins of ours (Matthew 3:15; John 1:29; Isaiah 53:1-7). When we believe in the Word of the water and the Spirit, and when we put our hands on the Lord who has become our sacrificial offering and thereby pass all our sins onto Him, we can receive the remission of sin by believing that the Lord who took upon our sins also bore the condemnation of sin in our place. By believing in the gospel of the water and the Spirit, we can pass all our sins onto the Lord who has become our sacrificial offering, and we can die with Him and live with Him (Romans 6:1-11, Galatians 3:27).

The spiritual lessons that we must realize from the offering of the Day of Atonement are, first of all, that we must recognize our sins and the condemnation of our sins, and that we must then give the offering of faith that God wants to receive—that is, we must have faith in Jesus who fulfilled our salvation with His baptism and bloodshed on the Cross. We must lay our hands on the head of Jesus by believing in His baptism. Why? Because only when we lay our hands on the offering of sacrifice by faith and draw its blood can we be saved from all our sins.

Like this, anyone who wants to be remitted from his/her sins before God must pay the ransom of life, for the wages of sin is death. Whether rich or poor, there must be the sacrificial offering that pays the wages of one's sins and the price of the atonement of life. Unless this is the case, no one can receive the remission of sin by faith.

The Old Testament's Offering of the Day of Atonement

Let us turn to Leviticus 16:6-10: *"Aaron shall offer the bull as a sin offering, which is for himself, and make atonement for himself and for his house. He shall take the two goats and present them before the LORD at the door of the tabernacle of meeting. Then Aaron shall cast lots for the two goats: one lot for the LORD and the other lot for the scapegoat. And Aaron shall bring the goat on which the LORD's lot fell, and offer it as a sin offering. But the goat on which the lot fell to be the scapegoat shall be presented alive before the LORD, to make atonement upon it, and to let it go as the scapegoat into the wilderness."*

To enable the people of Israel to receive the remission of their sins by faith, the High Priest, on their behalf, gave the offering that was accompanied by the laying on of hands and bloodshed. How, then, is the faith of today's Christians? Is it not a speculative and groundless faith whose offering seeks to receive the remission of sin without even passing their sins? If your faith is not the kind of faith that has passed your sins onto Jesus Christ through the laying on of hands, then you have a problem at hand. Unless your faith is the faith that believes in the baptism of Jesus and His blood on the Cross, it cannot be the true faith.

We could not but fail to keep the Law before God and committed all kinds of sins throughout the past year. So if we had lived in the Old Testament's time, we would have needed to receive the remission of our sins by believing in the sin offering that the High Priest would have given on our behalf. To give the offering of faith to God, we must first acknowledge that we are bound to be destroyed for our sins, and we must then believe in the laying on of hands that passes all our sins onto the sacrificial offering that God prepared for us and the bloodshed of this offering.

Because the laying of hands on the sacrificial animal and its bloodshed had the power of salvation, the people of the Old Testament could receive the remission of their sins through this offering that the High Priest gave according to the sacrificial system set by God. By laying his hands on the sacrificial offering, the High Priest passed a year's worth of his people's sins onto it, cut its throat and drew its blood, and sprinkled this blood before the mercy seat and on its eastside for seven times. By doing so, he never ceased to give the right offering to God every year. This is how the people of Israel could receive the perfect remission of sin in those days.

Like this, through the sin offering that the High Priest gave, the people of Israel believe and affirmed in their hearts that all their sins were thus remitted. What the Old Testament's offering of the Day of Atonement is showing us is that in the New Testament, Jesus Christ took upon the sins of the world by being baptized by John and shed His blood on the Cross, and that we must believe in this Jesus Christ as our Savior and receive the everlasting remission of sin by faith. All the souls of this world whose hearts are suffering and agonizing over their sins must realize that they can receive the eternal remission of sin by believing in the gospel of the water and the Spirit, and they must believe this in their hearts. Like this, the offering of the remission of all sins had been set by God beforehand and promised by Him to be fulfilled, and this promise of salvation is also manifested in the blue, purple, and scarlet thread and the fine woven linen that were used as the materials of the Tabernacle.

The Offering of the Day of Atonement Fulfilled in the Tabernacle

On the Day of Atonement, to take care of all the sins of the people of Israel, the High Priest laid his hands on the head of the sacrificial offering before the presence of all the Israelites (Leviticus 16:1-23). It was absolutely necessary for him to pass their sins onto the sacrificial offering by laying his hands on its head on their behalf. When the High Priest Aaron gave the offering of the Day of Atonement inside the Tabernacle for the people of Israel, no one else could enter into the Tabernacle. It was an extraordinary event, because there used to be many priests in the court of the Tabernacle except on the Day of Atonement.

The High Priest passed the sins of the people of Israel onto the sacrificial offering by putting his hands on its head, took the blood of this sacrifice into the Most Holy, and sprinkled it with his finger on the mercy seat on the east side;

and before the mercy seat he sprinkled it seven times (Leviticus 16:14).

At this time, the golden bells that were attached to the hem of the robe of the High Priest were bound to ring, and so each time he sprinkled the blood before the mercy seat and on the eastside, the bells rang and the people of Israel who were standing outside the Tabernacle could hear the sound of bells. When the Israelites heard this sound of bells, they realized that the High Priest was now giving the offering to God on their behalf. And having heard the sound of bells for all seven times, they then sighed in relief, for they knew that the giving of the offering of the Day of Atonement was now finished, confirming the completion of the offering that forgave a year's worth of their sins.

After this, the High Priest Aaron came out of the Tabernacle, took the other remaining goat as another offering, and gave this offering of the Day of Atonement before the presence of the people of Israel. God commanded the people of Israel to do nothing on the Day of Atonement (Leviticus 16:20-21, 29). With the huge crowd of the Israelites gathered around to see the giving of this offering outside the Tabernacle, the High Priest laid his hands on the head of the sacrificial goat to fulfill his duties and sent it away into the wilderness by the hand of a suitable man.

On the Day of Atonement, the High Priest brought the goat before the people of Israel, laid his hands on its head, and confessed all the iniquities and transgressions of the children of Israel, passing them onto the goat. "Lord, I confess all the sins that the people of Israel have committed during the past year. We have failed to keep all the Law wholly, we have committed countless sins against You and each other, we have failed to live the life that You had commanded us to live, and we have done those things which you commanded us not to do. We have broken so many of Your commandments during the past year. We have lied. We have murdered. We have committed adultery. We have stolen." Like this, the High Priest passed all the sins of the people of Israel onto the sacrificial goat by putting his hands on its head before their presence, and then sent it away into the wilderness by the hand of a suitable man.

Because the wages of sin is death, God could not let the sacrificial goat live after accepting the sins of the people of Israel. The scapegoat that was abandoned into the wilderness had to suffer and die in the wilderness, for it had shouldered all the iniquities, blemishes, and transgressions of the people of Israel. Now, all the people of Israel started to enjoy the Feast of Tabernacles (Leviticus 23:34) because they had discarded, through the offering of the Day of Atonement, the sins that had bound them for the past year.

The laying on of hands is the means by which the sins of all people are passed onto the sacrificial offering. When the High Priest laid his hands on the sacrificial animal, all the sins of the people of Israel that had accumulated for a year were passed onto it once for all. Every single sin of each and every Israelite was all at once passed onto the offering of sacrifice with the High Priest' laying on of hands.

Can all the sins of today's people also be passed onto the sacrificial offering with the laying on of hands, just as the iniquities of the people of Israel were passed with the laying on of the High Priest's hands in the Old Testament? If this were not possible, where is the way for today's people to receive the remission of their sins? Who passes the sins of today's people, how, and through whom? In accordance to the sacrificial system established by God in the age of the Old Testament, Jesus Christ took upon the sins of the world by being baptized by John the Baptist in the New Testament's time. Just as a year's worth of sins were passed onto the sacrificial goat once for all through the offering of the Day of Atonement that the High Priest gave for the people of Israel, so were our sins passed onto Jesus Christ who was baptized by John the Baptist, the last High Priest. Where, then, are all the sins of today's people? They are now on the head of Jesus Christ.

Just as the scapegoat accepted all the sins of the people of Israel through the High Priest with the laying on of his hands, Jesus became the sacrificial offering of the everlasting remission of sin for all of us who are now living in this present age. Jesus who became our own scapegoat offered Himself to God as the sacrificial offering for our sins. Jesus, in other words, was baptized by John and gave Himself up to be crucified, as in the Old Testament God had set the offering of sacrifice for the people of Israel and passed their sins onto this sacrificial animal and condemned it instead.

The scapegoat that was sent out into the wilderness could not survive, for there was no water but only burning sunlight in the sand desert. Likewise, Jesus, too, could not avoid but be crucified, for He had already taken upon mankind's sins of the world through His baptism. As the scapegoat was abandoned in the lifeless wilderness, Jesus who took upon the sins of the world was also hated and despised by many people. If the sacrificial goat were led into the desert and abandoned in the desolate, lifeless land, would it not have wandered around, only to die in the end from thirst?

In the same manner, Jesus who accepted our sins was rejected by many people, and He had to be crucified to bear the condemnation of our sins, shed His blood, and die. This was the salvation that Jesus Christ fulfilled to give us His true salvation in the gospel of the water and the Spirit.

The people of Israel saw the process of the atonement of the remission of sin with their eyes and believed in it in their hearts. Like them, we, too, can now receive the remission of our sins by seeing, hearing, and believing in the righteous works of Jesus Christ in our hearts. This tells us that Jesus Christ would be baptized by John, carry the sins of the world, be crucified, shed His blood, die, and rise from the dead again, and that we would be saved by seeing all these with our spiritual eyes and believing in them in our hearts.

This offering of the Day of Atonement will go on as long as the Israelites continue to exist. They still give the offering of the Day of Atonement on the 10th day of the seventh month in their calendar, because God had told them, *"This shall be an everlasting statute for you, to make atonement for the children of Israel, for all their sins, once a year" (Leviticus 16:34).* By making the people of Israel give the offering of the Day of Atonement like this, God bestowed His mercy on them so that all their sins would be washed away and they would be delivered from the punishment of these sins.

Just like this, for today's people also, God has enabled them to realize that Jesus bore all the sins of the world upon His own body by being baptized by John, was crucified, and has thereby wholly completed the everlasting cleansing of sin. Jesus Christ shouldered the sins of mankind with His baptism and has become the eternal High Priest of Heaven. Now, there is nothing else that remains for us to do for our own salvation but only to believe in this truth.

The Offering of the Great Atonement that the Messiah Gave to God the Father with His Own Body

Why did God command the people of Israel to give Him the offering of the Day of Atonement? He did this so that they would look forward, with their faith, to the day when God the Father would have His Son Jesus Christ offer the great atonement for the sins of all human beings with His baptism and bloodshed. This is why Jesus Christ, the only begotten Son of God the Father and the Savior of humanity, came to this earth to blot out all the sins of everyone, fulfilled everything with the love of God, and revealed salvation unto mankind. By being baptized by John to take upon all the sins of us mankind and shedding His blood on the Cross, Jesus has blotted out all the sins and inequities of the world, was condemned for them, and has thereby become our true Savior.

God called Moses and gave him the Law first. And then He ordered him to build the Tabernacle with such materials as blue, purple, and scarlet thread and fine woven linen, and He gave him the sacrificial system. By doing so, God enabled the people of Israel to realize the importance of the laying on of hands and bloodshed, and in turn He showed them Jesus Christ, the door of salvation prophesied in the Tabernacle, would come to this earth, take upon the sins of the world by being baptized, be crucified and shed His blood. The salvation of the washing of sin that God has given us is manifested clearly in the materials that were used for the door of the Tabernacle.

Among the materials used for the door of the Tabernacle, the meaning implied by the blue thread is that Jesus took upon the sins of the world once for all by being baptized by John; the purple thread shows that Jesus is the King of kings and the

Lord of lords, for He created the universe; the scarlet thread tells us that because Jesus had been baptized, He bore the condemnation of sin for all sinners by shedding His blood on the Cross; and the fine woven linen tells us that the Bible is describing elaborately about these three ministries manifested in the blue, purple, and scarlet thread, and God has given the remission of sin to those who believe in His Word.

Now, all must remind themselves once again and believe that this truth—that is, Jesus Christ is their Savior and He has washed away all their sins by being baptized by John and shedding His blood on the Cross—is also manifested in the blue, purple, and scarlet thread and the fine woven linen used as the materials of the Tabernacle, and they must thereby receive the remission of their sins. Through Moses, God established the law of salvation, the law of the remission of sin for mankind, and when the time came, He sent Jesus Christ to this earth and had Him be baptized by John and shed His blood on the Cross, so that Jesus would become the offering of sacrifice that would wash away the sins of the world. And by doing so, God has enabled all those who believe to be washed from all their sins by faith.

Therefore, when we profess to believe in Jesus Christ as the Savior, we must believe by knowing the baptism that Jesus received and His bloodshed on the Cross. Just as the sacrificial offering of the Old Testament accepted the iniquities of sinners with the laying on of hands and was vicariously condemned by shedding its blood in their place, Jesus Christ came as the sacrificial offering of sin for everyone living on this earth, took upon the sins of the world by being baptized, was crucified and shed His precious blood, and has thereby forever blotted out, all at once, the sins of those who believe.

We must believe in the truth of the written Word exactly

as it is. The biblical truth is that with the same method as the offering that the High Priest gave for his people in the Old Testament, Jesus came to this earth, was baptized and crucified, and shed His blood to save us from all the sins of the world once for all. We must therefore believe in the Bible exactly as it is written. We could not avoid but be forever condemned for our sins, but Jesus Christ came to this earth and has saved us from all our sins with His baptism and blood.

Not believing this, even though God has forgiven all our sins like this, is a sin that can never be forgiven by God. He has blotted out all the sins of the world except the only remaining sin, "the sin of blaspheming the Holy Spirit" (Mark 3:28-29). As such, those who truly want to receive the remission of sin must believe the truth that Jesus Christ was baptized, shed His blood, rose from the dead again, and has thereby delivered us from all the sins of the world. Apart from such faith, what good deeds would ever be necessary for our remission of sin? Now the time has come for us to know what the truth of the gospel of the water and the Spirit is, and to believe in this truth.

Everyone must realize and believe that the truth manifested in the door of the Tabernacle woven of blue, purple, and scarlet thread and fine woven linen is the gospel of true salvation, and the shadow of Jesus Christ to come. Insofar as believing in Jesus Christ is concerned, the baptism that He received and the blood that He shed on the Cross are essential to our salvation, and we must therefore believe in them. The indisputable and irrefutable truth is that Jesus has given salvation to those who believe in His baptism, His bloodshed on the Cross, and His resurrection from death, and that all of these were done to save us from the sins of the world.

The Sacrifice of the Son that God the Father Wanted

Let us turn to Hebrews 10:5-9: *"Therefore, when He came into the world, He said: 'Sacrifice and offering You did not desire, But a body You have prepared for Me. In burnt offerings and sacrifices for sin You had no pleasure. Then I said, 'Behold, I have come—In the volume of the book it is written of Me—To do Your will, O God.'" Previously saying, 'Sacrifice and offering, burnt offerings, and offerings for sin You did not desire, nor had pleasure in them' (which are offered according to the law), then He said, 'Behold, I have come to do Your will, O God.' He takes away the first that He may establish the second."*

What is it meant by the passage here that says that God did not desire sacrifice and offering? This passage quotes from Psalm 40:6-7. It means that all the sins of the world could not be completely blotted out with the daily offerings of the Old Testament, and that to give the everlasting sin offering, Jesus Christ therefore came to this earth, was baptized, shed His blood, rose from the dead again, and has thereby become the Savior of all of us. The meaning of Psalm 40:7, which says, *"Then I said, 'Behold, I come; In the scroll of the book it is written of me,'"* is that Jesus Christ came to this earth and washed away all sins with the laying on of hands and His bloodshed, exactly as written in the Old Testament.

In the age of the Old Testament, the sins of the people of Israel were remitted as the sacrificial animal was offered to God on the Day of Atonement with the laying on of the High Priest's hands and the bloodshed of the offering. Likewise, Jesus Christ who came to this earth to become the everlasting sacrificial offering for all mankind took upon the sins of the world by receiving baptism, a form of the laying on of hands, and bore all the condemnation of the sins of the entire mankind by carrying these sins of the world to the Cross, being crucified, shedding His precious blood and dying. By doing so, Jesus has given eternal salvation to all those who believe.

Exactly as God had promised through the Tabernacle system, in the New Testament Jesus came to this earth and has thereby fulfilled salvation once for all. Those who believe have therefore been saved from all sins. In the Tabernacle was the promise of God that Jesus would forever blot out the sins of all people once for all by being baptized and shedding His blood. And Jesus indeed came and fulfilled the promised salvation by actually being baptized and shedding His blood, and thereby fulfilling the Word of God to perfection. All God's promises of salvation, in other words, have indeed been fulfilled in Jesus Christ.

The people of Israel believe that the Old Testament's Law and the words of the prophets are the Word of God. But they are unable to believe in Jesus Christ who came to us in the age of the New Testament as God or the Savior. All the people of this world, including the people of Israel, must now realize that Jesus Christ is God Himself and accept into their hearts that He is the Messiah to come.

For What Did Jesus Come?

As Jesus came to fulfill the will of God the Father, He is the Savior of all those who believe in Him as such, and He came to this world to forever wash away all their sins. As Hebrews 10:10 states, *"By that will we have been sanctified through the offering of the body of Jesus Christ once for all."*

We must clearly realize and believe that it was by the will of the God the Father that Jesus Christ was born unto this earth, that He was baptized according to the Father's will, that by this will He was crucified, shed His blood to death on the Cross, rose from the dead again, and has thereby become the Savior of those who believe. To blot out all our sins according to the will of God the Father, Jesus Christ had to fulfill the salvation of mankind by blotting out all sins with the baptism that He received and His bloodshed. As such, He willingly gave Himself up to be sacrificed, thereby giving us perfect salvation.

Because Jesus Christ sacrificed Himself to blot out not only the sins of the people of Israel but also the sins of the entire mankind, we can be saved only if each of us believes in this in our own hearts. Through His 33 years of life, Jesus was baptized only once, sacrificed only once, and has thereby saved the sinners of the world once for all. This is the only and perfect salvation.

Just as Jesus has all at once blotted out all the sins committed by mankind from the beginning to the end of the world, He has also enabled us to be saved once for all by faith. By offering His own body once for all, Jesus Christ has made us forever perfect. As He was baptized by John and was condemned for all our sins by shedding His blood, we must now gladly believe in this gospel in our hearts and thereby be saved from all our sins. By the will of God the Father, Jesus Christ came to this earth to bear all our sins and pay the wages of life, and He successfully revealed His true salvation through the love of God in accordance to the Father's will.

This Word is surely the truth that you and I who are now living in this modern world must believe. We must bind the baptism of Jesus and His bloodshed on the Cross together and believe in them as the singular set of truth that saves us perfectly. If we fail to do so, we will then lose the everlasting remission of sin. As such, we must believe according to the written Word of God, according to the truth of the gospel of the water and the Spirit. The gospel of the water and the Spirit sheds the light of salvation, but if we add anything else to or subtract some essentials from the true gospel when we believe in God, or if we do not believe in the truth as it is, then this light of the gospel of salvation will be lost, only to be hidden and to disappear.

We must not fall under the illusion that the truth of the gospel of the water and the Spirit is also merely one of the worldly doctrines, as if it teaches that we can somehow receive the remission of sin through our prayers of repentance by asking God to forgive our sins daily. God said clearly in Hebrews 10:11, *"And every priest stands ministering daily and offering repeatedly the same sacrifices, which can never take away sins."* He told us, in other words, and the sins that we commit everyday cannot be washed away just because we ask God to forgive us of our daily sins with our faith in the blood of the Cross.

Because the offering of sacrifice that Jesus Christ gave to God the Father by being baptized by John and dying on the Cross was the perfect offering of salvation, it was by believing in this offering that we have been wholly saved. It was because the sins of the world were passed onto Jesus Christ once for all when He was baptized by John that Jesus could carry our sins to the Cross and die on it to end the condemnation of their sins, and it was because of this that the sins of those who believe in His baptism and bloodshed have been washed away.

By believing in the baptism that Jesus Christ received and the blood of the Cross, we, too, also died with Jesus Christ and have come alive with Him by faith. Romans 6:23 states, *"For the wages of sin is death, but the gift of God is eternal life in Christ Jesus our Lord."* The wages of sin is death, no matter what it may be, and therefore its wages must be paid with life. This is why it was necessary for Jesus Christ to come to this earth incarnated in the flesh, be baptized by John, and shed His blood on the Cross. The actual passing of your sins onto the body of Jesus was accomplished by His baptism, and by shouldering these sins and dying, Jesus paid the wages of your sins and has thereby blotted them out once for all. Yet despite this, even as God has given us this truth of the gospel, there are many people who still plead God to forgive their actual sins everyday—they are simply ignorant of the truth of the gospel of the water and the Spirit.

When people have sin in their hearts, they cannot help but be terrified before God for this sin. It is true that there are many who, still remaining ignorant of the gospel of the water and the Spirit and yet to be washed from their sins, are gripped by fear because of the sins of their consciences. However, Jesus came to this earth to deliver them from all their sins, was baptized by John, shed His blood on the Cross, and has thereby saved them perfectly. For what reason do we need to be worried then, when the gospel of the water and the Spirit, the gospel of God's salvation, has wholly saved us and taken care of our condemnation of sin?

Those who know and truly believe that Jesus has blotted out all the sins of mankind through the gospel of the water and the Spirit can indeed be saved perfectly by faith, just as God promised, *"Though your sins are like scarlet, they shall be as white as snow; Though they are red like crimson, they shall be as wool" (Isaiah 1:18).* We can all be saved by faith, for there was the baptism of Jesus who accepted the sins of this world according to the law of God set in the Old Testament that had passed all sins onto the sacrificial offering with the laying on of hands. It was because Jesus took upon the sins of the world by being baptized by John that He could die on the Cross, and it was because the salvation that God spoke of in the Old Testament was fulfilled that we can be saved from all our sins only by our faith.

Yet despite this infallible truth, we still see some people who believe in Jesus as if it were an exercise in empathy. They weep and cry everyday to enhance their faith because the basis of their faith is to sympathize with Jesus for the deadly sufferings that He endured on the Cross. The hearts of such people are thoroughly flawed, and they must abandon this mistaken faith.

It is you and I who need the baptism and blood of Jesus our Savior, not Jesus who needs our sympathy or devotion. The simple truth is that it is we who desperately need Jesus Christ the Savior, and yet there are many people who believe in God for no particular reason of their own, thinking that it is God who is lacking in something, as if He is begging them to believe in Him. But such faith that believes patronizingly is the kind of faith that is despised by God.

The hearts of those who condescendingly say to Jesus that that they would believe in Him, as if they are doing a favor for Him, are placed higher than even God, and so in their arrogance they can never accept into their hearts the gospel of the water and the Spirit that saves them perfectly from sin. They have so little regard for the Word of God that they consider it little different from what any of their neighbors say, scorning and patronizing it, as if to believe in it is doing a favor for God out of their sympathy.

In the end, they are the ones who do not believe in the baptism and bloodshed of Jesus as the remission of their sins and stand against God. They believe that their sins can be washed away through their agonizing prayers of repentance without even believing in the gospel of the water and the Spirit. Because they take the name of God in vain, they neither know nor believe that Jesus Christ the Savior has completely blotted out their sins, and they therefore cannot be saved.

God said, *"I will have mercy on whomever I will have mercy, and I will have compassion on whomever I will have compassion" (Romans 9:15).* If God decided to save sinners with the law of salvation out of His mercy, then He will do so exactly as He decided. We must therefore believe in the gospel of the water and the Spirit and thereby receive our true salvation.

Those who do not believe in this gospel Word of the water and the Spirit will personally discover just how great God's severity and His wrath really are. Those who believe in the gospel of the water and the Spirit, on the other hand, will see just how great and merciful God's love is. Whoever acknowledges his/her sins before God and recognizes and believes in the gospel of the water and the Spirit, God's gospel of perfect salvation, will be delivered from all sins.

Those who believe that Jesus Christ took upon all their sins by being baptized will be delivered from all their sins. Those who despise this truth, in contrast, will face the fearful condemnation of sin for their sins. All the people of this world must therefore believe in the gospel of the water and the Spirit, the real truth. Those sinners who do not fear God's judgment and do not believe in the gospel of the water and the Spirit will surely be condemned for their sins. But those who believe in the truth of Jesus' washing of sin will be saved from all their sins.

Everyone whose conscience has sin is ill at ease, and so

people come up with unfounded, groundless doctrines of salvation that are completely different from the gospel of the water and the Spirit, trying to comfort their distressed consciences. There are even those who say, "Since I believe in Jesus, it's okay for me to have sin in my heart." But we must not forget that all who have sin in their hearts will face the punishment of hell, for God will surely render His just judgment to such people for their sins. Because they are siding with Satan, God simply cannot leave them free from judgment.

But those who know about the justice of God, that there would be His judgment of sin, ask God for His merciful love, want to be saved from all sins, search for the truth, and desire to stand at God's side. For such people, here is the truth that Jesus Christ took upon the all the sins of mankind by being baptized. Every sinner must believe in it and receive the remission of sin. Through His baptism, Jesus Christ accepted all the sins of the entire world once for all, died on the Cross once, and has thereby blotted out all sins and made us righteous.

Through the gospel Word of the water and the Spirit, all of us must now realize what our true salvation is, and in our hearts we must all have the faith that truly believes in this gospel. All who believe in this truth in their hearts, no matter what kind of sins they might have committed, will indeed be washed from all their sins by faith and receive the true remission of sin and eternal life. Do you not want to believe in this gospel Word and take the gospel of the water and the Spirit by faith, the gospel that makes all the sins of your hearts disappear? Those who believe in the gospel of the water and the Spirit before God will surely receive the remission of sin.

Your Prayers of Repentance Cannot Save You

Today, many who profess to believe in Jesus give their prayers of repentance everyday, asking God to forgive their sins. They live their lives of faith by giving their sacrificial offerings to God everyday, like in the Old Testament's time. But this is not the life of faith that you would want to live. Does Jesus shed His blood on the Cross to wash away your sins whenever you give your prayers of repentance? This is not the case. Instead, you must wash away your sins once for all by believing that the power of the baptism and bloodshed of Jesus Christ lasts forever. Those who try to be washed from their sins by giving their prayers of repentance everyday cannot receive the everlasting remission of sin, nor do they have the faith that enables them to receive true salvation.

If everyone's sins could be forgiven through such prayers of repentance or any man-made rituals, then God would not have established the law that declares the wages of sin to be death. For people to be remitted of their sins, they must actually give the offering that passes their sins onto the body of Jesus by faith. What we must have is not the kind of faith that gives prayers of repentance everyday, but the faith that believes in the gospel of the water and the blood manifested in the blue, purple, and scarlet thread and the fine woven linen used for the door of the Tabernacle. In other words, we must realize that only the faith that believes in the gospel of the water and the Spirit can bring us the true washing of sin, and we must believe this in our hearts.

Just as the sinners of the Old Testament had passed their sins onto their sacrificial animal by laying their hands on its head when they gave their sin offering, we must also pass our sins onto Jesus Christ by believing in His baptism, and by this faith that believes in His baptism and His bloodshed on the Cross, we must come out to God and receive the everlasting remission of sin. God said, *"For with the heart one believes unto righteousness, and with the mouth confession is made unto salvation,"* and *"Faith comes by hearing, and hearing by the word of God" (Romans 10:10, 17).*

John 1:29 says, *"The next day John saw Jesus coming toward him, and said, 'Behold! The Lamb of God who takes away the sin of the world!'"* This passage describes the testimony that John the Baptist gave on the next day that He had baptized Jesus. When John the Baptist saw Jesus approaching him, he said, "Look people! There goes the One!" This caused a commotion among the crowd gathered around John. John shouted out, "Behold! Here comes the Lamb of God! He is none other than the Son of God, the very Lamb of God who took upon the sins of mankind through me. He is our Savior. He is Jesus Christ, the Lamb of God. Behold! The Lamb of God who takes away the sins of the world!"

It was because John the Baptist had baptized Jesus Christ and passed the sins of the world onto Him that John himself could personally bear witness to Jesus. Because John had passed our sins onto Jesus by baptizing Him, in other words, Jesus Christ became the Lamb of sacrifice who took upon our sins according to the will of God the Father.

In the Old Testament, the remission of sin was received by giving sacrificial offerings to God, but in the New Testament, it is only by the faith that wholly believes in the baptism of Jesus and His blood on the Cross that we can be remitted of our sins. Because God took such livestock as bulls, lambs, and goats as sacrificial offerings to blot out the sins of the people of Israel, countless animals were bled, cut into pieces, and burnt on the altar of burnt offering. Myriads of sacrificial animals were indeed killed because of the sins of people.

But in the age of the New Testament, Jesus did not offer such sacrificial animals, but He offered His own body for us. As Jesus the Lamb of God came to this earth, accepted the sins of the world onto His body through His baptism, and shed His blood on the Cross, He has enabled those who believe in this to be saved from all their sins once for all. It was to forever end our sins with the water, the blood, and the Spirit that Jesus came to us.

God is now commanding you and me to believe in this truth of real salvation. He is telling us, "I have blotted out all your sins, for I have loved you. I have saved you like this. So believe! I have blotted out your sins by giving My own Son as the sin offering for you. I let My Son live on this earth for 33 years of His life, I had Him baptized, I made Him shed His blood on the Cross for your sake, and by doing so I have wholly delivered you from all your sins and condemnation. Now, by believing in this truth, you can become My own children whom I love, and who can be embraced in My arms." Know and believe this in your hearts—that those who believe in the baptism that Jesus Christ received and the blood that He shed will not only be saved from all their sins, but they will also receive the right to become God's own children.

Did Jesus Really Remit All the Sins of This World?

Let us turn to Hebrews 10:14-18: *"For by one offering He has perfected forever those who are being sanctified. But the Holy Spirit also witnesses to us; for after He had said before, 'This is the covenant that I will make with them after those days, says the LORD: I will put My laws into their hearts, and in their minds I will write them,' then He adds, 'Their sins and their lawless deeds I will remember no more.' Now where there is remission of these, there is no longer an offering for sin."*

The passage makes it clear: *"Where there is remission of these, there is no longer an offering for sin."* Listen to this blessed news, that all our sins were passed onto Jesus through the baptism that He received! Not only was every sin that you and I commit in our entire lifetime passed onto Jesus, but all the sins of the entire mankind were passed onto Him as well. To fulfill all the righteousness of God, Jesus received the laying on of hands, being baptized into and out of water, and thereby allowed all sins to be passed onto Himself.

Shouldering all sins, moreover, He was crucified and thereby bore the condemnation of all the sins of mankind, and therefore those who believe have now been delivered from all their judgment. Just as the High Priest had passed the sins of the people of Israel to the sacrificial animal by putting his hands on its head, John the Baptist passed all our sins onto Jesus by baptizing Him. And Jesus, in turn, shouldered these sins and was crucified, and thus has delivered everyone who believes in Him from sin. Therefore, those who believe in this can receive the right to become God's own children.

Romans 10:10 states, *"For with the heart one believes unto righteousness, and with the mouth confession is made unto salvation."* For all, it is by believing in the righteousness of God with the heart that they can be justified, by believing in the truth of salvation with the heart that they can receive the remission of sin and enter Heaven. Brothers and sisters, have you been saved by believing with your hearts and confessing with your tongues that the baptism and blood of Jesus are the essential elements that constitute "the righteousness of God," "the truth of salvation," and "the gospel of the remission of sin"? Under the sacrificial system of the Old Testament, the sins of the Israelites were not blotted out just by killing the sacrificial animal without the laying on of hands that passed their sins onto the offering. Likewise, if we believe only in the blood of the Cross and leave out the baptism that Jesus received, then all our sins cannot be washed away.

"Their sins and their lawless deeds I will remember no more. Now where there is remission of these, there is no longer an offering for sin" (Hebrews 10:17-18). Why did God say here that He would no longer remember our sins? Though we cannot help but continue to sin until the day we die, because Jesus took upon all the sins of the world once for all by being baptized, our salvation is now accomplished and will last forever, and those of us who believe in this are now sinless. This is why God has no need to remember our sins.

The righteousness of God means His justice. The justice of God the Father dictates that just as He is holy, those who believe in the gospel of the water and the Spirit are also holy and sinless. From the very beginning, God loved us and desired to make us His own children. But no matter how much He wanted to make us His children, He could not do so because of our sins. So God the Father came up with a solution to resolve this problem.

Because God had set side an unblemished offering that would be vicariously sacrificed on our behalf and decided to wash away our sins by passing all sins onto this sacrificial offering, Jesus did not hesitate to be baptized, to become our own offering of sacrifice, to be vicariously condemned in our place, and to thereby give the everlasting sin offering. And through this sin offering, God fulfilled His providence to cleanse those who believe from their sins and make them His own children. Now, those who believe in this gospel of truth are remitted from all their sins before God. Because Jesus has already washed away all the sins of this world by being baptized, if we believe in this Jesus who has cleansed away mankind's sins by being condemned vicariously, we no longer need to give any offering for our sins. Do we still need to offer sacrifices for our sins, brothers and sisters? No, absolutely not!

Do you know why Jesus Christ was crucified, even as He was sinless and pure? Although Jesus was crucified, He had done nothing wrong at all, in fact. It was only because Jesus had accepted all the sins of mankind by being baptized in the Jordan River that He had to die in our place. The reason why He had to die on the Cross was because He had already accepted the sins of the world passed onto Him through His baptism and was ready to fulfill all righteousness.

When the Son of God was baptized to fulfill all righteousness in this way, how could we not thank Him? It was because Jesus had taken upon our sins that He, like a sheep before its shearer, quietly bore the suffering of the Cross. We must all remember His baptism and Cross forever, for had He not been crucified and condemned, then we ourselves would have had to be condemned for sure.

Our Lord not only took upon all our sins, but He Himself also bore all the condemnation of sin. Put differently, Jesus the Savior Himself, who had taken upon our sins, became our own sin offering and quietly bore the punishment of the Cross, all in order to save us from sin and thereby fulfill all God's will. This is why the Bible says, *"'Their sins and their lawless deeds I will remember no more.' Now where there is remission of these, there is no longer an offering for sin. Therefore, brethren, having boldness to enter the Holiest by the blood of Jesus"* (Hebrews 10:17-19).

Free book request www.bjnewlife.org

Do you now understand why Jesus Christ was crucified? We must not believe just in Jesus' blood of the Cross, but we must grasp the reason why He had to die on the Cross, and we must properly understand and believe that this reason lies in the baptism that He received. If you and I want to know and believe exactly where and how our sins were washed away, we must realize and believe that it was because our sins were passed onto Jesus when He was baptized by John in the Jordan River that we have been washed from our sins by faith.

By Knowing and Believing in the Truth of the Gospel of the Water and the Spirit, We Can Now Be Saved from All Our Sins

What I have told you so far is the truth of the gospel of the water and the Spirit that the Bible speaks of in elaborate detail. And this truth is the salvation that had been planned even before the foundation of the world, and this salvation is also manifested in the blue, purple, and scarlet thread, the materials used for the door of the Tabernacle. Together with my fellow workers, I have been preaching this truth manifested in the blue, purple, and scarlet thread to countless people in this world. And even now, at this very hour, this gospel is spreading throughout the entire world through our books.

Yet there are those who claim to believe in Jesus even as they are ignorant of the gospel of the water and the Spirit. I can dare to call such people fools, for this gospel of the water and the Spirit is the core truth that tells us of the true sacrificial system fulfilled through Jesus Christ, the actual substance of the shadow of salvation manifested in the Tabernacle. Now, it is your turn. If you had believed without knowing the real truth, it is now time for you to turn around, believe in the gospel of the water and the Spirit, and receive the remission of your sins.

The baptism of Jesus and His death on the Cross had been promised even before the foundation of the world, and they were manifested in the blue, purple, and scarlet thread and the fine woven linen also. To fulfill this promise, and to actually save you and me from our sins, Jesus was baptized, died on the Cross, rose from the dead again, and is now sitting at the right hand of God the Father.

Are you still trying to believe in Jesus by following your own experiences or emotions, without knowing this truth? There are many such people in this world, but they must now turn around from their flawed faith and wholeheartedly believe in the truth of the gospel of the water and the Spirit hidden in the blue, purple, and scarlet thread and the fine woven linen manifested in the door of the Tabernacle.

Hebrews 10:19-20 says, *"Therefore, brethren, having boldness to enter the Holiest by the blood of Jesus, by a new and living way which He consecrated for us, through the veil, that is, His flesh."* When Jesus Christ, having taken upon the sins of the world by being baptized, was crucified, the veil of the Temple was torn, and the sins of mankind were washed away with the baptism of Jesus and His blood on the Cross. The veil of the Temple, woven of blue, purple, and scarlet thread and fine woven linen, was so strong that it could not be torn even when pulled at its four corners by four horses.

That this sturdy veil of the Temple was nonetheless torn from top to bottom, even as it was touched by no one, reveals that the very moment Jesus Christ completed His mission, the gates of Heaven were opened wide. The tearing of the veil of Temple from top to bottom means that all the walls of sin were brought down, showing us that through Jesus Christ, God tore down these walls of sin.

What, then, does it mean that the walls of sin were torn down? This means that anyone can be remitted from all sins by believing in the baptism that Jesus Christ received and His blood on the Cross. What God sought to make manifest through the door of the Tabernacle is that the salvation of mankind has now been fulfilled once for all through the ministries of Jesus shown in the blue, purple, and scarlet thread and the fine woven linen. It was because our everlasting atonement promised by God to all of us was fulfilled that the veil door of the Most Holy woven of blue, purple, and scarlet thread and fine woven linen were torn into two from top to bottom, not by the hand of man, but by the hand of God Himself.

This reveals that Jesus Christ who has become the everlasting sacrifice for the sins of mankind has perfectly saved those of us who believe in the gospel of the water and the Spirit. God the Father has set that whoever believes in the baptism Jesus Christ received and His bloodshed on the Cross can receive the remission of sin and stand before His presence. Will you believe in this truth or not?

Just as God has loved you, so has Jesus Christ the Son of God loves you, and He has given you perfect salvation by being baptized by John and crucified. By receiving this love of God given to us through Jesus Christ, and by believing in the truth that enables us to enter the Kingdom of God, all our sins have disappeared. By believing in the gospel of the water and the Spirit, even all our actual sins have been taken care of, for all our sins and condemnation were already washed away with the baptism of Jesus and His blood on the Cross.

Hebrews 10:22 says, *"Let us draw near with a true heart in full assurance of faith, having our hearts sprinkled from an evil conscience and our bodies washed with pure water."* The Bible continues to speak of the washing of sin. We can be saved from all our sins by believing in the truth that Jesus Christ has washed away all the sins that we commit with our flesh and minds through His baptism.

Just as the High Priest also washed away his uncleanness at the laver of bronze after giving offerings, after cleansing away all our sins by believing in the baptism of Jesus, we, too, must remember this faith everyday. As the High Priest washed himself at the laver of bronze, we must wash away our actual sins by remembering and believing everyday that all our sins were cleansed away with the baptism of Jesus, for as we live in this world, there are times when we are exposed to its filthiness.

All sins, whether committed with the body, heart, or thoughts, belong to the sins of the world. With what faith, then, can we wash away all these sins of the world? We can wash them away only by the baptism that Jesus received. Those who have once become clean by believing in the baptism of Jesus must keep their clean hearts, and whenever they sin, they must wash them again by faith. Those who remember the baptism of Jesus everyday and wash the garments of their acts by faith are the blessed. Because all our sins were passed onto Jesus Christ through the baptism that He received from John, by ruminating on this truth and believing in it everyday, we can be wholly delivered from all sins forever.

You must believe in the gospel of the water and the Spirit, that your sins were also all passed onto Jesus Christ when He was baptized by John. You have nothing to lose from believing in this gospel, for the Omnipotent God had planned it even before the foundation of the world, before the age of the Old Testament. The truth that Jesus accepted your sins by being baptized in the Jordan River and bore all the condemnation of your sins by going to the Cross has enabled you to reach the righteousness of God and your salvation. The truth that has enabled you to realize that Jesus the King of kings has forever saved you from sin, and that has sprinkled your hearts from an evil conscience and washed your bodies with pure water, is this very gospel of the water and the Spirit. The gospel of the water and the Spirit is the indispensable Word for your life, and it shines even more brilliantly when you believe.

During the 3 years of His public life, the very first thing that Jesus did to save the entire mankind from sin was being baptized. Jesus Christ, in other words, had to take upon our sins, and to do so He had go to John and be baptized by him. So, all the Four Gospels write this critical incident at the beginning.

You and I, in fact, were all bound to die for our sins. But what happened? Our Lord came to this earth, took upon our sins by being baptized by John, became the Lamb of God, carried all the sins of the world to the Cross, was nailed on both His hands and feet for our sins, shed all the blood that was in His heart and died, and then rose from the dead again. This is why Jesus said, "It is finished," when He took His last breath on the Cross.

Everything that Jesus told and did is all true. Jesus became our sin offering to save us, and rose from the dead again in three days. And after rising from the dead, He bore witness to His resurrection for 40 days, ascended to Heaven, and now sits at the right hand of the throne of the Father. This Jesus Christ will come to this earth to take us away. Jesus came as the Savior when He first came to this earth, but when He comes again for the second time, He will come as the Judge to condemn all those who do not believe.

You must now realize that Jesus Christ will return to this earth as the Judge, to call and receive as the children of God those who believe in the salvation of the water, the blood, and the Spirit that He fulfilled through His 33 years of life on this earth and enable them to live in the Millennial Kingdom and the eternal Heaven, and to render His everlasting judgment on those who do not believe in the gospel of the water, the blood, and the Spirit and have rejected the love of God.

Now, you must no longer ignore the gospel of the water and the Spirit and pretend to be unaware of it, but you must believe in this truth of salvation. And you must realize that just as God had promised through the Tabernacle and the sacrificial system, Jesus Christ came to this earth, was baptized in a form of the laying on of hands, was crucified, and has thereby saved all the nations of the whole world from all sins, and you must receive the remission of your sins by believing in this truth with all your hearts.

Even so, the nation of Israel still has its back turned away from the truth and is waiting for another Messiah. But the Israelites must realize that regardless of how ardently they wait for a Messiah other than Jesus, there simply is no other Messiah apart from Jesus Christ. That there is no other Messiah but Jesus on the face of this earth is the self-evident truth, and as even the people of Israel are no exception when it comes to this truth, nor is there any other Savior for them either.

As such, the people of Israel must repent from their sin of not believing in Jesus Christ as the Son of God, and they must believe that Jesus Christ is indeed their true Messiah and accept this as the truth. By once again affirming and believing that Jesus Christ is the very Savior to come, the nation of Israel must become the true, spiritually chosen nation of God.

Even now, the people of Israel are still waiting for a majestic, capable, and powerful Messiah who can save them from the sufferings and miseries of this world. But Jesus Christ already came to this earth in the flesh of a man as the Messiah and has saved them, who cannot avoid but be judged by fire, from all their sins. As such, they must acknowledge this truth and believe in it. For their souls, Jesus Himself came to this earth as their sin offering of sacrifice promised in the Old Testament, has saved them forever from all their sins, and has made them God's own people.

Jesus Christ who came as the Savior has saved all of us through the gospel of the water and the Spirit, the truth manifested in the blue, purple, and scarlet thread and the fine woven linen. And He will surely enable those of us who believe this to reign over the Millennial Kingdom with Him. After this, He will also allow them to take part in the everlasting Kingdom of God and live forever with God Himself in happiness and glory.

As such, while we are still on this earth, all of us must believe in the gospel of the water and the Spirit with our hearts and become God's own children. Only those who believe in this gospel of truth can become the sinless children of God and are guaranteed to receive all the blessings that await them in the next world.

Hallelujah! I thank the Lord with my faith for giving us the spiritual blessings of Heaven. Our Lord promised that He would return soon; even so, come, Lord! ⊠

SERMON

12

You can download Rev. Paul C. Jong's Christian Books on iPhone, iPad, or Blackberry by going to Amazon's Kindle e-bookstore (www.amazon.com).

The Four Mysteries Hidden in the Coverings of The Tabernacle

< Exodus 26:1-14 >

"Moreover you shall make the tabernacle with ten curtains of fine woven linen and blue, purple, and scarlet thread; with artistic designs of cherubim you shall weave them. The length of each curtain shall be twenty-eight cubits, and the width of each curtain four cubits. And every one of the curtains shall have the same measurements. Five curtains shall be coupled to one another, and the other five curtains shall be coupled to one another. And you shall make loops of blue yarn on the edge of the curtain on the selvedge of one set, and likewise you shall do on the outer edge of the other curtain of the second set. Fifty loops you shall make in the one curtain, and fifty loops you shall make on the edge of the curtain that is on the end of the second set, that the loops may be clasped to one another. And you shall make fifty clasps of gold, and couple the curtains together with the clasps, so that it may be one tabernacle. You shall also make curtains of goats' hair, to be a tent over the tabernacle. You shall make eleven curtains. The length of each curtain shall be thirty cubits, and the width of each curtain four cubits; and the eleven curtains shall all have the same measurements. And you shall couple five curtains by themselves and six curtains by themselves, and you shall double over the sixth curtain at the forefront of the tent. You shall make fifty loops on the edge of the curtain that is outermost in one set, and fifty loops on the edge of the curtain of the second set. And you shall make fifty bronze clasps, put the clasps into the loops, and couple the tent together, that it may be one. The remnant that remains of the curtains of the tent, the half curtain that remains, shall hang over the back of the tabernacle. And a cubit on one side and a cubit on the other side, of what remains of the length of the curtains of the tent, shall hang over the sides of the tabernacle, on this side and on that side, to cover it. You shall also make a covering of ram skins dyed red for the tent, and a covering of badger skins above that."

The Coverings of the Tabernacle

We now turn our attention to the coverings of the Tabernacle. The Tabernacle's coverings were made in four layers. When God told Moses to build the Tabernacle, He gave him detailed instructions. Uniquely, the first covering could be seen only from inside the Tabernacle, covering over the boards of the Tabernacle and all its utensils inside. This covering draped over the boards of the Tabernacle, the Holy Place and the Most Holy, all the way down to the ground. And it was made of blue, purple, and scarlet thread and fine woven linen, and beautiful images of cherubim were also woven into it.

The first covering was made of two main sets of curtains attached to one another, each of which was made by coupling five smaller curtains to one another. To couple these two main sets of curtains to each other, fifty loops of blue yarn were made at each contacting edge of the curtains. Gold clasps were coupled to these loops of blue yarn, attaching the two sets of curtains to make a large, single covering.

The first covering of the Tabernacle was made with ten curtains, which were coupled into two sets of wider curtains. Its length was 28 cubits. A cubit is about 45 cm (1.5 feet), and so the length was about 12.6 m (41.6 feet) in today's measurement, while the width of each curtain was four cubits, 1.8 m (5.9 feet). Five curtains were first coupled together to make two sets of curtains, and then these sets were attached to one another with fifty loops of blue yarn and fifty clasps of gold. This is how the first covering of the Tabernacle was completed. But there were three more coverings. The first covering of the Tabernacle was made by weaving curtains with artistic designs of cherubim with blue, purple, and scarlet thread and fine woven linen.

This was to show us the way to the Kingdom of Heaven. For example, the blue thread used for the first covering of the Tabernacle refers to the baptism that Jesus received from John to take upon the sins of the world. By being baptized, Jesus took upon all the sins of the world (Matthew 3:15). Because Jesus took upon the sins of the world on His own body through His baptism, this baptism has now become the antitype of salvation (1 Peter 3:21).

The second covering of the Tabernacle was made of goats' hair (Exodus 26:7). Its length was longer than that of the first covering by 90 cm (3 feet). At 30 cubits, the length was 13.5 m (45 feet), and at 4 cubits, the width was 1.8 m (5.9 feet). The covering was made of eleven curtains, coupled to one another into two sets of curtains, one with five and the other with six curtains. These two sets were then coupled to each other with bronze clasps.

Free book request www.bjnewlife.org

This second covering of the Tabernacle, made of goats' hair, tells us that Jesus has made us holy with the righteousness of God. Coming to this earth, when our Lord turned 30, He was baptized by John out of His own volition, and He accepted the sins of the world onto Himself. As a result of this, the Lord carried the sins of the world to the Cross, was crucified, blotted out our sins once for all, and has thereby become our Savior. Therefore the second covering, the white covering of goats' hair, tells us that Jesus Christ who became the scapegoat made us sinless with His baptism and blood.

The third covering of the Tabernacle was made of ram skins dyed red, which tells us that Jesus shouldered our sins by being baptized, carried them to the Cross, shed His blood and was condemned, and has thereby delivered us from all our sins.

The fourth covering of the Tabernacle was made of badger skins. The meaning of the badger skins is that Jesus Christ, when looked at His outside appearance, had nothing desirable in Him. But He was actually God Himself. The badger skins shows us a portrait of Jesus Christ who lowered Himself all the way down to the level of human beings in order to save us from the sins of the world.

Let us now examine these four coverings of the Tabernacle in more detail.

The Spiritual Meaning of the First Covering of the Tabernacle

The materials used for the first of the four coverings of the Tabernacle were blue, purple, and scarlet thread and fine woven linen. It was made in such a way that the four colors would be clearly visible from inside the Tabernacle. Also, artistic designs of angels were woven into it, so that they would look down the Tabernacle from above. The spiritual meaning held in each of these four threads are as the following.

The mystery of the blue thread manifested in the materials of the first covering of the Tabernacle is that the Messiah, once for all, accepted all the sins of the whole world through His baptism. He came to this earth and was baptized by John the Baptist, the representative of mankind, to bear all the sins of the world, just as the sacrificial offerings of the Old Testament had accepted the iniquities of sinners passed onto them through the laying on of hands. And it also tells us of the truth that Jesus washed away all the sins of the world by bearing the condemnation of these sins all at once.

The purple thread, on the other hand, tells us that Jesus Christ who came to this earth is the King of kings and the absolute God Himself for us. It tells us that Jesus is God Himself in His essence. The scarlet thread manifested in the Tabernacle tell us that Jesus, having at once accepted all our sins through the baptism that He received from John, shed His blood on the Cross and thereby vicariously bore the sacrifice and condemnation of our sins in our stead.

The baptism of Jesus and His death on the Cross were the same as the sacrificial system of the Old Testament's time where unblemished offerings accepted the iniquities of sinners through the laying on of hands and bled to death to bear the condemnation of these sins. Like this, in the New Testament, Jesus was baptized, went to the Cross, and shed His blood and died on it.

The Bible refers to Jesus Christ as the sacrificial offering. The name "Jesus" means *"He who will save His people form their sins" (Matthew 1:21).* And the name "Christ" means "the anointed One." In the Old Testament, three kinds of persons were to be anointed; kings, prophets, and priests. Therefore, the name "Jesus Christ" signifies that He is the Savior, God Himself, the High Priest of the Kingdom of Heaven, and the Lord of the everlasting truth. By coming to this earth, being baptized by John, and shedding His blood, He has become our true Savior.

Like this, the first covering of the Tabernacle reveals that the Messiah would come through the blue, purple, and scarlet thread and the fine woven linen and thereby save all those who believe in Him from their sins and condemnation. These ministries are none other than the baptism of Jesus and His blood on the Cross. The mystery of salvation manifested in this four-colored first covering is that the Messiah came to this earth, took upon the sins of mankind by being baptized, was crucified to death, rose from the dead again.

With these ministries, Jesus Christ has saved those who believe in Him from their sins, and has made them God's people. Jesus Christ is the King of kings and the sacrificial offering that has blotted out the iniquities of sinners, and He has delivered those who believe from all their sins and condemnation.

The Spiritual Meaning of the Second Covering of the Tabernacle

The materials used for the second covering of the Tabernacle were goats' hair. This tells us that the Messiah to come would justify mankind by delivering them from their sins and the condemnation of these sins. It shows us, in other words, that for human beings to receive the righteousness of God, it is absolutely necessary for them to believe in the gospel of the water, the blood and the Spirit. The righteousness of God has washed away our hearts as white as snow, and it has thereby enabled us to received the remission of our sins.

The Spiritual Meaning of the Third Covering of the Tabernacle

The materials used for the third covering of the Tabernacle were ram skins dyed red. This manifests that the Messiah would come to this earth, take upon the sins of the world by being baptized, be crucified, and thereby become the sacrificial offering for the sins of His people. The blood that Jesus Christ shed on the Cross paid off the wages of death for the sins of the world. In other words, it tells us that Jesus Christ Himself became the sacrificial offering and has thereby saved His people from their sins (Leviticus 16).

On the Day of Atonement, two sacrificial goats were prepared to take upon the entire sins of the people of Israel. One of them was a sacrificial offering of atonement that was given to God for their sins. At that time, the High Priest laid his hands on the head of this first sacrificial goat, passing all the sins of His people onto it at once. He then took its blood, sprinkling it on the eastside of the mercy seat, and sprinkling it seven times before the mercy seat. This is how the offering of the atonement of the people of Israel was given to God.

Then, before the witnessing of the Israelites gathered around the Tabernacle, the High Priest put his hands on the other scapegoat and passed a year's worth of the sins of the people of Israel. This was to give all the people of Israel the conviction that all their sins of the past year were thus taken away from them through the laying on of the High Priest's

Free book request www.bjnewlife.org

hands. This scapegoat was then sent out to the wilderness to its death, carrying with it all their sins (Leviticus 16:21-22). This was the promise of God that the Messiah would come to this earth, take upon the sins of the world by being baptized by John the Baptist, the representative of mankind (Matthew 11:11-13, 3:13-17), bear the condemnation of these sins by being willingly crucified, and thereby save His people from all their sins.

The Spiritual Meaning of the Fourth Covering of the Tabernacle

Badger skins show our own image, as well as the image of the Lord when He came to this earth. Our Lord came to this earth in the flesh of a man to call on sinners and make them righteous. Badger skins also tell us that Jesus Christ did not raise Himself high when He came to this earth, but rather He lowered Himself as a man of humble birth.

In the Old Testament time, God said through His prophets that the Messiah would come and deliver the sinners of this earth from their iniquities. We can see that God fulfilled the Word of prophecy spoken through His servants with the baptism of Jesus Christ and His blood of the Cross. This promise of prophecy is the Word of the covenant that the Messiah would bear not only the sins of the people of Israel but also all the sins and condemnation of everyone in this world, and that He would save all His believers and make them His own people.

Exodus 25 speaks of the materials used to build the Tabernacle. These materials of the Tabernacle included blue, purple, and scarlet thread, fine woven linen, goats' hair, ram skins dyed red, badger skins, gold, silver, bronze, spices, oil, and precious stones. All these materials manifest that the Messiah would come to this earth and save His people from their sins through His baptism and bloodshed. As such, hidden in the coverings of the Tabernacle is the profound plan of salvation that God made to save His people from their sins.

Why did God command that blue, purple, and scarlet thread be used as the materials of the coverings of the Tabernacle? And why did He command to use goats' hair, ram skins, and badger skins? We must pay careful attention to the plan that God made to deliver us from the sins of the world. We must believe in the ministries manifested in the blue, purple, and scarlet thread, through which Jesus has saved His people from their sins, as they are, and we must thereby be saved from our sins and become God's people. We must, in other words, know and believe in the plan of God manifested in the coverings of the Tabernacle.

By Four Methods

The four coverings of the Tabernacle tell us of the way in which God has delivered us from our sins in detail: The Messiah would come to this earth in the flesh, take upon all the sins of the world with His baptism received from John, be crucified for the punishment of these sins, and remit the sins of His people and save them from their sins with His own blood. However, this salvation is fulfilled only to those who believe in the Messiah as their Savior. We must all believe that Jesus Christ, as manifested in the materials of the coverings of the Tabernacle, indeed came by His baptism and the Cross, and has thereby saved us once for all from all our sins.

Free book request www.bjnewlife.org

In accordance to the prophecies of the blue, purple, and scarlet thread manifested in the coverings of the Tabernacle, the Son of God came to us as the sacrificial offering of the New Testament's time, was baptized, and shed His blood crucified to the Cross. Moreover, by believing in the Messiah revealed in the coverings of the Tabernacle, we can give to God the offering of faith that saves us.

As such, we must believe in the truth manifested in the blue, purple, and scarlet thread. If anyone does not come out before God and fails to give the offering of faith by believing in the ministries of Jesus manifested in the blue, purple, and scarlet thread, he/she will surely be destroyed for his/her own sins. But if one believes in this truth, then by his/her faith of salvation he/she can go before God at all times as His child. The Tabernacle shows us that no one who does not believe in Jesus Christ who became the sacrificial offering and was manifested in the blue, purple, and scarlet thread can ever enter the Kingdom of God.

The Tabernacle's coverings thus show us the way to Heaven. We must find the way to enter the Kingdom of Heaven by believing in the truth revealed in the blue, purple, and scarlet thread. Anyone who wants to enter the Kingdom of God must first have his/her problem of sin resolved by believing in the truth of the remission of sin manifested in the blue, purple, and scarlet thread. As such, whether people enter into God's Church by believing in this truth, or whether they are rejected by God for not believing, is a choice that they must make.

Of course, our consciences are at liberty to believe or not to believe in the truth of salvation revealed in the coverings of the Tabernacle. But you should also recognize that the result of not believing in this truth will be too catastrophic for anyone to endure. However, for us to enter the shining House of God according to His will, we must be forever saved from our sins by believing in the baptism that the Messiah received from John and the blood of the Cross. All must accept and believe in their hearts that this baptism of the Messiah and His blood on the Cross have remitted all their sins. Only when they believe so can they receive the everlasting remission of sin and enter into the glory of God.

The first covering of the Tabernacle was woven of four different threads, and it was laid under the second covering made of goats' hair. This shows us that the fact that we were able to receive the remission of sin is based on Jesus' ministries: His baptism and His own blood. As such, the remission of sin that we have received by believing in the righteousness of God is based on our faith in the blue, purple, and scarlet thread and the fine woven linen manifested in the first covering. To see just how certain this fact is, let us turn to the Word of the Bible below.

Isaiah 53:6 states, *"The LORD has laid on Him the iniquity of us all."* Hebrews 9:28 declares, *"So Christ was offered once to bear the sins of many."* And 2 Corinthians 5:21 states, *"For He made Him who knew no sin to be sin for us, that we might become the righteousness of God in Him."* All these passages therefore tell us that our salvation has been fulfilled based on Jesus' ministries of salvation manifested in the fine linen and the blue, purple, and scarlet thread used for the first covering of the Tabernacle. That Christ Himself was hung on the tree and vicariously bore the condemnation of our sins onto His own body was made possible by the fact that He had first taken upon our sins by being baptized by John, and it is not only on the Cross that He bore the sins of the world.

When Jesus took all the sins of the world by being

baptized and thereby bore deadly sufferings on the Cross to atone them, He had no fear. On the contrary, He was rejoiced! Why? Because that was the very moment for Him *"to fulfill all righteousness" (Matthew 3:15)*. To deliver us from our sins, Jesus was baptized and shed His blood on the Cross. He did so because He loved us. This is why He came to this earth, was baptized by John, and willingly drank from the cup of sacrifice. It is because the Lord took upon our sins and blemishes through His baptism that He could shed His blood on Calvary and vicariously bear the condemnation of our own sins.

The Clasps That Coupled the First Covering of the Tabernacle together Were Made of Gold

The Tabernacle's first covering was made of two sets of five curtains, which were coupled to each other with gold clasps. This actually shows us that we can enter the Kingdom of Heaven only when we believe in the truth of the remission of sin manifested in the blue, purple, and scarlet thread. That the two sets of five curtains were coupled to one another with fifty gold clasps shows us that we can be saved from all our sins only when we have thorough faith in His salvation. In the Bible, gold denotes the true faith that believes in the Word of God.

As such, each and every one of us must surely believe in all the Word of God. It is particularly important for us to have faith in the truth manifested in the blue thread. Jesus' crucifixion alone has, in and of itself, no effect whatsoever on our salvation. Why? Because prior to His crucifixion, there first had to be a process of Jesus' baptism by which sinners could pass their sins onto Jesus Christ through. The Cross is effective for our salvation only when we believe that God the Father made Jesus Christ accept the sins of the world by being baptized.

What Does the Fine Woven Linen Tell Us in the Tabernacle?

It tells us that God has worked among us all according to His elaborate Word of truth. The Messiah actually came to this earth and bore our sins and condemnation through the baptism that He received from John and the blood of the Cross. And it tells us that His salvation has already been fulfilled just as He promised in His Word.

In the New Testament's time, our Lord did in fact come to this earth, took upon our sins by being baptized by John, bled to death, bore all the condemnation of our sins, and has thereby kept all the promises of salvation. By being baptized by John and crucified, our Lord completed and fulfilled the will of God the Father. The covenant that God had made with His people of Israel was all fulfilled through His Son Jesus.

Who, then, should actually pay close attention to this truth? Is it the people of Israel only? Or is it you and I?

The fact that the first covering of the Tabernacle was coupled together with fifty gold clasps demands the real faith from us. It shows us that we can enter the Kingdom of God only when we know and believe that Jesus has washed away all our sins through His ministries manifested in the blue, purple, and scarlet thread and the fine woven linen used for the first covering of the Tabernacle.

In other words, it shows us that the remission of sin is received only by believing in the Word of the truth. Through the Word of the Old and New Testaments, God is actually showing us in detail that we can attain our true salvation only by believing that the baptism and the blood of the Cross manifested in the coverings of the Tabernacle have saved us from all our sins.

God has indeed enabled us to be washed of all our sins and become as white as snow by believing in the truth revealed in the blue, purple, and scarlet thread and the fine woven linen used for the Tabernacle's first covering. And God has allowed only those who have this faith to enter into His Kingdom. We must know about the coverings of the Tabernacle and believe in them. By believing in Jesus Christ who has come to us through the ministries of the blue, purple, and scarlet thread, we can actually attain the qualification to become God's children and receive the glory of entering into His Kingdom.

When the Messiah has saved us from all our sins through His works manifested in the blue, purple, and scarlet thread, how could we not believe in God's profound and vast love of salvation and reject it? How could we reject the remission of our sins and the Kingdom of Heaven, which can be attained only by faith? We must all believe in Jesus Christ as our own Savior who has saved us from the sins of world by being baptized and shedding His blood on the Cross. Only then can we become the people of God.

Those who do not believe in the truth of the blue, purple, and scarlet thread manifested in the first covering of the Tabernacle cannot actually wash away their sins by faith. Those who do not believe in this truth cannot become God's children. This is why we must believe in the truth of salvation revealed in the blue, purple, and scarlet thread used for the Tabernacle's coverings, and we must thereby receive eternal life.

The Covering of Goats' Hair Was Made Bigger Than the First Covering of the Tabernacle

The second covering made of goats' hair was bigger than the first covering of the Tabernacle. This means that those who stand against God cannot see even a part the truth revealed in the Tabernacle's first covering. There was actually a need to hide the mystery of the remission of sin manifested in the blue, purple, and scarlet thread of the first covering of the Tabernacle. This was because God has set that only those who revere and fear Him can enter His Kingdom by believing in the ministries of Jesus manifested in the blue, purple, and scarlet thread.

This also is why God placed cherubim at the east of the garden of Eden, and a flaming sword which turned every way, to guard the way to the tree of life, after He drove out the man who had fallen into sin (Genesis 3:24). The truth that enables one to enter the Kingdom of Heaven is not allowed to be seen by just anyone without first believing in God. This is why God made the second covering made with goats' hair slightly bigger than the first covering of the Tabernacle.

The second covering of the Tabernacle shows us that we can become righteous only when we receive the remission of sin manifested in the first covering. Put differently, God has allowed only those who believe in His Word with fear and reverence, and who thereby hold the gospel of truth, to become His people. Because this is how God has determined it to be, He does not allow just anyone to become His child without first believing in the blue, purple, and scarlet truth of the remission of sin set by Him. The will of God is that those whose hearts are evil can never realize even a bit of the mystery of the blue, purple, and scarlet thread.

The Second Covering of the Tabernacle Was Made of Goats' Hair, and Its Clasps Were Made of Bronze

The spiritual meaning of the bronze clasps denotes the judgment of people's sins. The bronze clasps tell us that all sins require the payment of their just wages. As such, the bronze claps contain the truth that the Messiah had to shed His blood on the Cross because He had come to this earth and taken upon the sins of the world all at once by being baptized. Because the Messiah had first taken upon our sins of the world through the baptism that He received from John, He could then bear the condemnation of these sins of the world with the blood that He shed on the Cross.

From the bronze clasps, we can discover God's law that tells us that the wages of sin is death (Romans 6:23). Therefore, we must recognize that God fulfilled the judgment of our sins through the Messiah. Since Jesus Christ was baptized by John and bled to death on the Cross, the judgment of all the sins of mankind was wholly completed.

When we go before God, you and I must think in our consciences about what the truth is. We live this world committing actual sins everyday with our hearts, thoughts, and acts. Nevertheless, the Messiah accepted all these actual sins that we commit everyday also, paid the wages of these sins with the price of His own life, and has thereby completed our salvation for us. Our consciences before God are bound to wither and die away, if we have no faith in His truth. Therefore, all of us must now believe in this truth, so that our dying souls can be saved and live again.

Do our hearts desire to believe in the truth manifested in these bronze clasps? The truth that the bronze clasps are telling is that while we could not avoid but be condemned for our sins, the Messiah took upon our sins by being baptized and was vicariously condemned for all these sins on our behalf. Jesus actually bore all the condemnation of sin once for all with His baptism and the blood of the Cross. By doing so, Jesus Christ has given us faith and enabled us to enter the Kingdom of God.

When someone has sin in his/her heart before God, then he/she must be cast out to hell. Because of our sins, all that we deserved to receive was only eternal death. But the Messiah became the offering of vicarious sacrifice for our sins and has thereby saved us from all their condemnation. We were supposed to be punished to hell for our sins, yet by believing that the Messiah was vicariously punished instead, we can now enter the Kingdom of God.

By believing in this truth in our hearts, we must be remitted of our sins of the world and escape from the condemnation of our sins. It is to do these works of salvation that the Messiah accepted the sins of the world by being baptized by John, and was crucified for these sins of the world. By knowing and believing in this truth, we must not only receive the remission of sin, but we must also be saved from the condemnation of sin.

We have to believe that the Messiah could accept our sins onto Himself and bear the condemnation of these sins only by coming to this earth and first receiving His baptism in a form of the laying on of hands. If the Messiah took upon all our sins of the world through the baptism that He received from John, and if He was crucified to pay the wages of these sins, then we must also believe so. To those who thus believe, God gives new life.

Because we were bound to hell for our sins, the Messiah accepted our sins and died in our place, thereby bearing the condemnation of our own sins. For us who were supposed to die from the condemnation of our sins, our Lord instead bore this condemnation for our sake. If the Lord was crucified to death to save us from the judgment of our sins, we must believe so.

We must accept the Lord's salvation into our souls, into the depth of our hearts, not by our carnal volition but by our spiritual faith in His Word. Each and every one of you, who have now heard this message, must believe in this truth in your hearts. Because the Messiah has saved us with His baptism and bloodshed, those who believe can indeed be saved.

If people do not believe that they are bound to hell, then they would see no need to be saved by believing in the Messiah who came by the blue, purple, and scarlet thread. But if people do believe that they are indeed bound to hell, then they would clearly see their need to be saved by believing in this Messiah who came by the blue, purple, and scarlet thread. This is why Jesus says, *"Those who are well have no need of a physician, but those who are sick. I did not come to call the righteous, but sinners, to repentance" (Mark 2:17)*. When they thus believe in this truth in their hearts, they will then receive the remission of sin into their hearts.

If we look at ourselves measured by the Law before God, then we would not be able to deny that we are utterly sinful, and that they we are to be cursed forever for our sins. Not only must we admit to ourselves that we are bound to hell because of our sins, but we must also have an earnest desire to avoid such condemnation, so that we may be washed of all our sins by believing in this message. This is the only way of life to bear the just condemnation of all our sins by faith.

Without our faith in the ministries of Jesus manifested in the blue, purple, and scarlet thread used for the first covering of the Tabernacle, we would most certainly be facing hell now. The baptism that the Messiah received and the blood that He shed on the Cross are intimately related to the salvation of our souls.

Because we were born as the descendants of Adam and therefore sinful, we were bound to hell. We must therefore admit before God that we are all sinners heading straight to hell, but do you admit this? When God looks at us, He see that we had been bound to hell, and when we look at ourselves before God as well, we, too, see that we had been bound to hell. It is because you and I were destined to hell that our Savior came to this earth to save us from our sins.

By coming to this, being baptized, and shedding His blood and dying, our Lord fulfilled His works of saving us. Had we not been fundamentally bound to hell, there would have been no need for the Lord to do these works of salvation. But clearly, even though we the born-again have no sin in our hearts now, we, too, all were sinful before.

Whoever is sinful must surely go to hell. The wages of sin is death. This means that sinners are most certainly cast out to hell. But those who, by faith, receive the gift of the remission of sin given by our Lord Jesus Christ attain eternal life. When you and I believed in Jesus the Messiah as our Savior, the Lord saved us from all our sins condemnation in His love for us. Amen! Hallelujah!

We Must Examine Ourselves and See If We Have in Our Hearts the True Faith Given by the Lord

Let us take a look at ourselves. Have you and I believed accordingly to the law of God's Word? If so, then what would have happened to us before God? Were we not to be condemned by God for our sins? Our God is not an unjust God who does not punish the sinful. Because God is holy and righteous, He does not tolerate the sinful. God has told us that He would surely cast into hell all those who are sinful before Him by not believing.

He has told us that He would cast them into the fiery hell burning with fire and brimstone where even the worms would not die. God will throw to hell all those who try to wash away their sins on their own and comfort their hearts by themselves. This is why the Lord said to such people, *"Depart from Me, you who practice lawlessness!" (Matthew 7:23)*

As such, we must believe in the Messiah, and we must believe in the baptism that He received when He came to this earth, in the blood of the Cross, and in His resurrection from the dead. Why? Because fundamentally speaking, we were all sinful before God and were therefore all bound to hell. This is why the Messiah came of the blue, purple, and scarlet thread, gave the sacrificial offering of salvation with His own body, and has thereby blotted out all our sins. We must therefore believe that the Lord was baptized and sacrificed all for our sake. If we cannot realize ourselves that we are all bound to hell, then we have nothing to do with the Lord.

However, so many people do not think themselves as to be doomed to hell for their sins. They think they are too well to consult their doctors. Such people are the ones who regard Jesus only as a gentle and well-behaving man, a man of respect and a teacher, and they also are the ones who believe in Jesus only to pretend themselves to be people of character. Our Lord said to such people, *"Those who are well have no need of a physician, but those who are sick" (Matthew 9:12)*. They have to examine their hearts thoroughly from the biblical standpoint right now, lest they should end up in hell.

The reason why we believe in the Messiah is to be remitted of our sins by believing in Him as our Savior. It is not to build our own virtue that we believe in the Messiah. Rather, it is because of our sins that it is absolutely necessary for you and I to believe in the Messiah. This is why we believe: That Jesus the Messiah was born unto this earth; that He was baptized by John at the age of 30; that He carried the sins of the world and shed His blood with His crucifixion; that He rose from the dead again in three days; that He ascended to Heaven; and that He now sits at the right hand of God the Father—all these things bear witness to our remission of sin. Because all these things were the works of the Savior who has delivered us from our sins, we need to surely believe in all of them, leaving out nothing.

In our own thoughts, it may seem okay to make the coverings of the Tabernacle just by weaving some thick thread, but in the Bible God explicitly gave the detailed specifications as to how they were to be made, how some clasps were to be made of gold and others of bronze. Why do you think God commanded so? He commanded so because all these things were meant to reveal their spiritual significance to us. This is why we cannot overlook any of them.

We Must Surely Believe in the Baptism and Blood of Jesus Christ Who Has Become the Messiah

Because of our sins, we had to be cast out to hell, but Jesus Christ the Messiah came to this earth and has saved us from our sins. Jesus was actually baptized, crucified, and shed His blood. As such, it is lawless for us to just say that we are sinless without first believing in our hearts in the baptism of Jesus and the blood that He shed on the Cross. Jesus, who has become the Messiah, did indeed come to this earth to save us, did actually accept the sins of mankind onto His own body through His baptism, bore our punishment and died, rose from the dead again, and has thereby become our true and eternal Savior. Jesus has saved us in this way because only then can we be remitted of all our sins by believing in this Jesus.

To compete the works of salvation, the Messiah had to be baptized by John the Baptist and then die on the Cross. This means that from the beginning, we were to be condemned for our sins. But in fact, now we no longer need to bear this condemnation. Why? Because the Messiah who was sinless and therefore did not have to be condemned actually accepted our sins passed onto Him, and He was vicariously condemned for all our sins. Therefore, it is by wholeheartedly believing in Jesus' baptism and His blood of the Cross that we have been delivered from all the condemnation of our sins.

We can see "Jesus loves you!" stickers on the back windows of many cars. Is that all Jesus wants you to know? Our Lord's salvation was not something that was made only by such words. He wants to let you know, "I love you so much. Therefore, I have forgiven your sins. Just believe in Me, and I will make you My children." The Messiah was actually baptized and crucified, and shed His blood and died, all in order to deliver us from our sins. The Lord has indeed saved us and delivered us from the judgment awaiting us.

The Lord became our physician to heal the illness of our sins. Coming to this earth, He actually accepted our sins onto His body by being baptized, was crucified and bled to death, rose from the dead indeed, and has thereby saved us. When we were surely bound to hell for our sins, the Lord has already healed us from the illness of all our sins. We must be healed of our sins through the right faith.

If people were not to be cast into hell even as they are sinful, then there would have been no need for the Messiah to come to this world and shed His blood. But the reason why people absolutely must believe in Jesus is because they actually have the fearful illness of sin that leads them to hell. Indeed, people who have this fearful illness of sin cannot avoid but be cast into hell, and this is why unquestionably they must believe in the baptism and blood of Jesus who has become the Messiah.

All who have sin in their hearts are to receive the punishment of hell for sure, for when it comes to the law of God, the wages of sin is death for everyone. Simply put, if one has even the slightest bit of sin in his/her heart, then he/she will be cast into hell. This is why Jesus had to come to us. So when we truly believe in the Messiah who has perfectly blotted out all our sins, we can then be saved from all our sins. We must believe in Jesus as our Savior, and we must believe exactly according to what He has done for us.

Jesus is indeed God Himself. He is the actual Creator. But He set aside His divine glory and actually incarnated into the flesh of man for a while, all in order to deliver you and me, whom He loved, from the fearful punishment of sin and hell, destruction, and curses. And He was actually baptized, crucified, resurrected, and then ascended to Heaven. This is the truth. We cannot not regard this actual truth lightly, as if it were only a joke. To believe this factual truth is not something optional for you. We must surely believe in this actual truth in our hearts, and we must know it for sure.

Did the lambs and goats used as sacrificial offerings have any sin? No animal has even the remotest idea of what sin is. But because these animals accepted the sins of the Old

Testament's people of Israel through the laying on of hands, they actually had to be put to death vicariously instead of them. Why? Because the wages of sin is death, and this was what God had determined. So the offering of sacrifice of the Day of Atonement that had accepted all the sins of the people of Israel also had to die for sure. So was it for the same reason that Jesus Christ had to die, for He had already borne all the sins of the world through His baptism.

For whom were theses works actually done? They were actually for you and me. Is this, then, something that we can either believe or not believe? People do not believe because they are completely oblivious to the seriousness of their illness of sin. But had they known the fact that they are to be cast into hell even for the tiniest bit of sin, then they would not be able to regard the salvation of Jesus Christ the Messiah as something that is optional, something that they can either believe or not believe without any consequences.

If people have sin, even as tiny as a grain, then they will be cast into hell. They will be destroyed. Everything they do on this earth will eventually all end with their everlasting curse. Those who think that it's okay to have sin are deeply hallucinated. The consequence of sin is unquestionably death. Of course, there are still many people who apparently live their successful lives even though they have sin in their hearts. Youngsters are apt to worship celebrities, dreaming of meeting them someday. But will their seemingly splendid lives last forever? Many of them turn into miserable ones when their fifteen minutes of fame fades away.

There are some people for whom everything that they do turns out badly. Before you met the Lord, you, too, were probably like this also, when nothing really went quite as well you had wanted. As if you were living a cursed life, what you thought were a sure thing never quite turned out to be, and what you thought were going well ultimately fell apart. You might have dreamt big, but nothing actually materialized, and the dream kept getting smaller and smaller, until it ultimately disappeared. When you realized that even the smallest of all your dreams cannot be actualized, then your dream was completely shattered in the end.

Why was this the case? It was because of the sins that were in your hearts. People who have sin in their hearts can never be happy. God never blesses them, no matter how hard they try. If there are some people who seem to be successful despite being sinful, you must realize that God has abandoned them. You should know that although their present lives may be successful, God has given up on them to cast them into hell. Had this world been filled with only the sinless, there would have no need the existence of hell. But God has actually made hell, and He has made it for those who have sin in their hearts.

God commanded to make the first covering of the Tabernacle with blue, purple, and scarlet thread to actually give the remission of sin to our hearts. And it also reveals that when the New Testament's time comes, Jesus Christ would take upon the sins of the world by being baptized by John, and that He would then be crucified to death to bear the condemnation of these sins. Our Lord has indeed become the Savior of sinners.

This is why He has given the remission of sin to sinners through His works of the blue, purple, and scarlet thread. Do you realize this now? Jesus Christ was actually baptized in the Jordan River to take upon our sins, and He was crucified and shed His blood to pay the wages of these sins. That He was baptized was to bear our sins. Do you believe that Jesus died on the Cross because He had first taken upon our sins through the baptism that He received from John?

In Our Flesh, You and I Had Been Like Badger Skins

The fourth covering was made of badger skins. Badger is the translated name of a mammal called "Tachash" in Hebrew in the Old Testament. It has been translated into some different mammals—for example, "sea cow" (NIV), "seal" (ASV), "fine goat skin" (NLT), and "porpoise" (NASB). We cannot identify exactly what this mammal is. Biblical philologists assert that the origin of this word "Tachash" is probably of foreign derivation. At any case, the mammal "Tachash" was the animal whose skins were used to make the fourth covering of the Tabernacle. And it is probably safe to assume that this covering was not beautiful and offered no attractive qualities.

This fourth covering of badger skins implies that Jesus Christ came to this earth in the flesh of a man. Moreover, He had nothing attractive in His countenance. The Bible describes His appearance by saying, *"He shall grow up before Him as a tender plant, and as a root out of dry ground. He has no form or comeliness; and when we see Him, there is no beauty that we should desire Him" (Isaiah 53:2).*

That the Son of God came down onto this earth in the flesh of a man of humble birth was to save all of us who cannot but live shameful lives until the day of our death. When God sees us, the descendant of Adam, He sees that we also are unattractive like this skin covering. Moreover, we only like to commit sin. Just like filthy badgers, human beings are only interested feeding their own bellies, from their very birth to their end. This is the actual reason why Jesus came in the flesh of a man, and was inflicted with suffering.

Only those who really know the seriousness of their sinful nature can believe in the Messiah and be saved from their sins and condemnation. As such, those who are ignorant of their own sins, and those who do not know and believe in the condemnation of their sins, are not qualified to receive the remission of sin. God tells us that such people are no better than beasts (Psalm 49:20).

Although we have been made in the likeness of God's images, not everyone accepts God's love. Those who do not believe in God's plan of salvation cannot receive the remission of sin into their hearts, and therefore are to be destroyed like the beasts that perish. It is because God had a plan for human beings that He made them in the likeness of His images.

Take a closer look at what everyone does or thinks. I am not referring to you in particular, but I am referring to the whole mankind. Most people do not even know their own Creator who made them. Furthermore, many of them claim that they do not commit sin, and that they are better than everyone else. How obtuse and foolish are human beings? Those who do not know God are full of arrogance. When we compare ourselves to another other, what actual difference can we really find? How much better or worse are we really? And yet people still harm others just to pursue their own selfish interests—how wrong is this?

We cannot even fathom just how many sins everyone commits against God in a lifetime. I am not saying this just to despise human character, but I am only pointing out the fact that although God has created human beings to be precious, most of them do not still realize that they are actually to be destroyed for their sins. People do not know how to take care of their souls; they cannot prepare their future for themselves;

they do not recognize the Word of God; and they do not want to believe in Him even though they have no other option to avoid their eternal destruction. None other than these people are the ones who are no better than the beasts that perish.

But God Did Not Leave Us to Our Destruction

To save us from our sins, in fact, Jesus came to this earth, and to blot out all our sins, He was baptized, shed His blood on the Cross, and rose from the dead again. The Lord has thereby become our true Savior. We must believe in this truth. Do you believe? By any chance, are you not saying, out of your ignorance and lack of biblical knowledge, "What's the big deal? If we believe in Jesus somehow, then we will all go to Heaven"? And there are those who also say, "If we believe just in the blood of the Cross, then Heaven is ours." But is this kind of faith really right?

God is, in fact, the God of truth. He is the One who spoke to us about His plan, who fulfilled the works of salvation exactly according to His Word, who has given us the remission of sin, and who meets us through this truth. God is alive. God is here even now, with each and every one of us. People who have sin in their hearts should not try to deceive God. If people have sin in their hearts and their consciences are eating them away, then they must get this problem solved by believing in the baptism that He received and the blood that He shed. The sinful must believe in the truth that because they were bound to hell, the Lord has saved them from all their sins through His baptism and His blood on the Cross.

There is absolutely no one who is unable to solve the problem of their sins by believing in the water and the blood.

But even as our Lord has saved us through the water, the blood, and the Spirit (1 John 5:6-8), if on our side we do not recognize and believe in this fact and are therefore destroyed, then we are entirely responsible for this outcome. All of us must confess before God, "I am bound to hell for I am sinful. But I believe in the gospel of the water, the blood, and the Spirit." We must have such faith. We must believe in our hearts that the Lord has saved us from all our sins through the water, the blood, and the Spirit. With our sincere hearts and faith, we must unite ourselves with the truth manifested in the gospel of the water and the Spirit. Only then can we be saved from all our sins.

As such, we must understand all these things, and we must believe in their truth. Without even knowing the truth that is manifested in the Tabernacle and the gospel of the water and the Spirit, some people believe, "Because I believe, I'm going to Heaven even as I still have sin." But God said that all who have sin will be cast into hell; He did not say that they will not be cast into hell even as they have sin just because they believe in Jesus. This is akin to becoming the greatest fool of all. Saying that they would go to Heaven just because they believe in Jesus, when, in fact, they believe in whatever way they like, is the reflection of a foolish, ignorant, and completely blind faith.

Some others say, "I haven't seen a single person who was cast into hell, nor have I seen anyone who entered Heaven. We won't find out until the Day of Judgment." But there actually are Heaven and hell. Are there in this world only the things we can see with our eyes? Can you see air with your eyes? There surely is also the realm of the unseen. All sinners who do not believe in God because they cannot see Him are like the beasts that perish.

As such, people must realize that if they have sin in their

hearts, they will be destroyed, and they must therefore believe in the gospel of the water and the Spirit and escape from the judgment of God. The wise are those who, even if they have not done many wrongs toward people around them, nevertheless recognize that they have done many wrongs against God, and therefore admit that they will surely be judged when they soon stand before Him.

We should not perish on account of our ignorance and disregard of God and His just judgment. He will surely condemn each and every sinner with the everlasting fire of hell. If people are destroyed for not believing in the truth manifested in the Tabernacle even as they have heard it, then they must be Satan's children. What the Messiah wants from us is for all of us have the faith that enables us to receive the remission of sin and enter the Kingdom of Heaven.

God Did Not Make Us As Toys

When God made us the human beings, His purpose was to enable us to live without being tormented by sin, but forever enjoying eternal life, splendor, and glory with God as His own children. To not to send us to hell, the Messiah was baptized, took upon the sins of the world, shed His blood on the Cross, and has thereby blotted out all our sins. When God has loved us this much, if we do not acknowledge this love but only half-heartedly believe in the salvation that He has given us, then we will surely not escape from God's wrath.

God has delivered us from our sins by sacrificing His own Son. It is because the Messiah was baptized to bear all our sins onto His own body and gave Himself up as the sacrifice of our sin offering that He has actually saved us from all the sins of the world. It is because we were bound to hell from our sins that our Lord had mercy on us, and it is because of this that He was baptized, bled to death, rose from the dead, and has thereby saved us from all our sins and made us God's children. God did not make us as His toys.

A while ago, when a sister of my church was in college, I had a chance to attend her graduation exhibition. There, in this art gallery, I came across various paintings. One of the works painted by the graduating class was a canvas portraying Adam and Eve eating from the tree of the knowledge of good and evil, titled, "Did God make human beings as toys?" Someone scribbled an answer to this question below the canvass, saying, "God was bored, and so He made us as His toys."

Nothing could be more wrong than this answer. Why, then, did God make the tree of the knowledge of good and evil and then tell Adam and Eve not to eat from it? After all, He knew already that they were going to eat the fruits, and yet He still made the tree and told them not to eat from it. When they did eat, then He drove them out of the Garden of Eden for falling into sin. He then said that the sinful will be sent straight to hell. Why did God do this? Did God really make us because He had no toy and was bored? Did He make mankind because He was just too bored and couldn't stand it anymore? Of course not!

Brothers and sisters, what God actually wanted to do was to turn us into His own people, to make us immortal, and to live with us happily forever. God's providence in permitting all these things to mankind was to make us immortal beings who enjoy everlasting splendor and glory and who live forever glorified. Thus, when you and I, deceived by Satan, had fallen into sin and were destined to hell, God sent His only begotten Son to this earth to save us. And by having the Son be baptized and take upon the sins of the world, shed His blood, and rise from the dead again, God has saved us from Satan.

However, countless people have this grotesque misperception that God somehow made us as toys to beat His boredom. Among both those who ceased to believed in Jesus and those who never believed in Him from the beginning, there are those who, in their bitterness to God, say, "Why did God create me and then make me suffer? Why does He insist that I have to believe? Why does He say that He will give me salvation if I believe, but not if I don't?" They say such things because they do not know the profound providence of salvation that God has given to mankind.

This profound providence of the Messiah was to accept us as God's people and thereby make us His own children, allowing us to enjoy all the glory and splendor of Heaven as His family. This is the purpose of God's creation of mankind. I, myself, also could not understand this truth until I was born again of water and the Spirit. But after I received the remission of sin and was born again, I came to know, "Ah! So this is why the Lord made me!"

What is it that the Messiah actually did to take upon our sins when He came to this earth over 2,000 years ago? What is it that He did to bear our sins? He received baptism and shed His blood! And these were all righteous acts and righteous sacrifices meant to blot out our sins.

Herein lies the reason why we must actually believe in God, and why we must believe in Jesus Christ as our God the Savior. It is because you and I had been bound to hell that God Himself had to actually come to this earth to save us. In other words, Jesus had to be baptized by John, had to die on the Cross, and had to rise from the dead again. The reason why we actually believe in the remission of sin revealed in the blue, purple, and scarlet thread is so that we can be remitted of all our sins. It is to fulfill the providence of God toward us that we must have faith. And when we do believe in the Lord's salvation, we do so not for the benefit of someone else, but for our own benefit.

Now Is the Earliest Time to Believe in the Truth of God's Salvation

If anyone wants to reach the following realization, then this person must cast aside his/her mistaken faith right now and believe in the gospel of the water and the Spirit in the heart: "I didn't know that I was bound to hell. I just believed because I was told that Jesus blotted out my sins. But my faith was all based on faulty understanding! I should now learn what is correct and base my faith on sound knowledge. Up to now, I have believed wrongly, but it's not too late yet. All that I have to do is realize, from now on, that I am destined to hell for my sins, believe in my heart that the Messiah has saved me through His baptism and bloodshed, and then receive the remission of my sins. So I was bound to hell!"

As a matter of fact, only a handful of Christians had the proper and exact understanding of the gospel of the water and the Spirit when they first began believing. For myself, too, it actually took 10 years since I first became a Christian to fully realize that Jesus took upon the sins of the world with His baptism and was crucified to death on the Cross, and only then was I really saved by believing again in Jesus as my own Savior. And so 10 years after becoming a Christian, I threw out my mistaken faith, and came to the proper understanding of the gospel of the water and the Spirit and believe in it correctly. But for others, perhaps, it might even take more than 20 years to know the truth and believe again.

When such people come to realize, even after 20 years, that God had planned to save them through the water and the Spirit, they must then believe that Jesus was baptized and crucified for their own sins. Nothing could be more evil before God than knowing the truth and yet refusing to believe. But if they were to believe in the gospel of the water and the Spirit now, even after having lived 10, 20 years as Christians, is this somehow bad? Of course not! There is absolutely nothing wrong or shameful about this. When people actually know and believe in the remission of sin manifested in the blue, purple, and scarlet thread, then they will actually be saved. Faith in the gospel of the water and the Spirit is what pleases God. I hope that you would all believe in this salvation that has actually been achieved, whose fulfillment came through the blue and scarlet thread.

The coverings of the Tabernacle were made in elaborate detail. Just by looking at the fact that ram skins dyed red were placed on the covering made of goats' hair, and that badger skins were then laid on top of this, we can see the clear manifestation of the truth that we are all bound to hell, but our Lord came to this earth, actually took upon our sins by being baptized, and became the sacrificial offering for these sins of ours by shedding His blood and dying on the Cross. We can all believe in the gospel of the water and the Spirit. What the Lord has actually saved us through is the works of Jesus manifested in the blue, purple, and scarlet thread. The coverings of the Tabernacles hold none other than this mystery of salvation.

What is important is not just learning about the Bible. What pleases God is to not only to learn, but to believe—that is, if the Bible tells us that God determined to save us through the works of Jesus revealed in the blue, purple, and scarlet thread, then you and I must actually accept this into our hearts and believe so. This is how we can please God. If in our hearts we actually hear the Word of God, recognize our own sins, and believe in the baptism of the Lord and the blood of the Cross, then we can also actually receive the remission of our sins. But if we do not believe in this remission of sin given by the Lord, and instead believe in Him only as a theoretical matter, then we will continue to be tormented by a guilty conscience.

If we do not solve the problem of our actual sins by believing in the water and the Spirit, then this guilty conscience will continue to eat away at our hearts. However, if we believe in the gospel of the water and the Spirit, then we will be freed this guilty conscience, for when we become sinless by receiving the perfect remission of sin, how could we ever be tormented by sin again? This is how we must actually believe. We must believe in the gospel of the water and the Spirit and have the problem of all our sins solved. Those who fail to do so have no choice but to continue in the bondage of sin.

Life is very short, and full of suffering. God allows suffering to every human being. What is the reason God allows suffering to us? It is because through our suffering of sin, He wants us to realize the preciousness of the gospel of the water and the Spirit, to believe in this gospel, and to thereby be actually absolved of our sins. He brought the suffering of sin to you so that you would come to believe in your hearts that the Messiah has washed away all your sins through His baptism and the blood of the Cross. Not believing in the gospel of the water and the Spirit as the truth is the most foolish thing to do. The sins of mankind can be wiped out clean only by the faith that actually believes in the gospel of the water and the Spirit.

God is telling us to solve the problem of our sins by believing in the true gospel. We must therefore believe in Jesus, the real Savior. You, too, must actually believe in Jesus Christ as your own Savior in your hearts. You must admit your sins before God, believe in the gospel of the water and the Spirit, and thereby be saved. When in your hearts you believe in the baptism of Jesus the Savior and His blood of the Cross, then you will actually be remitted of all your sins. Only when we believe in the baptism of Jesus and the blood of the Cross as the truth can we be saved from all our sins.

The Order of the Coverings Coincides Exactly with the Order of Our Salvation

When it comes to the order of our salvation, the priority is to first recognize truthfully that from the very moment we were born into this world, we have all been sinful like badgers, the beasts that perish. And we must believe that we surely are to be put to death and cast into hell for our sins. Furthermore, we must also believe that to be delivered from our sins, we actually need a sacrificial offering, and as such, the Messiah has to actually come and bear our sins by being baptized. We must believe that our Savior must be not a human being, but God Himself. And we must believe that Jesus the Savior has indeed saved us from all our sins through His baptism and the Cross.

If this were not the case, then God would have made only two coverings over the Tabernacle. If salvation could be reached by leaving out Jesus' baptism, then there would have been no need to make four separate coverings of the Tabernacle, and God would have covered it with only badger skins and ram skins. But were only these two coverings actually used? No! The Tabernacle had to be covered by four different coverings; the curtains woven of blue, purple, and scarlet thread and fine woven linen; another curtains made of goats' hair; yet another covering made of ram skins; and the last one made of badger skins.

We must believe in the truth as it is—that is, Jesus accepted all our sins by being baptized, died on the Cross, and has thereby saved our filthy and pitiful souls bound to hell for our sins, making us God's own people. This is the mystery hidden in the four coverings of the Tabernacle, and the order in which these four coverings were laid on the Tabernacle is none other than the very order of our salvation.

To couple the first and second coverings of the Tabernacle together, gold and bronze clasps were needed. And at the edge of the two sets of curtains that together made up each covering, loops of blue yarn were made. But for those who believe only in the blood of the Cross, it is impossible to know what these gold and bronze clasps attached to the loops of blue yarn actually mean. Only those who believe in the gospel of the water and the Spirit can understand and believe in the truth hidden in the four coverings.

The loops of blue yarn refer to the baptism that Jesus received in the Jordan River. Why, then, do people not believe in the baptism through which Jesus accepted the sins of the world, but believe only in the blood of the Cross? It is because they do not believe in God's Word as it is. When we profess to believe in Jesus, we cannot believe in Him correctly by adding to or subtracting from the Word of God. We must believe in God's Word exactly as it is, with a "yes."

Among the many people who claim to believe in Jesus, most of them believe only in the blood that He shed on the Cross, leaving out the baptism that He received. This is why so many Christians cannot understand the mystery of the truth manifested in the coverings of the Tabernacle. And this is why today's Christians do not believe in the real remission of sin that the Messiah has perfectly fulfilled. They believe in Jesus, all in vain, just as one of the founders of the religions of the world. As such, many Christians are in fact walking on the wrong path. They sin everyday, and yet claim that they can go to Heaven just by repenting everyday. This explains why the secular people of the world so often denounce Christians.

When we ask Christians, "How, and with what kind of faith, can we really solve the problem of your sins?," then most of them say, "We can solve it by offering prayers of repentance while believing in Jesus' bloodshed on the Cross." When we then ask them, "Have your sins then actually been solved away in your heart?," they reply, "Actually, I still have sin left in my heart." People who have sin in their hearts are still not the people of God. Such people are outside Jesus Christ. They must come into Jesus Christ by believing in the gospel of the water and the Spirit soon.

We must know in detail with what exact method our Lord has blotted out all our sins, as it really is. It is by carrying the sins of the world to the Cross through the baptism that He actually received from John and shedding His blood that the Lord has indeed blotted out all our sins. If we want to enter into God's presence, then we must enter by believing in our salvation woven of the blue, purple, and scarlet thread. No matter how devotedly one might actually have believed in God, it is still possible for him/her to have misunderstood and misbelieved the whole time. For us to enter into the Kingdom of Heaven, we must accept salvation made of the blue, purple, and scarlet thread, through which the Messiah has actually blotted out our sins, as the truth, and believe in it.

If our faith before God is wrong, then we must fix it and

believe again correctly, no matter how often. We must believe in salvation, that the Lord actually took upon our sins and washed them all away through His baptism, as the truth. We must actually believe that the Lord took upon all our sins once for all with His baptism, and that He bore all the condemnation of our sins through the blood of the Cross.

With the real faith in the ministries of Jesus manifested in the blue, purple, and scarlet thread of Tabernacle, we can meet the Messiah. Through the Tabernacle, we have now been able to grasp the gospel of the water and the Spirit more definitely, and to realize that its faith is founded on the truth manifested in the blue, purple, and scarlet thread and the fine woven linen. The faith of critical importance that we must all now have is the one that actually believes in the heart in salvation made of the blue, purple, and scarlet thread.

We are now hearing and learning about the truth that is held in the Tabernacle made of blue, purple, and scarlet thread and fine woven linen. The Messiah is waiting for us now, having actually remitted all our sins already through His works manifested in the blue, purple, and scarlet thread.

God is admonishing you to believe in this truth with all your hearts. Do you still have sin in your hearts? Then, you must all clearly recognize before God just how dark and filthy the sins in your hearts are, confess your sins, believe in the truth revealed in the blue, purple, and scarlet thread, and thereby receive the remission of all your sins. When you truly believe that Jesus has already remitted all your sins, you can then pass all the sins found in your hearts onto Him and receive His perfect remission of sin.

We must all believe, in our hearts, in the remission of sin made of the blue, purple, and scarlet thread and the fine woven linen that God actually planned for us. God has given us the gospel made of these marvelous ministries of Jesus, of the blue, purple, and scarlet thread, and has thereby enabled us to receive the remission of sin and enjoy all power and authority as His own children. The Lord has enabled us to be saved from all our sins and condemnation, and to receive eternal life, by believing in the works of salvation given to us and manifested in the blue, purple, and scarlet thread.

I thank the Lord for making it possible for us to be saved by believing in the truth manifested in the blue, purple, and scarlet thread and the fine woven linen. By believing in this truth, we can be remitted of all our sins and enter the Kingdom of Heaven by faith. Halleluiah! ✉

READERS' REVIEWS

You can download Rev. Paul C. Jong's Christian Books on
iPhone, iPad, or Blackberry by going to Amazon's Kindle
e-bookstore (www.amazon.com).

Readers' Reviews

Reviewer: Valeria Jones
Hammond, Indiana, USA

Rev. Paul C. Jong, I have never really heard about the blue, purple, and scarlet threads and the fine woven linen of the gate of the Tabernacle before, so naturally I was bewildered to learn and understand the significance they have concerning my salvation! I was told not to believe everything that I read because of so much false information circulating, and I was struggling with repentance daily so much that it was like living under the old law of Moses. However, I came to know something concerning Jesus' baptism that has a profound meaning towards my salvation.

I am 55 years old now, but no one has ever told me the reason for Jesus' baptism. The only thing that I was taught was that it was just an outward sign for us. But my common sense told me different. Why? Because the Lord manifested Himself and many heavenly signs appeared that day, and Jesus Himself spoke. But nobody had an answer for His baptism. I was led to pray for repentance whenever I did any wrong. But this only took me back to Moses' law. The only difference with the Old Testament's sacrifice was that I did not offer clean animal sacrifices.

We perish because of the lack of knowledge. After I told a person about what the book said, he said if this was true, why no one has preached it in the churches I have attended. But all that I could say was that the baptism of Jesus did seal our salvation and I believe in this truth. I don't ever want to stop loving the Lord or living a faith-filled life. Jesus knew our flesh is weak. It was becoming such a struggle for me to live a perfect life, and I knew there was something I didn't understand, even though my heart and mind told me that Jesus' baptism had a profoundly significant meaning.

I just don't know in what way I can express how I feel truly blessed in possessing this knowledge. I have come into much criticism when explaining this, but I will continue to plant the seed of the truth in the blue, purple, and scarlet thread and the fine woven linen of the gate of the Tabernacle. And I will also preach the significance of Jesus' baptism. Thank you so much for your research and being obedient to the Holy Spirit! I want to distribute your books.

Reviewer: Robert Cohn
New Bern, North Carolina, USA

This is a book of freedom. Freedom from the way of the world. Freedom from sin through Jesus Christ. When I started reading the collection of books from Rev. Jong, I felt a peace from within. As everyone has had at one time or another a feeling inside that you knew it was just right. This is how I feel. I feel a spirit of peace from knowing that all my sins have been forgiven, the past, present and future. My God, my Abba, my Savior loved me so much that He sent His only begotten Son to take my sins and pay the price for me, and all He is asking in return is for me to just believe in Him.

FAITH in the Water and the Spirit. We as human beings want to make such a big deal and make everything hard when our God has made it so easy. Remember He is not the God of chaos, but the God of peace and love. Believe and He shall set you free... Have faith and He shall set you free... Revelation 3:20 states, "Behold, I stand at the door, and knock: if any man hear my voice, and open the door, I will come in to him, and will sup with him, and he with me." This book is our Lord knocking in your life. Will you open the door?

Reviewer: Rev. Jason Blakeman
Sanford, North Carolina, USA

In this book, Rev. Paul Jong has taken the inspired Word of God and has shown us clearly a failsafe way to eliminate the sins of the past, present, and future. Rev. Jong reveals the common misconceptions that most Christians make in believing the false doctrines of justification and sanctification. He clearly shows the reader how to accept the gospel of the water and the Spirit to receive the elimination of all sins, and how to know if the Holy Spirit dwells within you.

I have been a Christian for years. I believed that I was saved by the doctrine of justification. Rev. Jong's books pulled me away from that path leading to hell and placed me in the light. I prayed to the Lord to know if the gospel of water and the Spirit is true and I was answered. Now I'm eager to share it with the world. I recommend this book to Christians of all ages to read, and I pray that you will accept the true gospel of the water and the Spirit.

Reviewer: Pastor Timothy Katola
Nairobi, Kenya

God bless Rev. Paul C. Jong for bringing the born-again gospel more clearly to the readers of his book, *Have You Truly Been Born Again of Water and the Spirit?* After I read this book a few weeks ago, the message of redemption through the death of our Savior Jesus Christ became more vivid in my life. The laying of the sins of the world on Jesus at His baptism at the Jordan River by John the Baptist gives every human being the assurance that all burden (sin) is off our lives, once we believe in the gospel.

John the Baptist was an antitype of the High Priest of the Old Testament, e.g. Aaron who sacrificed for the sins of the Israelites. Aaron offered sacrifices to God, every time pleading for the forgiveness of the sins committed by the Israelites. Jesus at His baptism took all our sins when John the Baptist laid his hands on Him. He signified the scapegoat of the Old Testament. But He did it once for all for all humanity. Once we believe in the Lord Jesus Christ, we become forgiven all at once.

Rev. Paul Jong shows clearly how our sins are put on Jesus and that sin should no longer be a problem in our lives. I am no longer a sinner now, because I am forgiven as JESUS TOOK MY SINS ON HIMSELF and died in my place.

Man's greatest problem today is freedom from sinful nature. This book shows us clearly how we can live a life free of sin, guilt and condemnation as we believe in the true gospel of Jesus. Thank God for His revelation on His servant Paul C. Jong.

Reviewer: Linda Liu
Beijing, China

I am very glad to have the opportunity to read this book. It gives me a better understanding about the relationship between Jesus' baptism and our salvation. Also, it gives me a new concept about my identity in Him, which really brings me a big release and joy.

As a Christian for many years, I had never got a clear teaching about it like this book. I only knew that Jesus set a good example for us to be baptized by John the Baptist, even though He had no sin at all. If His purpose was just to set an example for us, we should unconditionally accept the water baptism just like Him. In this case, for those who have not been baptized, they have not been saved. This causes confusion and makes people feel that our personal salvation is so related to our baptism.

I believe that most Christians think that they are sinners, but the only difference between them and other non-Christian sinners is that they are given the grace of God and their sins can be forgiven by Him. Before I read this book, I really struggled a lot whenever I sinned, as I was afraid that He would change His view towards me and I would no longer be saved every time I sinned. This book gave me a complete deliverance from this struggle, because I know He foreknew that I would sin even if I became a Christian, and He would never change the salvation that He gave to me since the day I confessed and repented in front of Him. In His eyes, I am no longer a sinner but a righteous person. I just need my faith to accept this truth. What a wonderful message it is! I think it will set more people free from many of today's unclear and flawed teachings.

Reviewer: Martin Wilde from Shelby,
North Yorkshire, United Kingdom

Before reading Rev. Paul C. Jong's book, *Have You Truly Been Born Again of Water and the Spirit?*, I was unsure about my daily sins and mistakes. I knew God would forgive me, but I still struggled with condemnation after I repented—BUT NOT ANYMORE! Now I know for sure after reading this book that Jesus did take all the sins of the world upon Himself when He was baptized by John the Baptist in the Jordan River, so now there is no condemnation for those who are in Christ Jesus! WHY? Because Jesus bore all the sins of the world when He was baptized in the Jordan River and He paid the price in full on the Cross by shedding His blood and giving His life, and was raised from the dead in three days. Glory to God! Thank you Rev. Paul C. Jong for writing this book and making it clear. And thank You Jesus for saving me, through the Water, the Blood, and the Spirit

Reviewer: Nadene Reynolds,
Kingston, Jamaica

I was always taught that Jesus did not need to be baptized as He was without sin. I was also taught that the only reason He was baptized was to set an example for us so that we would know that it is important for us to be baptized. After reading this book I realized that I had been brainwashed. Jesus had to be baptized so that our sins could be washed away. Jesus took on our sins at His baptism and He was judged for them on the Cross. He took the judgment that was meant for us as a result of our sins being passed onto Him at His baptism. The Holy

Spirit opened my eyes by using this book as a tool to let me see the real truth.

Reviewer: P. Square
Aiken, SC, USA

This book is truly magnificent. Every Christian and non-Christian needs to read this book. Rev. Jong explains very clearly and in easy English language, referencing the Biblical Scripture, of how we must be born of water and the Spirit. If you don't believe in Jesus, John the Baptist, water baptism, the Spirit and the Blood of Jesus now, you will do when you finish this book. The book is written so that it flows with the knowledge of God's Word, and the more you read, the more intrigued and excited you are by its message. I never knew how important John the Baptist was to Jesus' baptism, why he was born 6 months earlier than Jesus, and that his mother and Jesus' mother were so similar in how they conceived all according to God's plan.

Q&A section is great, along with a glossary in the back of the book that explains some of the important terms used in it. It is a must-read for everyone. Get the book, and you will end up recommend it to everyone after reading it. Rev. Jong explains the Tabernacle and how it typifies Jesus. He teaches the same truths that I learned in my Bible College—for example, the colors of the veil, the pieces of equipment in the Tabernacle (the laver, the altar of burnt offerings, the Holy of Holies, etc.) and what they meant (typified in Jesus). I strongly recommend you to read the book. You will not put it down until you finish.

Reviewer: Gabriel Tchede
Porto-Novo, Benin

To give the knowledge of sin to man, God gave us 613 articles of the Law. The Law teaches us that the wages of sin is death and judgment drives us directly to hell. But at the time of His baptism, Jesus Christ removed all the sins of the past, present and future of the world. He took our sins to the Cross of Golgotha and paid the wages of our sins by the blood of His death. Hallelujah! Jesus has saved the world. All those who believe in His birth, His water baptism, His blood on the Cross, and His resurrection have no sin in their hearts and will greet Jesus without sin when He comes again. The Holy Spirit dwells within them. They are the children of God and the heirs of His Kingdom.

This is the grace that is given by faith. The materials that were used in the Tabernacle and the colors of the threads used symbolize the ministry of Jesus Christ who has washed away all the sins of the world. The water, the blood, and the Spirit agree as one and the three elements are a must for our salvation.

Pray for me so that I can preach this beautiful gospel as much as the Apostles did. Thank you very much. ✉

Before Creation, God Planned Salvation

Composed by Min-woo Kim
Song written by Ji-hye Kim

Copyright © The New Life Mission, 2003

HAVE YOU TRULY BEEN BORN AGAIN OF WATER AND THE SPIRIT?

HAVE YOU TRULY BEEN BORN AGAIN OF WATER AND THE SPIRIT?

PAUL C. JONG

Among many Christian books written about being born again, this is the first book of our time to preach the gospel of the water and the Spirit in strict accordance with the Scriptures. Man can't enter the Kingdom of Heaven without being born again of water and the Spirit. To be born again means that a sinner is saved from all his lifelong sins by believing in the baptism of Jesus and His blood of the Cross. Let's believe in the gospel of the water and the Spirit and enter the Kingdom of Heaven as the righteous who have no sin.

RETURN TO THE GOSPEL OF THE WATER AND THE SPIRIT

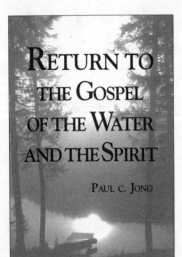

RETURN TO THE GOSPEL OF THE WATER AND THE SPIRIT

PAUL C. JONG

Let's return to the gospel of the water and the Spirit. Theology and doctrines themselves can't save us. However, many Christians still follow them, and consequently have not been born again yet. This book clearly tells us what mistakes theology and doctrines have made and how to believe in Jesus in the most proper way.

The Fail-safe Way for You to Receive the Holy Spirit

In Christianity, the most significantly discussed issue is salvation from sins and the indwelling of the Holy Spirit. However, few people have the exact knowledge of these two topics. Nevertheless, in reality people say that they believe in Jesus Christ while they are ignorant of true redemption and the Holy Spirit.

Do you know the true gospel that makes you receive the Holy Spirit? If you want to ask God for the indwelling of the Holy Spirit, then you must first know the gospel of the water and the Spirit and have faith in it. This book will certainly lead all Christians worldwide to receive the Holy Spirit through the remission of all their sins.

Our LORD Who Becomes the Righteousness of God (I) & (II)

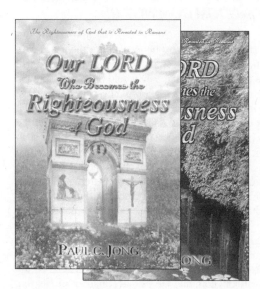

The teachings in these books will satisfy the thirst in your heart. Today's Christians continue to live while not knowing the true solution to the personal sins that they are committing daily. Do you know what God's righteousness is? The author hopes that you will ask yourself this question and believe in God's righteousness, which is dealt in detail in these books.

The Doctrines of Predestination, Justification, and Incremental Sanctification are the major Christian doctrines, which brought only confusion and emptiness into the souls of believers. But, dear Christians, now is the time when you must continue in the Truth which you have learned and been assured of.

These books will provide your soul with a great understanding and lead it to peace. The author wants you to possess the blessing of knowing God's righteousness.

IS THE AGE OF THE ANTICHRIST, MARTYRDOM, RAPTURE AND THE MILLENNIAL KINGDOM COMING? (I)

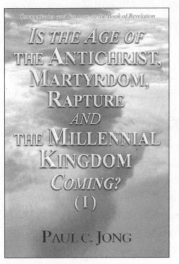

After the 9/11 terrorist attacks, traffic to "www.raptureready.com," an Internet site providing information on the end times, is reported to have increased to over 8 million hits, and according to a joint survey by CNN and TIME, over 59% of the Americans now believe in apocalyptic eschatology.

Responding to such demands of the time, the author provides a clear exposition of the key themes of the Book of Revelation, including the coming Antichrist, the martyrdom of the saints and their rapture, the Millennial Kingdom, and the New Heaven and Earth-all in the context of the whole Scripture and under the guidance of the Holy Spirit.

This book provides verse-by-verse commentaries on the Book of Revelation supplemented by the author's inspired sermons. Anyone who reads this book will come to grasp all the plans that God has in store for this world.

IS THE AGE OF THE ANTICHRIST, MARTYRDOM, RAPTURE AND THE MILLENNIAL KINGDOM COMING? (II)

Most Christians today believe in the theory of pre-tribulation rapture. Because they believe in this false doctrine teaching them that they would be lifted before the coming of the Great Tribulation of seven years, they are leading idle religious lives steeped in complacency.

But the rapture of the saints will occur only after the plagues of the seven trumpets run their course until the sixth plague is all poured-that is, the rapture will happen after the Antichrist emerges amidst global chaos and the born-again saints are martyred, and when the seventh trumpet is blown. It is at this time that Jesus would descend from Heaven, and the resurrection and rapture of the born-again saints would occur (1 Thessalonians 4:16-17).

The righteous who were born again by believing in "the gospel of the water and the Spirit" will be resurrected and take part in the Rapture, and thus become heirs to the Millennial Kingdom and the eternal Kingdom of Heaven, but the sinners who were unable to participate in this first resurrection will face the great punishment of the seven bowls poured by God and be cast into the eternal fire of hell.

The TABERNACLE: A Detailed Portrait of Jesus Christ (I)

How can we find out the truth hidden in the Tabernacle? Only by knowing the gospel of the water and the Spirit, the real substance of the Tabernacle, can we correctly understand and know the answer to this question.

In fact, the blue, purple, and scarlet thread and the fine woven linen manifested in the gate of the Tabernacle's court show us the works of Jesus Christ in the New Testament's time that have saved the mankind. In this way, the Old Testament's Word of the Tabernacle and the Word of the New Testament are closely and definitely related to each other, like fine woven linen. But, unfortunately, this truth has been hidden for a long time to every truth seeker in Christianity.

Coming to this earth, Jesus Christ was baptized by John and shed His blood on the Cross. Without understanding and believing in the gospel of the water and the Spirit, none of us can ever find out the truth revealed in the Tabernacle. We must now learn this truth of the Tabernacle and believe in it. We all need to realize and believe in the truth manifested in the blue, purple, and scarlet thread and the fine woven linen of the gate of the Tabernacle's court.

The TABERNACLE: A Detailed Portrait of Jesus Christ (II)

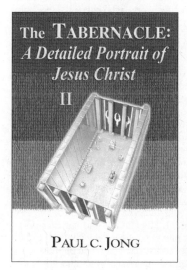

As God had commanded Moses to build the Tabernacle in the Old Testament, in the New Testament, God wants us to also build a Sanctuary in each of our hearts so that He may dwell in us. The material of faith with which we can build this Sanctuary in our hearts is the Word of the gospel of the water and the Spirit. With this gospel of the water and the Spirit, we must wash away all our sins and be cleansed. By telling us to build Him a Sanctuary, God is telling us to empty our hearts and believe in the gospel of the water and the Spirit. We must all cleanse our hearts by believing in the gospel of the water and the Spirit.

When we cleanse away all the sins of our hearts by believing in this gospel Truth, God then comes to dwell in them. It is by believing in this true gospel that you can build the holy Temples in your hearts. It is highly likely that until now, at least some of you have probably been offering your prayers of repentance to cleanse your hearts, trying to build the Temples by yourselves. But now is the time for you to abandon this false faith and be transformed by the renewing of your minds by believing in the gospel of the water and the Spirit.

The Elementary Principles of CHRIST

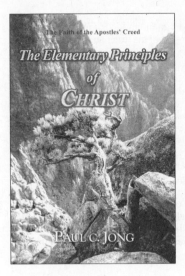

We must have the faith that the Apostles had and believe as they did, for their faith and beliefs came from the Holy Spirit. The Apostles believed in Jesus Christ, His Father, and the Holy Spirit as their God.

The Apostle Paul confessed that he died with Christ and was brought to new life with Him. He became an instrument of God by believing that he was baptized into Jesus Christ (Galatians 3:27). In God's gospel are found the baptism that Jesus received, the blood that He shed on the Cross, and the gift of the Holy Spirit that He has bestowed on everyone who believes in this true gospel of the water and the Spirit.

Do you know and believe in this original gospel? This is the very gospel that the Apostles had also believed. We, too, must therefore all believe in the gospel of the water and the Spirit.

The Gospel of Matthew (I), (II), (III), (IV), (V), (VI)

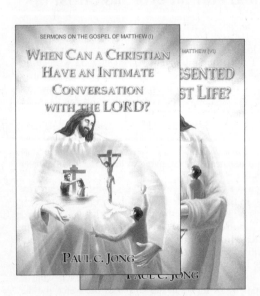

There are countless new Christians throughout the world, who have just been born again by believing in the gospel of the water and the Spirit that we have been spreading. We are indeed yearning to feed on the bread of life to them. But it is difficult for them to have fellowship with us in the true gospel, for they are all far away from us.

Therefore, to meet the spiritual needs of these people of Jesus Christ, the King of kings, The author proclaims that those who have received the remission of their sins by believing in the Word of Jesus Christ, must feed on His pure Word in order to defend their faith and sustain their spiritual lives. The sermons in these books have been prepared as new bread of life that will nourish the born-again to edify their spiritual growth.

Through His Church and servants, God will continue to provide you with this bread of life. May God's blessings be on all those who have been born again of water and the Spirit, who desires to have true spiritual fellowship with us in Jesus Christ.

The First Epistle of John (I) & (II)

He who believes that Jesus, who is God and the Savior, came by the gospel of the water and the Spirit to deliver all sinners from their sins, is saved from all his sins, and becomes a child of God the Father.

The First Epistle of John states that Jesus, who is God, came to us by the gospel of the water and the Spirit, and that He is the Son of God the Father. The Book, in other words, mostly emphasizes that Jesus is God (1 John 5:20), and concretely testifies the gospel of the water and the Spirit in chapter 5.

We must not hesitate to believe that Jesus Christ is God and to follow Him.

Sermons on Galatians: From Physical Circumcision to the Doctrine of Repentance (I) & (II)

Today's Christianity has turned into merely a world religion. Most Christians nowadays live in a situation of being sinners because they haven't been born again by spiritual faith. It is because they have only relied on Christian doctrines without being aware of the gospel of the water and the Spirit until now.

Therefore, now is the time for you to know the spiritual fallacies of the circumcisionists and keep distance from such faith. You have to know the contradictoriness of the prayers of repentance. Now is the time for you to stand firmer than ever on the gospel of the water and the Spirit.

If you haven't believed in this true gospel so far, you have to believe in our Savior who came to us by the gospel of the water and the Spirit even now. Now, you have to be complete Christians with the faith of believing in the gospel Truth of the water and the Spirit.

The Love of God Revealed through Jesus, The Only Begotten Son (I), (II), (III)

It is written, "No one has seen God at any time. The only begotten Son, who is in the bosom of the Father, He has declared Him" (John 1:18).

How perfectly did Jesus reveal the love of God to us! How perfectly did Jesus deliver us! What perfect Truth of salvation is the gospel of the water and the Spirit! We have never regretted receiving our salvation through our faith in Jesus, who came by water and blood (1 John 5:6).

Now, we have become His sinless people. Whoever believes in the gospel of the water and the Spirit can receive the eternal remission of sins and earn eternal life.

Eat My Flesh And Drink My Blood

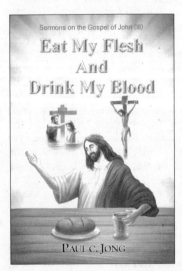

Until now, most Christians have not known the Truth, but only inherited religious acts. From the gospel to Holy Communion, today's Christianity maintains its orthodoxy not through the knowledge of the Truth, but by emphasizing only formal procedures and consecrated rites.

As a result, when today's Christians come across the bread and wine that signify the flesh and blood of Jesus during Communion, they are thankful only for the sacrifice of His blood, and they can't help but remain completely ignorant of the fact that Christ took upon Himself all their sins once and for all by being baptized by John the Baptist.

Therefore, I admonish all Christians throughout the whole world to learn, even from now on, what the flesh and blood of Jesus mean within the gospel of the water and the Spirit, to believe in it, and to thereby receive their salvation and also partake in Holy Communion with the right faith.

The Relationship Between the Ministry of JESUS and That of JOHN the BAPTIST Recorded in the Four Gospels

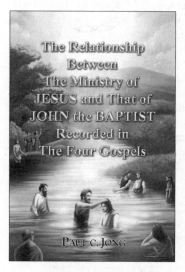

Do you perhaps think that it doesn't matter whether there needs to be the ministry of John the Baptist or not? You must believe according to the written Word of God. We must understand and believe in the ministry of John the Baptist within the frame of the ministry of Jesus Christ. John the Baptist in the New Testament was the prophet Elijah promised to be sent down to this earth according to the Book of Malachi chapter 4, verses 4-5. As the prophet Elijah to come, John the Baptist was born six months before Jesus, and he was the one who passed on the sins of this world at once by giving Jesus the baptism at the Jordan River at the age of thirty. Thus, we must become the recipients of God's blessing by knowing the ministry of John the Baptist and accepting the ministry of Jesus Christ.

THE WILL OF THE HOLY TRINITY FOR HUMAN BEINGS

Through the Book of Genesis, God wants us to realize His good intentions toward us. Where is God's will for us revealed? It is revealed in the gospel Truth of the water and the Spirit that God accomplished through Jesus Christ. We must come into this good intention of God by faith, manifested in the gospel of the water and the Spirit. To do so, when we consider God's Word, we need to cast aside our existing carnal thoughts we have had, and believe in God's Word exactly as it is. All of us must throw away our mistaken knowledge accumulated until now, and open our spiritual eyes by placing our faith in the righteousness of God.

The Fall of Man and the Perfect Salvation of God

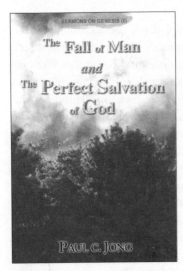

In the Book of Genesis, the purpose for which God created us is contained. When architects design a building or artists draw a painting, they first conceive the work that would be completed in their minds before they actually begin working on their project. Just like this, our God also had our salvation of mankind in His mind even before He created the heavens and the earth, and He made Adam and Eve with this purpose in mind. And God needed to explain to us the domain of Heaven, which is not seen by our eyes of the flesh, by drawing an analogy to the domain of the earth that we can all see and understand.

Even before the foundation of the world, God wanted to save mankind perfectly by giving the gospel of the water and the Spirit to everyone's heart. So although all human beings were made out of dust, they must learn and know the gospel Truth of the water and the Spirit to benefit their own souls. If people continue to live without knowing the dominion of Heaven, they will lose not only the things of the earth, but also everything that belongs to Heaven.

Heretics, Who Followed the Sins of Jeroboam (I) & (II)

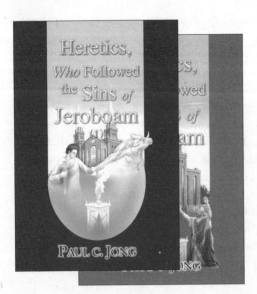

Christians today do not know what the gospel Truth of the water and the Spirit that the Lord has made and given us is. Thus, they continue to believe in the doctrines of Christianity and not the gospel of the water and the Spirit. For that reason, the fact of the matter is that despite their claim of having faith in Jesus, they continue to believe in and follow golden calves.

We must discern those that worship golden calves as God within Christianity. And by coming back before God of the Truth, we must offer the sacrifices of righteousness to God. The sacrifice that God receives with rejoice is the sacrifice of righteousness that people offer by faith after having received the remission of sin by having faith in the gospel of the water and the Spirit. Before God, you must seriously think about whether or not you are offering the sacrifice of God-given righteousness by the faith of believing in the gospel of the water and the Spirit.

The Lord's Prayer : Misinterpretations and Truth

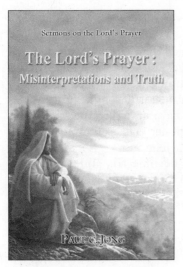

In order to interpret the Lord's Prayer correctly, we must first correctly understand the gospel of the water and the Spirit, which was spoken to us by the Lord. We have Truth in us when we not only know and understand the gospel of the water and the Spirit but also believe it with our hearts. The true gospel, which we believe in, has led us so far, so that we can lead truly faithful lives that the Lord wants from us in the Lord's Prayer.

Exegesis on the Book of ROMANS (I)

The righteousness of God is transparent. God's righteousness cannot be substituted by anything. That is because His righteousness is different from the righteousness of man. We need to know what God's righteousness is, and we need to believe in it.

God's righteousness is fundamentally different from human righteousness. The righteousness of mankind is like a filthy rag, but the righteousness of God is like a brilliant pearl shining forever. God's righteousness is the Truth that is absolutely needed by every sinner, transcending all ages.

HAVE YOU MET JESUS WITH THE GOSPEL OF THE WATER AND THE SPIRIT?

It is written, "No one has seen God at any time. The only begotten Son, who is in the bosom of the Father, He has declared Him" (John 1:18).

How perfectly did Jesus reveal the love of God to us! How perfectly did Jesus deliver us! What perfect Truth of salvation is the gospel of the water and the Spirit! We have never regretted receiving our salvation through our faith in Jesus, who came by water and blood (1 John 5:6).

Now, we have become His sinless people. Whoever believes in the gospel of the water and the Spirit can receive the eternal remission of sins and earn eternal life.

Sermons on the Gospel of Luke (I), (II), (III), (IV), (V), (VI), (VII)

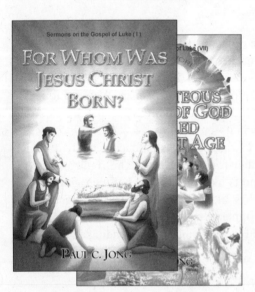

It is Jesus Christ who moves the entire history of this world. Our Lord came to this earth to save all humans from the sins of the world, and He has become the bread of new life for those of us who believe in the gospel of the water and the Spirit. In fact, it was to give this new life to us, who were all destined to hell for our sins that our Lord came looking for you and me.

No More Chaos, Void or Darkness Now (I) & (II)

Although we may be powerless and because the Word of God has power, when the Word falls to the ground it bears fruit without fail. Further, because the Word of God is alive we can see for ourselves that it is the same today and tomorrow, and forever unchanging. Unlike the words of man, God's Word never changes, for it is ever faithful. When God speaks, He fulfills exactly according to His Words.

For the Word of God has power, so when God said, "Let there be light," there was light, and when He said, "Let there be a greater light and a lesser light," it was fulfilled just as He had commanded.

THE DIFFERENCE BETWEEN ABEL'S FAITH AND CAIN'S FAITH

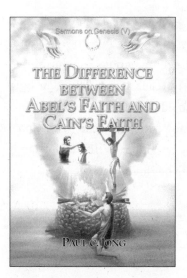

Whenever we stand before the presence of God to glorify Him, we should not approach Him through some religious rituals, but instead we have to approach Him by trusting in what He has done for us and thanking Him for His love. Only then does God accept our worship and pour the Holy Spirit on us abundantly.

FOR THE LOST SHEEP (I) & (II)

What God wants to do is to make us into His children by making us born again through the gospel of the water and the Spirit.

We humans are born as God's creations first, but if we receive the remission of sins by believing in the gospel of the water and the Spirit, we are born again as the children of God. This means that, after the Lord came and remitted all our sins, we who were blind could now obtain our sight.

WISDOM OF THE PRIMITIVE GOSPEL

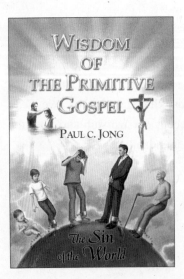

The primitive gospel is the Truth of salvation that's absolutely indispensable to everyone. Transcending all denominations, this primitive gospel will clearly teach every Christian how God's blessings could be bestowed on them. This true gospel will now fill your heart with God's overflowing love. And it will be the most precious gift to all your loved ones.

BE A GOSPEL WITNESS WHO SAVES
THE HUMAN RACE FROM DESTRUCTION

Mankind, who had eaten the fruit of the knowledge of good and evil, came to have the different standard for good and evil from God's. Then, which is correct, God's Word or our judgment? Our standard is always relative and selfish. Therefore we should cast away our own ideas and simply trust and follow God's Word focusing on "What does the Word of God say?" Ignoring God's Word and seeking self-righteousness is Cain's faith and religious belief. Abel put his faith in the Word of God he heard from his father, Adam, and offered the firstborn of his flock and of their fat. But self-conceited Cain brought an offering of the fruit of the ground to the Lord. God accepted Abel's offering but refused Cain's offering. It is God's lesson that faith in man-made religions cannot bring salvation.

THOSE WHO POSSESS ABRAHAM'S FAITH

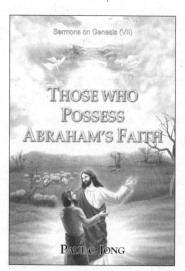

There are two kinds of righteousness in this world which are constantly in conflict and struggle with each another; these are the righteousness of God and the righteousness of man. Although God's righteousness faces many obstacles, it always prevails over the righteousness of man and leads us to the victorious way. That's because the Word of God is almighty. Because God's almighty power is with us, we are able to taste His blessings, for the Word of God has the power to reach our hearts, thoughts and souls, and brings all His blessings to us.

WHAT SHOULD WE STRIVE TO BELIEVE AND PREACH?

The Gospel of Mark testifies that Jesus Christ is the Son of God and God Himself. And it also testifies that He is our Savior. So we can see the writer of the Gospel of Mark bearing witness of Jesus forcefully, testifying that He is the very God and our Savior. This is why I would like to bear witness of this Jesus Christ who is manifested in the Gospel of Mark as much as possible based on the gospel of the water and the Spirit. What is obvious is that the core Truth of Christianity is found in the gospel of the water and the Spirit. Jesus said to Nicodemus, "Most assuredly, I say to you, unless one is born of water and the Spirit, he cannot enter the kingdom of God" (John 3:5).

FROM THIS CORRUPTED WORLD TO HEAVEN ABOVE

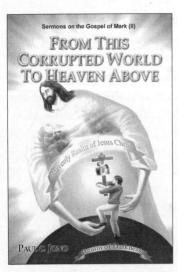

We must open our spiritual eyes and clearly see the wonders and beauty of this world. This is possible only when we escape from darkness through the Lord and live out our faith with the conviction that we have no sin. When you are born again through the gospel of the water and the Spirit and open your spiritual eyes, your life in this world will be more enjoyable than anyone else's life. So you must escape from darkness and dwell in the light, taking and enjoying everything the Lord has given you in your life, for the Word of God says, *"Let the hearts of those rejoice who seek the LORD!" (Psalm 105:3).*

THE BLESSING OF FAITH RECEIVED WITH THE HEART

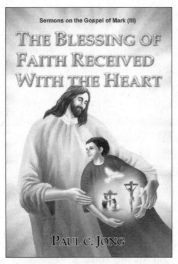

This special day of amnesty, when the remission of sins and the blessings of faith are received by believing in the gospel of the water and the Spirit with the heart, is found in no country in this world, but it is the greatest holiday that can be celebrated together with people from any country in the world. Today is the day you can receive the remission of sins, and it is the only common holiday celebrated together with God's people from all over the world.

The TABERNACLE (III): A Prefiguration of The Gospel of The Water and the Spirit

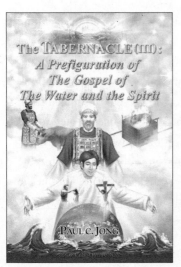

All Christians should stand firm in the faith of the gospel of the water and the Spirit. They will then understand the gospel of the water and the Spirit through the revelations which are manifested in the Tabernacle system as written in the Old Testament. They also can be sure of having received the remission of sins by faith. If you have as yet not possessed such faith, you need to strive to get it as soon as possible.

You should receive the remission of sins first if you want the Holy Spirit to abide in your heart. To do so, you need to put your faith in the righteousness of God fulfilled by the Lord. This is the only way the Holy Spirit can dwell in your heart.

WHAT GOD IS SAYING TO US THROUGH THE EPISTLE TO THE EPHESIANS

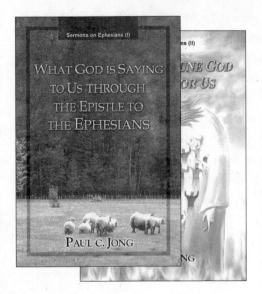

Today God has founded His Church on the faith of the believers in the gospel of the water and the Spirit. God's Church is the gathering of those who have been saved by believing in the gospel of the water and the Spirit. Therefore, if your hearts now have faith in the gospel of the water and the Spirit, you can then lead the true life of faith. Such a life of faith is possible only in God's Church. Furthermore, only such faith qualifies us to live forever in the Kingdom of the Lord. Through this faith we must receive the love of salvation and all the spiritual blessings of Heaven from God the Father, Jesus Christ and the Holy Spirit.

HOW CAN YOU STRENGTHEN YOUR FAITH?

Every sinner must now believe in the genuine gospel. The God-given gospel of salvation is the gospel of the water and the Spirit that is manifested in the righteousness of God. The writer of the Book of Hebrews is trying to correct your misguided faith. Therefore, our faith needs to be deep rooted in the foundation of the gospel of the water and the Spirit. Those who are standing sure-footed on this absolute gospel Truth abide most certainly in the faith in the righteousness of Jesus Christ.

SERMONS FOR THOSE WHO HAVE BECOME OUR COWORKERS (I), (II), (III), (IV)

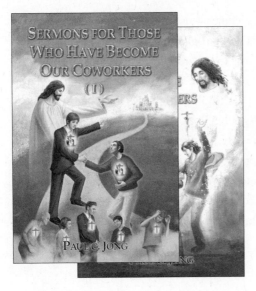

This book is a collection of sermons that have been written to direct our fellow coworkers and saints and to show them how to lead a life as a true servant of God. For this reason, these books are entitled *"Sermons for Those Who Have Become Our Coworkers."*

The author earnestly desires to share fellowship with coworkers within the faith, those who believe wholeheartedly in the righteousness of Christ, excluding personal interests. He does really desire this because he has met them by faith in the Lord's righteousness and they are also preaching it now.

ARE YOU NOW LIVING AS THE OBJECT OF GOD'S AFFECTION?

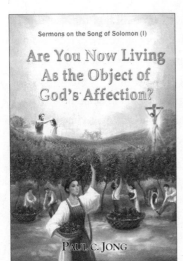

If you want to experience the Lord's love in your life always, listen closely to His voice. If you want to be loved by the Lord in your ministry, accept the God-given gospel of the water and the Spirit into your heart and then carry out the Lord's work. The Lord loves us precisely because we believe in and serve the gospel of the water and the Spirit. Our Lord cannot help but love whoever believes in His gospel of the water and the Spirit and serves Him faithfully to spread this gospel all over the world.

DO YOU KNOW THE INTENTION OF THE AUTHOR OF THE BOOK OF HEBREWS?

Every sinner must now believe in the genuine gospel. The God-given gospel of salvation is the gospel of the water and the Spirit that is manifested in the righteousness of God. The writer of the Book of Hebrews is trying to correct your misguided faith. Therefore, our faith needs to be deep rooted in the foundation of the gospel of the water and the Spirit. Those who are standing sure-footed on this absolute gospel Truth abide most certainly in the faith in the righteousness of Jesus Christ.

GOD HAS SOLVED AWAY ALL YOUR TRANSGRESSIONS

The Book of Leviticus explains the sacrificial system through which the people of Israel received the remission of their sins when they sinned against God or man. Addressing the problem of sin for every human being, God is pointing out in detail how we can all obtain the remission of our sins by giving a specific sacrificial offering according to the requirements of the God-established sacrificial system. From both the Old and New Testaments, you can now find the Truth that has solved away the problem of your sins There is therefore only one thing remaining for you to do now, and it is receiving the remission of all your sins by believing in the justice of God and the merciful and righteous love He has fulfilled for you.

WHAT IS REQUIRED OF YOU TO BE BORN AGAIN?

Christians today need to change their thoughts. They must believe in the God-given gospel of the water and the Spirit as their true salvation. We all ought to thank the Lord for giving us this gospel of the water and the Spirit. How can we instead say that the Lord's work of salvation that has delivered us from all the sins of the world is flawed?

Through this book on the gospel of the water and the Spirit, everyone must now be born again by believing in the salvation the Lord has fulfilled once and for all. If you are still unsure about this, you need to once again contemplate deeply on the righteousness of God that the Lord has given to you.

Paul C. Jong's Christian books have been translated into 76 major languages at this point: Afrikaans, Albanian, Arabic, Asante, Bengali, Bulgarian, Burmese, Cebuano, Chichewa, Chin, Chinese, Croatian, Czech, Danish, Dioula, Dutch, English, Fongbe, French, Georgian, German, Greek, Gujarati, Hebrew, Hindi, Hungarian, Indonesian, Iranian, Italian, Japanese, Javanese, Kannada, Khmer, Kirghiz, Kirundi, Kissi, Latvian, Luganda, Luo, Madi, Malagasy, Malayalam, Marathi, Mindat, Mizo, Mongolian, Nepali, Oriya, Polish, Portuguese, Punjabi, Romanian, Russian, Serbian, Shona, Slovak, Slovene, Spanish, Swahili, Swedish, Tagalog, Taiwanese, Tamil, Telugu, Thai, Turkish, Ukrainian, Urdu, Vietnamese, and Zou. They are also available now through our free e-book service.

E-book is digital book designed for you to feel a printed book on screen. You can read it easily on your PC monitor in your native language after downloading the viewer software and a text file. Feel free to visit our web site at http://www.nlmission.com or http://www.bjnewlife.org to download our e-books, and you will get the most remarkable Christian e-books absolutely for free.

And, would you like to take part in having our free Christian books known to more people worldwide? We would be very thankful if you link your website to ours so that many people get an opportunity to meet Jesus Christ through our inspired Christian books. Please visit our site at http://www.bjnewlife.org/english/about/take_banners.php to take our banners to your website. In addition, we would also be very grateful if you introduce our website to the webmasters around you for adding our link.

The New Life Mission
Contact: John Shin, General Secretary
E-mail: newlife@bjnewlife.org

The Official Website of The New Life Mission

www.nlmission.com *or*
www.bjnewlife.org

Worldwide websites of

The New Life Mission

Please find your vernacular websites below.
You can download Christian e-books and request Christian books for free.
Feel free to visit our websites below right now!

A
www.nlmafghanistan.com
www.nlmafrikaans.com
www.nlmalbania.com
www.nlmamharic.com
www.nlmangola.com
www.nlmarabemirates.com
www.nlmarabic.com
www.nlmargentina.com
www.nlmarmenia.com
www.nlmaruba.com
www.nlmaustralia.com
www.nlmaustria.com

B
www.nlmbahamas.com
www.nlmbahrain.com
www.nlmbangladesh.com
www.nlmbelarus.com
www.nlmbelgium.com
www.nlmbengali.com
www.nlmbenin.com
www.nlmbhutan.com
www.nlmbolivia.com
www.nlmbotswana.com
www.nlmbrasil.com
www.nlmbriton.com
www.nlmbrunei.com
www.nlmbulgaria.com
www.nlmburkinafaso.com
www.nlmburundi.com

C
www.nlmcameroon.com
www.nlmcanada.com
www.nlmcebuano.com
www.nlmchichewa.com
www.nlmchile.com
www.nlmchin.com

www.nlmchina.com
www.nlmcolombia.com
www.nlmcongo.com
www.nlmcostarica.com
www.nlmcotedivoire.com
www.nlmcroatia.com
www.nlmczech.com

D
www.nlmdenmark.com
www.nlmdioula.com
www.nlmdominica.com
www.nlmdrcongo.com
www.nlmdutch.com

E
www.nlmecuador.com
www.nlmegypt.com
www.nlmelsalvador.com
www.nlmequatorialguinea.com
www.nlmethiopia.com

F
www.nlmfinland.com
www.nlmfrance.com
www.nlmfrench.com

G
www.nlmgabon.com
www.nlmgeorgian.com
www.nlmgerman.com
www.nlmgermany.com
www.nlmghana.com
www.nlmgreek.com
www.nlmgrenada.com
www.nlmguatemala.com
www.nlmgujarati.com

H
www.nlmhaiti.com
www.nlmhindi.com
www.nlmholland.com
www.nlmhonduras.com
www.nlmhungary.com

Turn over

Some of these websites may not work because they are still under construction.

Worldwide websites of
 The New Life Mission

I www.nlm-india.com
www.nlmindonesia.com
www.nlmiran.com
www.nlmiraq.com
www.nlmisrael.com
www.nlmitaly.com

J www.nlmjamaica.com
www.nlmjapan.com
www.nlmjavanese.com

K www.nlmkannada.com
www.nlmkazakhstan.com
www.nlmkenya.com
www.nlmkhmer.com
www.nlmkinyarwanda.com
www.nlmkirghiz.com
www.nlmkirundi.com
www.nlmkorea.com

L www.nlmlatvia.com
www.nlmluganda.com
www.nlmluo.com

M www.nlmmadi.com
www.nlmmalagasy.com
www.nlmmalayalam.com
www.nlmmalaysia.com
www.nlmmarathi.com
www.nlmmauritius.com
www.nlmmexico.com
www.nlmmindat.com
www.nlmmizo.com
www.nlmmoldova.com
www.nlmmongolia.com
www.nlmmyanmar.com

N www.nlmnepal.com
www.nlmnewzealand.com
www.nlmnigeria.com
www.nlmnorthkorea.com
www.nlmnorway.com

P www.nlmpakistan.com
www.nlmpanama.com
www.nlmperu.com
www.nlmphilippines.com
www.nlmpoland.com

www.nlmportugal.com
www.nlmportuguese.com
www.nlmprcongo.com

Q www.nlmqatar.com

R www.nlmromania.com
www.nlmrussia.com
www.nlmrwanda.com

S www.nlmsaudiarabia.com
www.nlmserbian.com
www.nlmshona.com
www.nlmsingapore.com
www.nlmslovakia.com
www.nlmslovene.com
www.nlmsolomon.com
www.nlmsouthafrica.com
www.nlmspain.com
www.nlmspanish.com
www.nlmsrilanka.com
www.nlmsuriname.com
www.nlmswahili.com
www.nlmswaziland.com
www.nlmsweden.com
www.nlmswiss.com

T www.nlmtagalog.com
www.nlmtaiwan.com
www.nlmtamil.com
www.nlmtanzania.com
www.nlmtelugu.com
www.nlmthailand.com
www.nlmtogo.com
www.nlmtonga.com
www.nlmturkey.com

U www.nlmuganda.com
www.nlmukraine.com
www.nlmurdu.com
www.nlmusa.com

V www.nlmvenezuela.com
www.nlmvietnam.com

Z www.nlmzambia.com
www.nlmzimbabwe.com
www.nlmzou.com